CONTEMPORARY NEON

BY RUDI STERN

Retail Reporting Corporation, New York

For Moira, Mingus and Else...
and for Jeff Friedman—and the promise of new adventures...
and to my good friend Mel with whom I started the trip...

Retail Reporting Corporation
101 Fifth Avenue
New York, NY 10003

Copyright 1990 by Rudi Stern
All rights reserved. No part of this book may be reproduced
in any form, by mimeograph or any other means,
without permission in writing from the publisher.

Distributors to the trade in the United States and Canada:
Van Nostrand Reinhold
115 Fifth Avenue
New York, NY 10003

Distributors outside of the United States and Canada:
Hearst Books International
105 Madison Avenue
New York, NY 10016

Library of Congress Cataloging in Publication Data:
Main Entry under the title: Contemporary Neon

Printed and Bound in Hong Kong
ISBN 0-934590-37-0

Designed by Bernard Schleifer

Endpaper:
SATURN: Designed and painted by Nils Eklund: 1980
30″ Horizontal x 16″ Vertical x 8″ Deep
Wooden disc airbrushed, metal box, neon
Neon by: Let There Be Neon, Inc., New York

INTRODUCTION	7
GRAPHICS	8
ARCHITECTURE	40
PRODUCTS	80
SCULPTURE	92
INDEX	191
ACKNOWLEDGMENTS	192

Introduction

Neon is coming into its own. It is starting to fulfill its promise. In sculpture, architecture, graphics and products the creative potentials are being actively explored and realized. The better that it is being used, the more sophisticated are the demands placed on its potential. The public is beginning to know what neon is all about. They are beginning to differentiate neon from other light sources. They begin to understand that neon can write itself. The artist, the architect, the lighting and graphic designer and finally the consumer are beginning to take serious notice of it.

The ingenuity of the examples I have chosen for this book attest to a range of expression that is remarkable. I don't know of another medium that has this vigor, intensity, scope and vitality. I think neon is unique today in its fertility. I especially enjoy the maverick "neon freaks" who have no inhibitions about experimenting and who are entranced by the mysteries of the "bright lights." Without apparent public recognition, grants, or visible financial support they explore the limits of the process itself. They are searching areas of the craft that have been unknown or sometimes considered to be "mistakes" by the signmakers. There is an increasingly open neon "network" where information is available for the asking or in exchange from one cluster of activity to another. New techniques and fresh applications are eagerly encouraged. Technical information is free to those who can benefit from it. Geographic distance melts in a supportive, inter-active and international neon community. Paranoia and competition, so common in evolving media pursuits, is not in evidence as everyone involved seems inspired by a shared sense of discovery.

We are at a moment where each fresh design direction and technical development leads almost immediately to another as mutually beneficial experiences are shared. Crossing as it does all areas of technical and design activity, neon enjoys the richness of its own creative discoveries. This book is an attempt to survey this process. Wherever possible, I wanted the designers and artists to describe in their own words the nature of this exploration. Collectively, they speak of the excitement of invention.

The field shows little of the pretension which routinely inhibits evolution. Rather, there is a sense of craft-conscious modesty. Mostly ignored and therefore left alone to develop, there is a sense of pioneering. As it comes into its own aesthetically and as financial support grows, I hope that the field can maintain the energy that it now has.

The purpose of this book is to further build and support the growing neon network with its branches in places like Vienna, Amsterdam, Tokyo, Paris and Cincinnati. It is meant to encourage growth and to furnish even the skeptical with enough curiosity so that the flow continues. I feel most fortunate in having been a catalyst in this very kinetic and organic process.

RUDI STERN

Graphics

It was never the intention of George Claude, who is generally acknowledged to be the inventor of the modern neon process about 1910, that neon should be exclusively associated with signage. He never considered the modest hair salon sign at the Palais Coiffeur on the Boulevard Montmartre or even the bold white neon advertising on the Champs Elysees to be a definition of the medium's potential. Claude felt that neon was a light source — and an important one at that. His colleagues and business associates, in their efforts to sell franchises, discouraged Claude from pursuing his initial intuitions about neon.

The tradition of neon as signage was established at the beginning and the perception continued in the public's mind until very recently. It was, of course, for this reason that the electric sign manufacturers felt proprietary about neon. They felt that the medium was entirely in their domain and under their control. We know now that the medium and craft can be used in many other ways and for many other purposes. Neon has been liberated world-wide from those old constraints. Now, with this new freedom, signage made with neon is breaking all the traditional boundaries formerly imposed primarily by those who controlled its manufacture. The customer never was privy to enough information about the process or its possibilities to ask for more than was evident or readily available. As a rule, the manufacturer never offered more. Thus, when neon was almost extinct in the 1960's, a good part of its decline was due to ignorance, misinformation and confusion.

The signage in this chapter is representative of fresh air that has blown into the sign shop. Its diversity is the result of a more sophisticated specifier, the greater freedom of the younger poeple who have entered the field, and the encouragement of new directions by suppliers. Many of the old and large sign companies have seen their neon production revived — often far beyond what it ever was. They no longer close their ears to questions from designers, architects and "peopleoff the street" as they used to. They listen carefully now to the aesthetic requirements of the customer. And where for years they would laugh at refuseor requests for innovation or turn down projects as being not "do-able" they have learned, through economics, to open their ears and eyes to the market as it is evolving. These examples of signage are indicative of how far the craft has traveled in the area of most resistance. It was in this area that the electric sign trade was most intransigent — would insist "your might have all that weird art stuff but we know how to make signs . . . that's our business. We've been doing it since before you were born."

No longer do the neon schools (not that there ever were more than one or two in this country) insist as they once did that students *only* make signs. No longer do young people think that neon is *only* for signs and no longer is there any inhibition about trying new approaches, new techniques, new hardware or pursuing however "crazy" an idea. Virtually nothing is rejected as being too strange, too novel or too complicated. With this new affirmative spirit, the medium is at the wonderful and precious moment where everything is considered possible, every idea worth trying, any experimentation encouraged. There is no longer a wall of resistance — either on the part of the manufacturer (no matter how large or conservative) or the public or the designer/specifier. All is open and a fresh page has been turned. The future of the medium of neon has begun. We are all fortunate to be a part of it and to enjoy the freedom which this marvelous craft offers. We are lucky to be working with neon at a moment when everything is possible and there are no academic or economic restrictions on what can be done. What a pleasure to work with a craft that is in the flush of youth and utopian freedom!

The urban environments where these signs live are the beneficiaries of this bright freedom. Cities, often composed of grimly mundane and anti-human architecture, are brought to street-level life by these signs and symbols which become important and meaningful landmarks by virtue of their freshness and energy. The arbitrary lines between "high art sculpture" and "commercial art" dissolve in the face of creative graphics which remain purely visual and enjoyable experiences even though they advertise or promote. Their life, while paid for by a client who wants attention, is not predicated on the message but rather now by the medium itself and the vitality it has come to symbolize.

Overleaf:
6 LEVEL RETAIL MALL PROJECT
One Broadway Place, Times Square, New York, N.Y.
Rendering: Communication Arts, 1989
Designer: Ferren, Wainscott, N.Y. Associates and Ferren
John Jerde: Jerde Partnership of L.A.
Joint Venture: Eichner Properties, VMS Development Corp., American Hazana Inc. and the Hahn Company

This multi-level collage of signs and symbols is related stylistically to Hong Kong's City Plaza II project which is a three-dimensional checkerboard of animated graphics. The center of attraction will be a computer-controlled multimedia audio-visual system called Whiz Bang. It will use automated lighting fixtures, elaborate trusswork with neon signs and a large-scale, full animation display system with liquid crystals, visible through a 6-story cylindrical glass wall.

Marketplace at the Grove, San Diego, CA
Owner: William J. Stone & Associates, San Diego, CA
Architectural Design: SGPA/Architecture and Planning, San Diego
Environmental Graphic Design: Richard Benson, SGPA and Integrated Signs, San Diego, Ca.
Fabrication: Integrated Signs
Photo: Courtesy: Integrated Signs, Curt A. Bauer
Photographer: Jim Simon

CAMPUS LEVEL SIGN
Bridgewater Commons, Bridgewater, New Jersey, 1988
Owner/Developer: The Hahn Company
Dimensions: 6'3" in diameter and 30" deep
Art Director: Henry Beer
Designer: Bryan Gough
Fabricator: Nordquist Sign Company
Photo: R. Greg Hursley, Inc. courtesy Communication Arts, Inc.
Materials: vacuum-formed acrylic, painted sheet metal, polished brass and neon.

This innovative mall signage utilizes neon in a multi-dimensional application. Freed from the constraints of traditional neon signage, talented designers are opening many new avenues of expression. The best examples, like this animated sign, are sophisticated sculptural statements.

TIME MAGAZINE COVER
Japan issue, August 1, 1989
Kimono: Nigel Holmes, Parsons-Meares Ltd.
Neon: Let There Be Neon Inc., New York, N.Y.
Photo: Ulf Skogsbergh

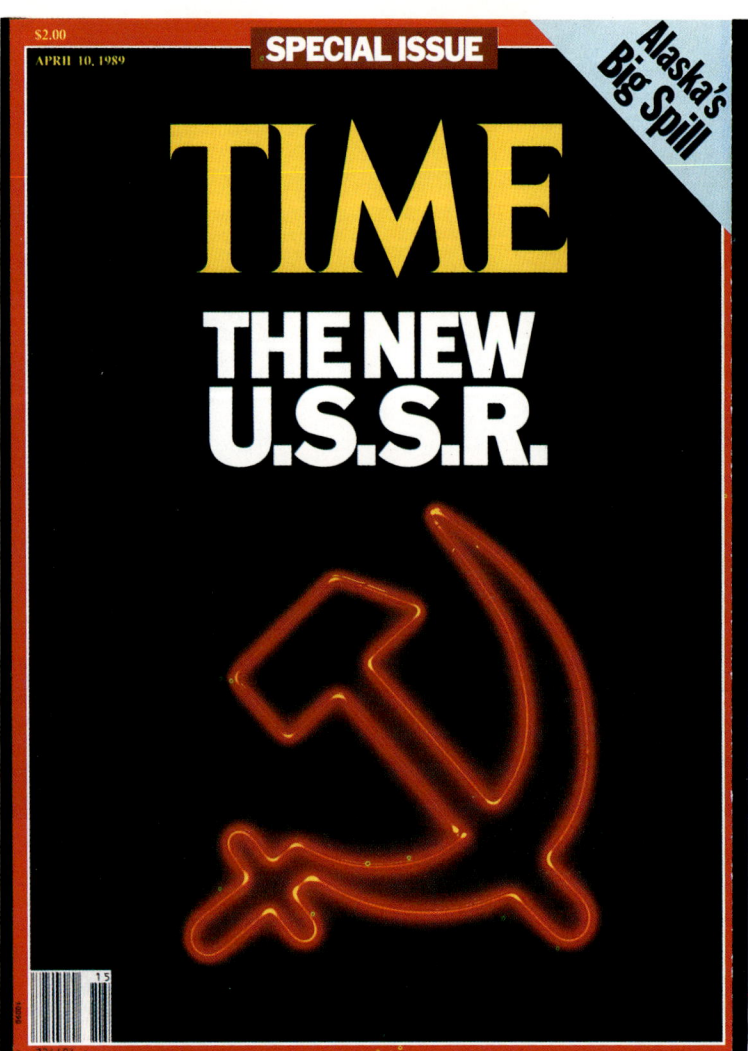

TIME MAGAZINE COVER
Soviet Union issue, April 10, 1989
Neon Sculpture: Let There Be Neon Inc., New York, N.Y.
Photo: Roberto Brosan
Art Director: Rudy Hoglund, "Time" Magazine
Photos courtesy Linda Freeland

MAIDEN FORM AD
c 1980
Photographd at: Let There Be Neon Gallery, New York, N.Y.

RADIO PACIFIC
Three Lamps, Ponsonby, New Zealand, 1986
Dimensions: 2.4 m high x 2.4 m wide
Materials: channel metalpan painted blue with remote transformer
Designer: Stirling Thomas
Neon fabrication and installation: Paul Hartigan, Gone on Neon Ltd.
Photo: Hamilton Lund

After half a century of conservative English neon signage by the original Claude Neon franchise in New Zealand, progressive "new wave" graphics have been promoted by Paul Hartigan and his Gone on Neon group in Auckland. These are examples of the fresh approaches he has set in motion.

SAKS: EXTERIOR SIGN
Auckland, New Zealand
Designer: Paul Hartigan, 1985
Dimensions: 3.2 m high x 5 m wide
Fabrication and installation: Gone on Neon Ltd., Auckland, New Zealand
Photo: Paul Hartigan

DETAIL FROM PLATO'S CAVE
The New Museum, New York, N.Y.
Designer: Remo Campopiano, 1983
Dimensions: 12′ diameter semi-circle
Fabrication: Neon Design in Minneapolis, Herb Jones, Prop.
Photo: Till Bartels

This was an art installation in the window of The New Museum that brings attention to a neglected U.S. Constitution.

BRIGHT CIGARETTES
Lieber/Katz Advertising, 1983
Dimensions: 8′ horizontal mock-up for a 48′ horizontal x 14′ vertical billboard
Consultants and manufacturers: Neon New York, Michael Hauenstein, Dir.
Client: R.J. Reynolds
Photo: Michael Hauenstein

This project was planned for a five city campaign. It involved a 28 channel computer-controlled animation program. Michael Hauenstein began working with Let There Be Neon, Inc. in 1972. His company, Neon New York, which was active between 1978 and 1985 was known for its experimental and innovative research. This project took two months of development with special emphasis on the animation effects. At the final presentation the client requested all the neon be turned on at the same time which killed the animation and thereby the entire project. The campaign moved into print and away from outdoor advertising.

MASSÉ BILLIARD CENTER
St. Pollen, Austria, 1987
Design, fabrication, installation: Neon Line, Vienna, Austria; Dusty J. Sprengnagel, owner
Photo: Dusty J. Sprengnagel

Green lacquered metal frame installed 2 1/2 meters from the building creates an interesting contrast and juxtaposition of neon letters against the Jugendstil facade. Neon Line's work is characterized by a sensitivity to style and composition.

CRAZY WEEKEND
Design, fabrication, installation: Neon Line, Vienna, 1987
Dimensions: 1.8 m. high x 2.8 m. wide
Photo: Dusty Sprengnagel

Designed for a young people's theater group in Vienna. It was used in 1989 for a French film production called "Eye of the Widow."

OMRON
Installed at Shibyua, near Hachiko Square, Tokyo
Client: Omron
Planning: Omron Communication Creates Co., Ltd. and
  Saiback Co. Ltd.
Design: Katsuhiko Hibino
Supervisor: Orikomi Co. Ltd.
Design/construction: Taisei Neon Co. Ltd.
Sizes: company name 15m (49′) wide x 4 m (13′) high.
  Display: 15 m (49′) wide and high. Neon tube total length
  3,300 m (3,608 yards). 335 Transformers
Photo: Shogo Togashi
Courtesy of Nobuyuki Sasaki, Sun Neon, Tokyo

A new style of Japanese neon influenced by U.S.A. street art.

CASA ROSSO
"de Wallen" Amsterdam's Red Light District, 1990
Installation: Neon Weka Amsterdam
Size: 10′ high
Director: Rob Nolte
Photo: Rob Nolte

ROCK CITY
Location: Cincinnati, Ohio
Copyright 1988
Fabrication: City Lights Neon
Dimensions: 42″ h x 60″ wide

The sign conveys the Rock & Roll attitude of the store and its contents: music fashion. The neon design evolved into "Flintstone"-like letters made with gradual undulations and surface bends of the clear glass with Argon/Hg. The skull's teeth are a tight series of double backs over double backs. The nasal and ocular cavities are intensified by black acrylic shapes.

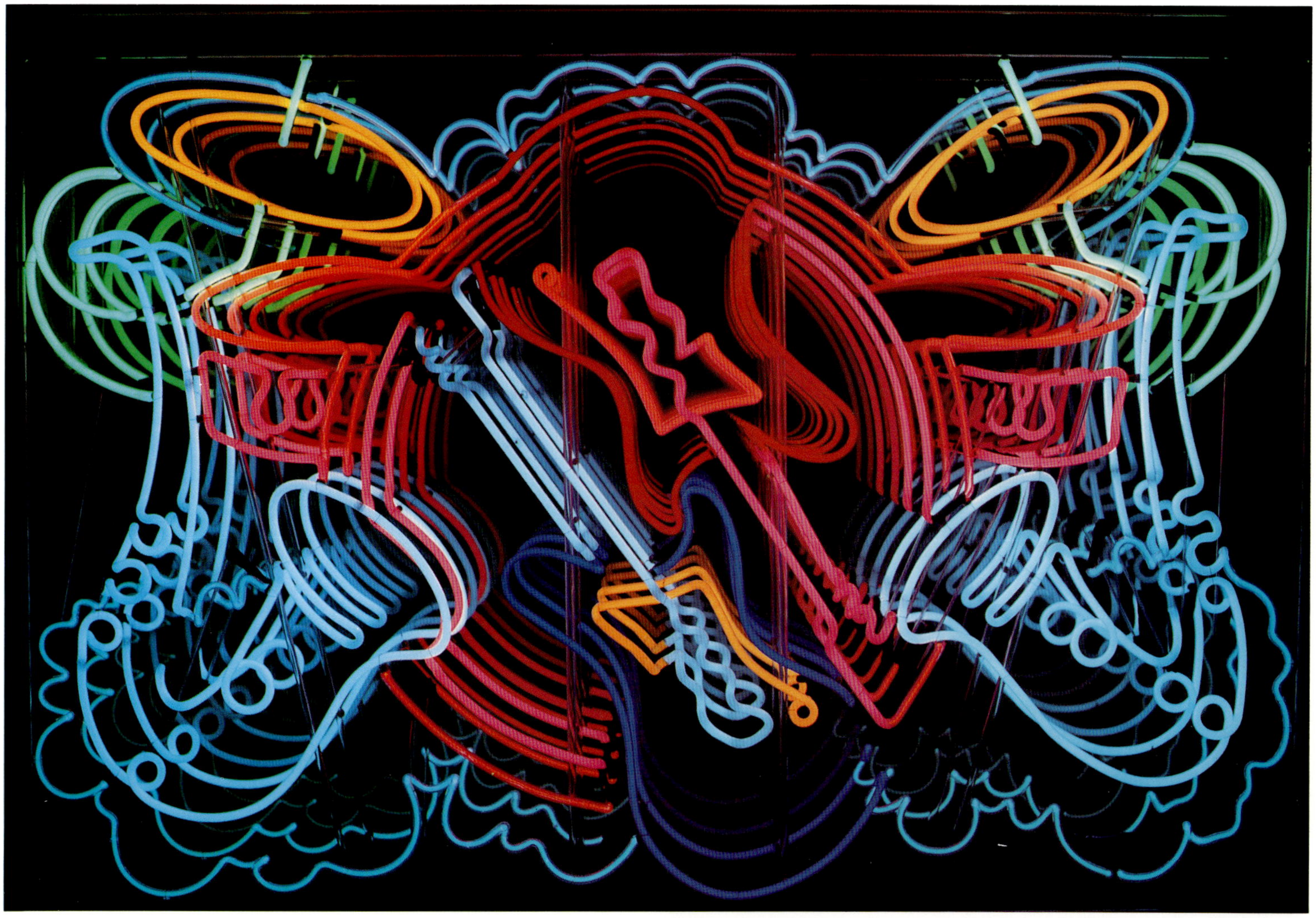

INFINITY IN SEE MAJOR
Design, fabrication, installation: Leland Johnson, 1981
Dimensions: 4.5′ high x 6′ wide
Materials: neon and mirrors
Photo: Leland Johnson

The artist describes it this way: "This piece is organized around the principle of infinite regression, where light bounces between mirrors until it dissipates. I meant to create a visual analogy to music using symmetry as a prime component. The viewer initially perceives chaos, similar to hearing an unfamiliar passage of jazz. As he moves past the sculpture, the image of instruments resolves itself into order."

MEMORIAL; KENT STATE 5/4/70
Artist: Bill Concannon, 1987
Photo: Bill Concannon

A site-specific installation at Kent State University, Kent, Ohio, employing neon, plywood and spray paint. This piece commemorates four students shot to death by the Ohio National Guard in 1970 in the wake of the U.S. invasion of Cambodia and the subsequent student demonstrations.

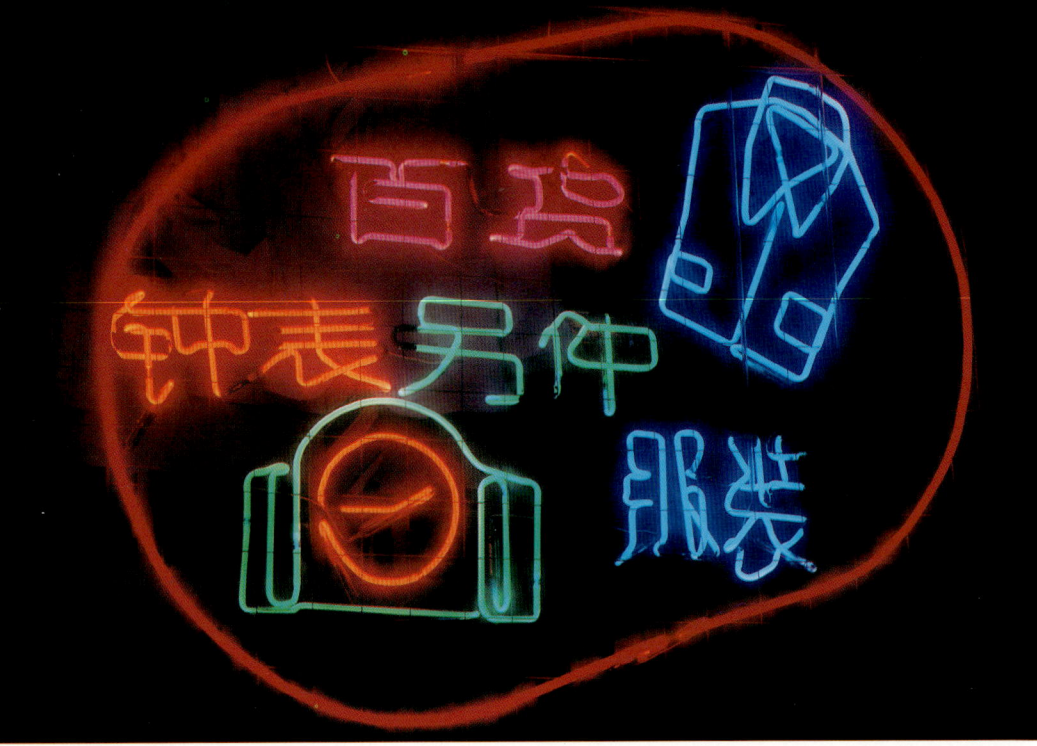

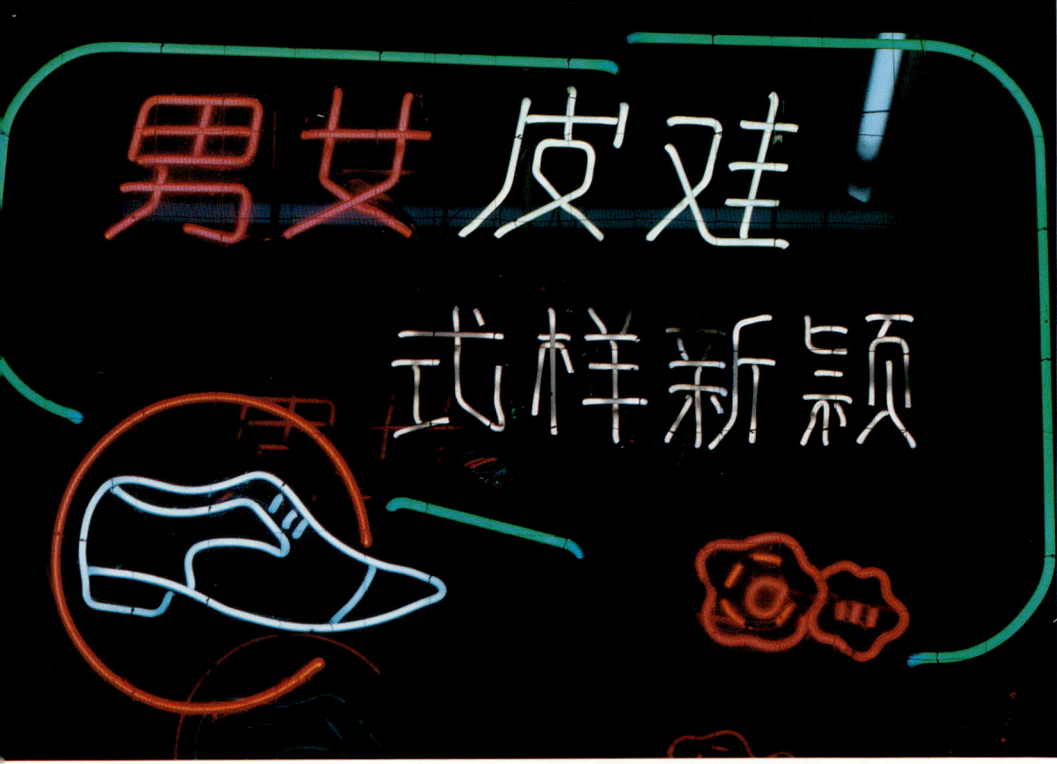

WINDOW SIGNS
Xian, China
Photos: Tom Sobolik/Black Star

A variety store selling watches and clothing. The greatest amount of neon activity in China is evidently still in Shanghai where the first Claude franchise was established in 1928. In a consumer economy that is struggling with other priorities, most of the neon activity (what little there is currently) is in what is known as the "private sector" which means private enterprise under state scrutiny. I have been working with a factory in Tianjin on developing some projects and have had an opportunity to marvel at their ingenuity and resourcefulness in the face of great difficulties. The skill of glass bending has a great tradition with only a straight-up torch in use, fueled by diesel oil. The streets of China tend to be quite dark and somber at night and the "neon people" are anxiously awaiting the time when they can put their skills to full use.

A men's and women's shoe store. Graphic representation has often the look of American 1940's neon with crisp, short-hand symbols and coloring book depictions. Many of the old neon craftsmen learned the trade from American correspondence courses. 8 and 10 mm tubing is, surprisingly, very much in use with hand coating giving a wider variety of colors than is normally available in other parts of the world. The signs, because of this, have very often a kind of hand drawn watercolor quality — quite delicate and fluid. The proximity of such a neon capital as Hong Kong has, because of import restrictions, been of no benefit to the craft in mainland China except as a manufacturing resource for assembled export products.

Opposite:
NEW WAVE NEON
Hong Kong
Photos: Dusty Sprengnagel
Top: Swing sign for video games, 12' wide.
Bottom: Swing sign for a real estate agency, 12' wide.

Stylistically somewhere between Las Vegas and Tokyo, these new Hong Kong signs are a break from the Crown Colony's tradition of Suzie Wong-type stage sets.

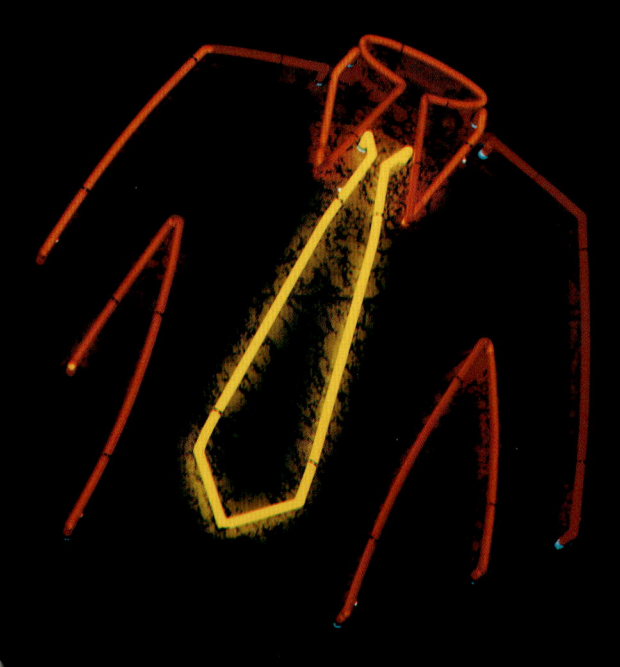

NECKTIES
Budapest
Photo: Till Bartels

3' square sign near Pariser Passage, an old shopping arcade from the turn of the century. Neon from the 1950's.

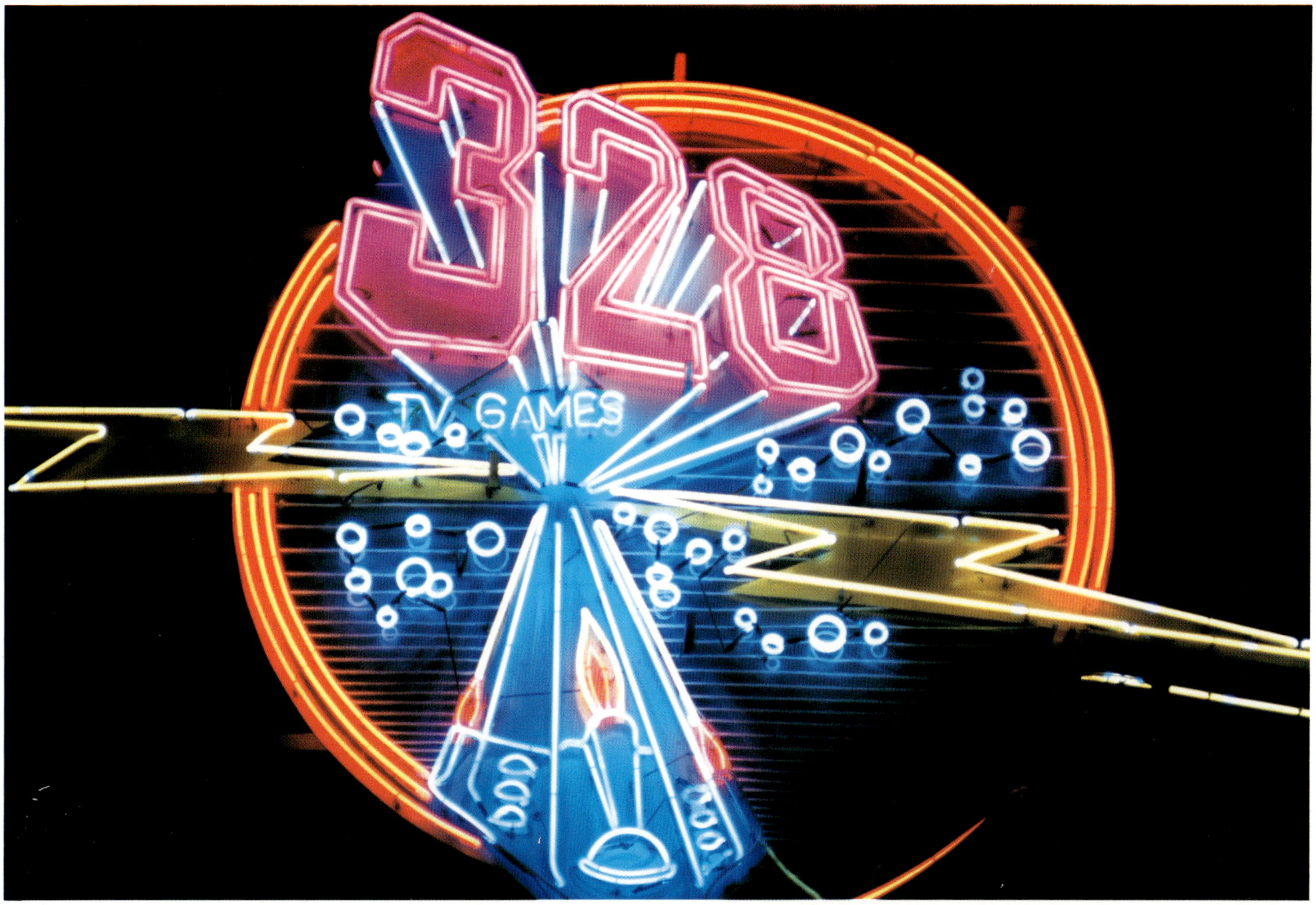
328
TV GAMES

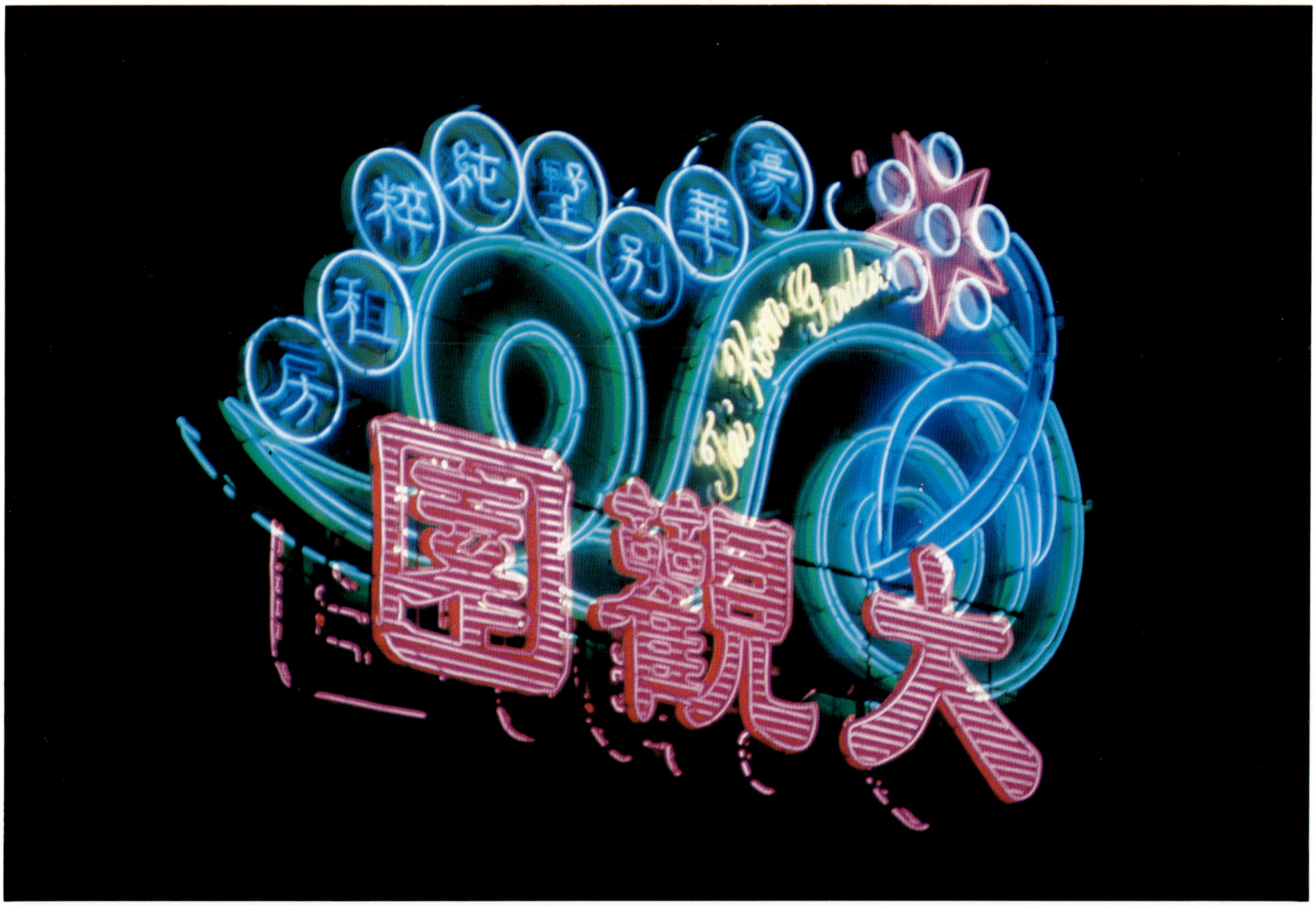
豪華別墅純粹租房
大觀園

ERROL CARROL'S HOLLYWOOD RESTAURANT SIGN
Re-creation by Richard Jenkins and his
 U.C.L.A. Extension Neon Design Class,
 1984
Dimensions: 13′ high x 8′ wide
Photo: Richard Jenkins

Richard Jenkins, a founder, with Lili Lakich, of the Museum of Neon Art is active as a teacher, consultant and neon artist in Los Angeles. This class project reflects his interest in neon's past and his teaching of design to students who will be drawing on the craft's traditions in their graphics and art work.

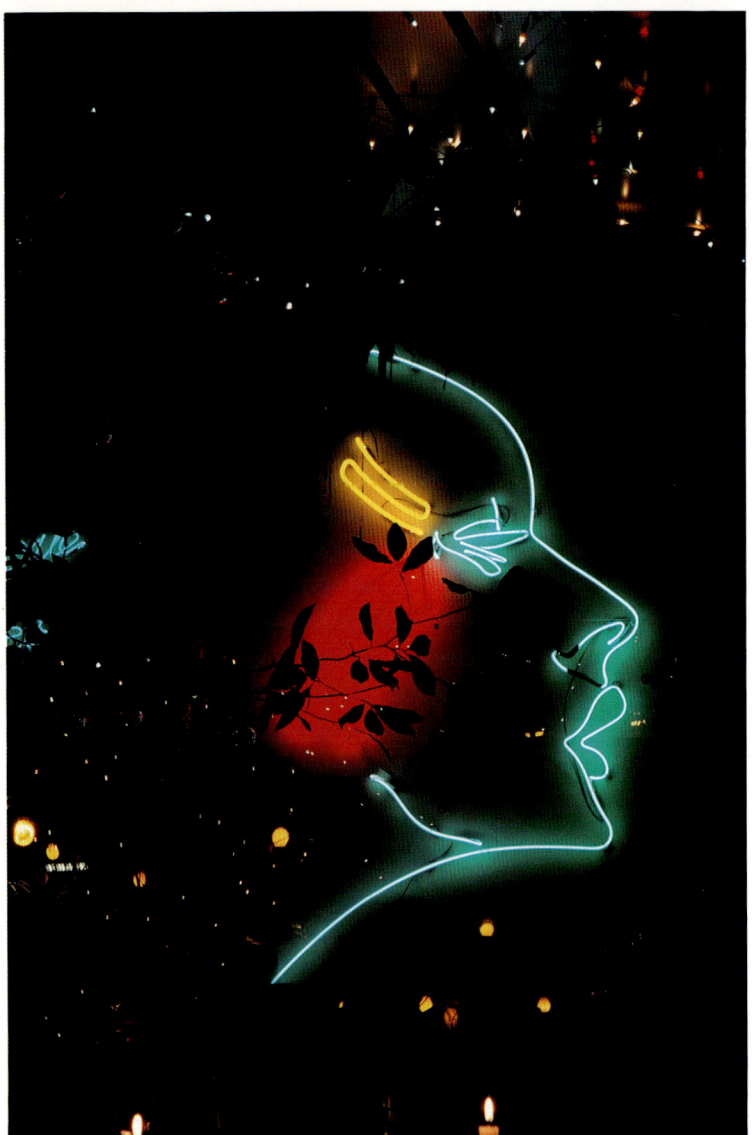

WOMAN'S FACE: RESTAURANT/BAR
Munich
Dimensions: 1.80 m high
Fabrication and installation: Simone and
 Olivier Michel, 1984
Photo: Till Bartels

This simple and elegant Schwabing neon design is an example of the work of Simone and Olivier Michel whose neon activities are now expanding beyond Germany.

BOGARD
Espace Neon, 114 Rue de Bagnoler, Paris
Dimensions: 24″ high
Designer, fabricator: Denis Lambert
Photo: Denis Lambert

Denis Lambert was a student at the state-run technical school in Paris when I asked him to work with us at Let There Be Neon in New York. He returned to Paris to become the "Professor of Neon" at the same school. In addition to this, he and his wife Martine have a custom neon company called Espace Neon in Paris.

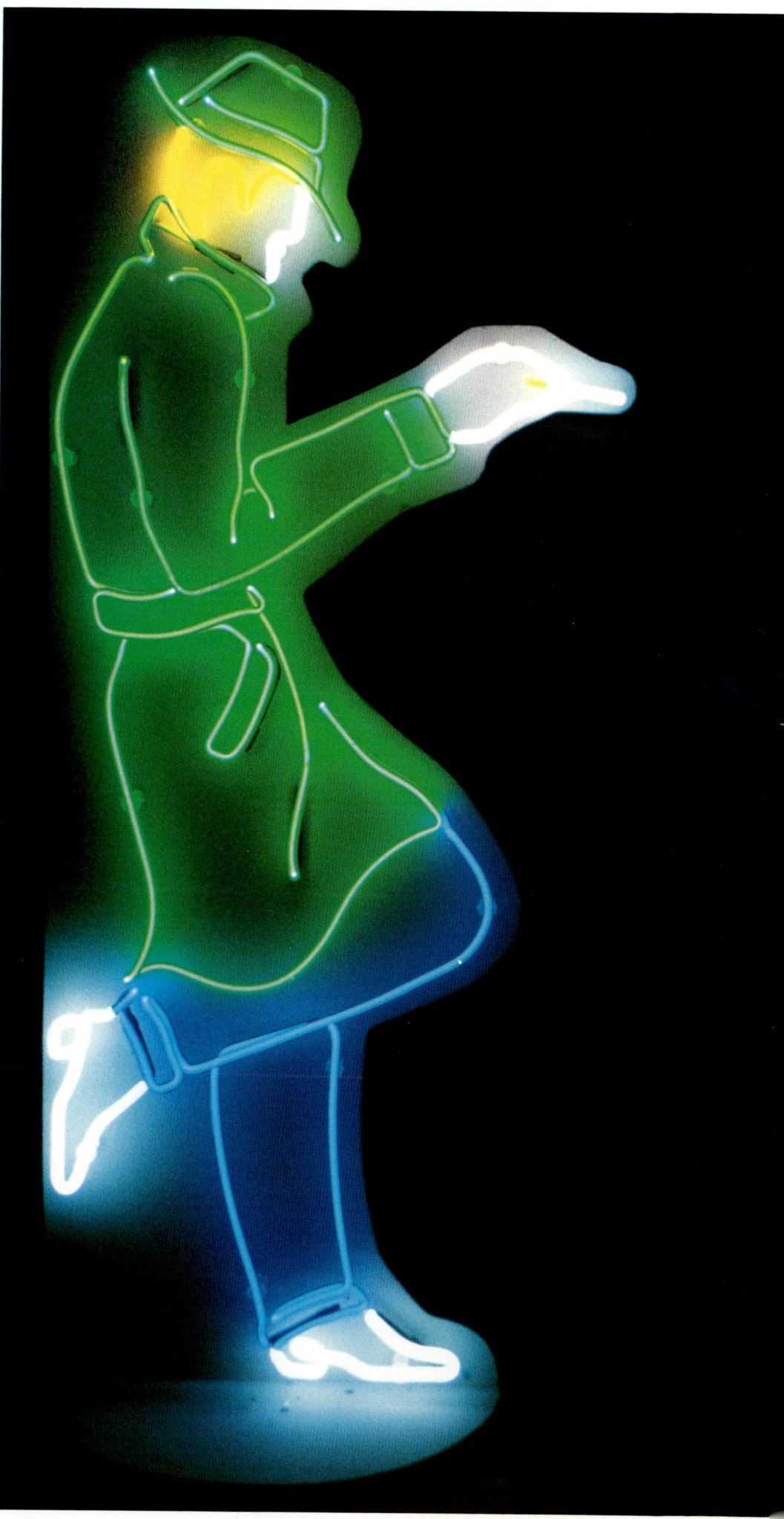

LOURNETTE
Stadtoptik, Ebreichsdorf, Austria, 1988
Acrylic form with neon sandwiched between transparent surfaces.
Planning and concept: Roderich Proksch, Architect
Design: H. Erwig Kucera and Dusty J. Sprengnagel, Neon Line, Vienna
Installation: Neon Line, Vienna
Photo: Dusty J. Sprengnagel

Beginning as a window trimmer, Dusty went on to work as a freelance decorator with projects for retail as well as trade shows. He had extensive film experience with design. It was after a world trip that Dusty came to specializing in neon design. He now directs Neon Line, which creates innovative design for the Austrian market and also, increasingly, for all of Europe.

"When dusk comes to a city, contours disappear and the great neon silhouettes prevail; the very heartbeat of the city is made visible," says Dusty.

THE MOONDANCE DINER
New York, N.Y., 1983
Designer: Alan Buchsbaum
Animated logo: Tim Fening
Fabrication: Jim Rogers in collaboration with Larry Hellenberg, who did the steel work.
Dimensions: 6′ diameter circle
Photo: John Stuart
Courtesy Larry Panish, Owner of The Moondance Diner

ED'S EASY DINER
King's Road, London
Designer: Design House, Camden, 1988
Dimensions: 500 mm high capitals and lower case letters
Materials: stainless steel and neon
Manufacturer and installation: Electroneon Signs Ltd.
Photo: Dusty J. Sprengnagel

LOMBARD STREET GARAGE
San Francisco, CA
Construction: neon and glass brick
Dimensions: 50′ vertical x 10′ horizontal
Commissioned by the San Francisco Art Commission for the San Francisco Parking Authority.
Fabrication and installation; Neon Neon
Photo: Melissa Hawkins

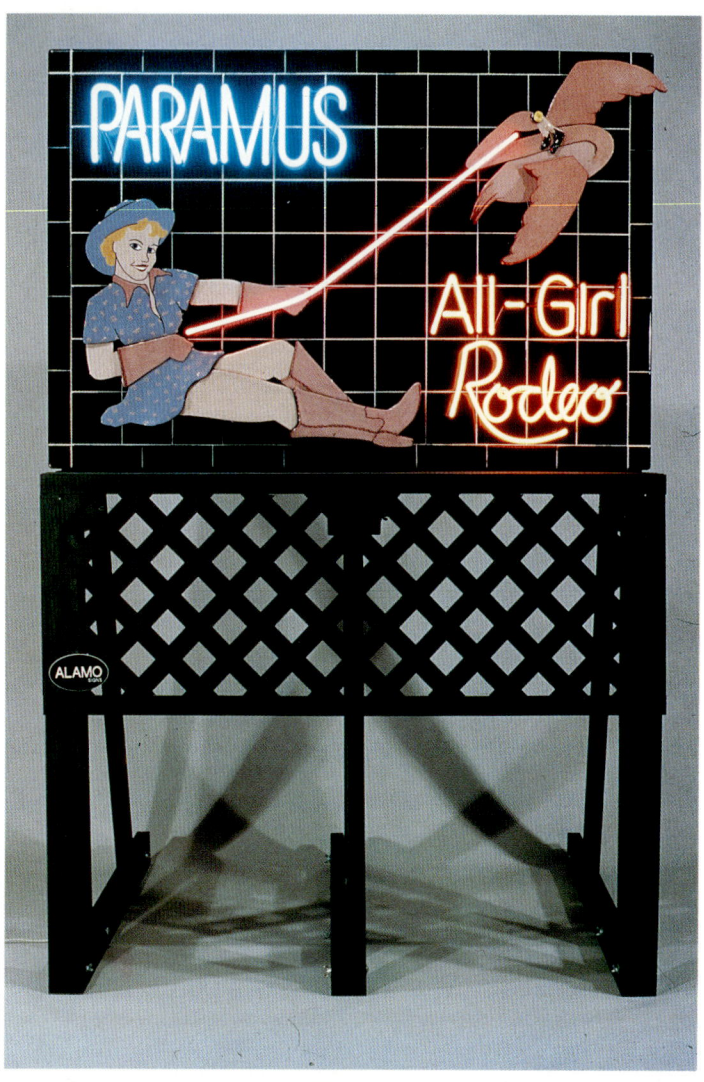

PARAMUS ALL GIRL RODEO
Designer: Tim Goeke

NOODLES RESTAURANT
New York, N.Y.
Designer: Allen Bank Associates, Allen Bank and Joseph Mastaduno, 1987
Fabrication and engineering: Joseph Mastaduno
Dimensions: 8′ high x 22′ horizontal
Photo: Aaron Rezny

This design was created to be both the interior's focal point and the restaurant's logo. The wall was surfaced with black leather and the bowl (which houses the transformer) was constructed of fibre glass. The gold neon "noodles" were bent three dimensionally, wrapped around the chopsticks, and extend 2′ out of the bowl.

PIZZA-A-GO-GO
Ted Bonar, Neon Projects, Washington, D.C., 1987
Dimensions: 40" high x 31" wide
Photo: Larry Kanter

This mounted interior sign is backlit acrylic with screen printing, cut-out and heat-formed acrylic shapes based on a logo design by Tom Snorek.

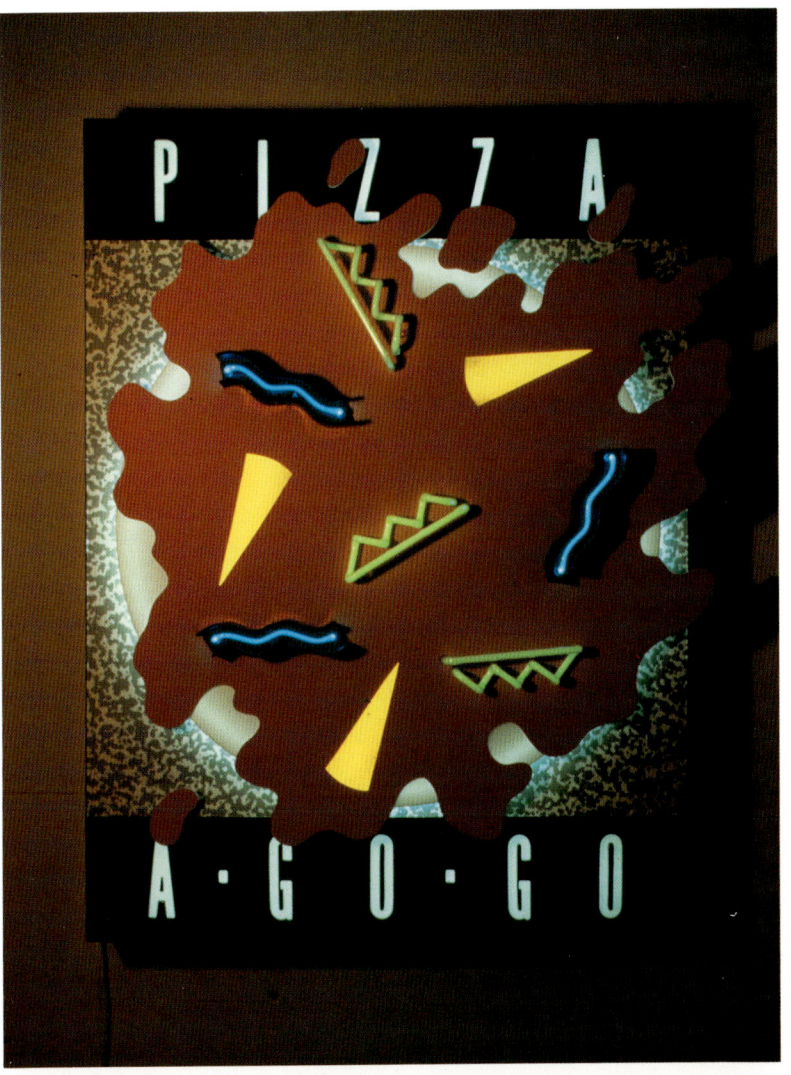

SCHWARZE'S CAFE
Berlin
Design: Christian Schneider, early 1980's
Dimensions: 4' horizontal x 3' vertical window sign
Photo: Till Bartels, Berlin

In a country that is not known for the dramatic excitement of its neon, Berlin stands out for a finesse and a sense of composition that is unique in Germany.

CLARION ANIMATED SPECTACULAR
Shibuya, Tokyo
Designer: Masao Omuku, President of Union Plan Co., Ltd., Tokyo
Photo: Masao Omuku, Union Plan Co., Ltd.
Courtesy Nobuyuki, Sasaki, Sun Neon, Tokyo

This animated sequence demonstrates the ingenuity of Japanese neon displays. Carefully conceived and executed, these spectaculars lend a memorable kinetic excitement to Japanese urban environments. They all seem to work together in clusters and have, collectively, such visual intensity that the entire cityscape becomes a cinematic fantasy of light and motion.

THE RED BALLOON
Kamiooka-Yokohama, Japan
Designer: Masao Omuku, President of Union Plan Co., Ltd., Tokyo
Photo: Masao Omuku, Union Plan Co., Ltd.
Courtesy Nobuyuki, Sasaki, Sun Neon, Tokyo

This is an example of the sculptural, three-dimensional rooftop signange which has been evolving in Japan. Emphasis is on the kineticism, not the particular product being advertised. The viewer is credited with enough sophistication to "read" the visual excitement and to thereby remember the sponsor. Visual impact secures response in the marketplace and advertising becomes an architectural feature rather than an imposition. Let us hope U.S.A. advertisers will also learn to trust the American consumer's intelligence!

OYAMA LIGHTING
Client: Oyama Lighting Co. Ltd.
Customer: Dentsu Sales Promotion Div.
Designer: Mr. Fumaki Nakamura, of Nakamura-ya
Installed at Ginza 4-chome. (Main intersection.)
Size: Front 8 m (26'3") wide, 6 m (19'8") deep 12 m (29'4") high.
Construction: 88 poles on a box frame with 400 flashing lamps and projection lights underneath.
Photo: Mike Marklew, Tokyo
Neon tube total length 1,500 m (1,640 yards).

The client is a manufacturer of lighting and wanted to highlight the light itself not the maker's name. The title of the sign is "Light Communication." There are 3 cyclic series of flashing lights, gradual illumination of the interior and a series of various colored neons. Each cycle lasts for 30 seconds.

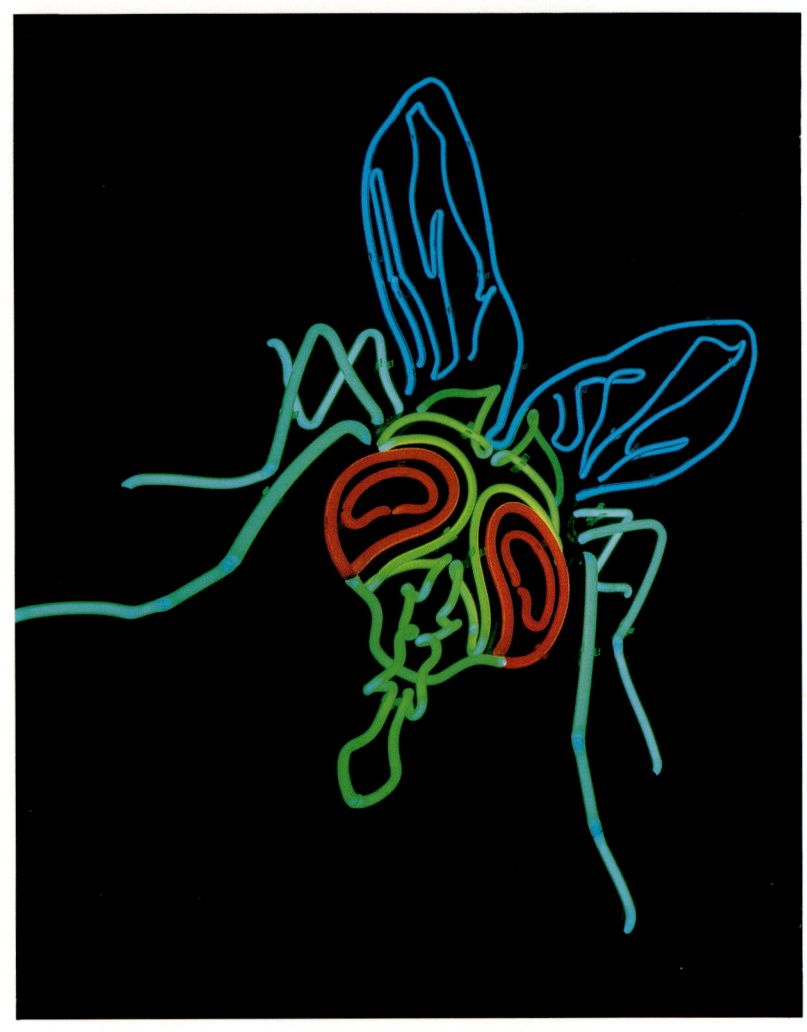

FLY IN THE OINTMENT
Cincinnati, Ohio
Fabricator: City Lights Neon
Designers: Dennis Dix and Dana Burton, c. 1988
Dimensions: 44" h x 33" w.

"The Fly," its designers tell us, "was originally a promotional piece which stated our credo in relation to the majority of the sign industry and was later purchased by the advertising agency, Sheppard & Associates." The Green Bottle Fly was displayed as if it were a huge, mutant fly form crawling up the glass of a hotel's atrium window.

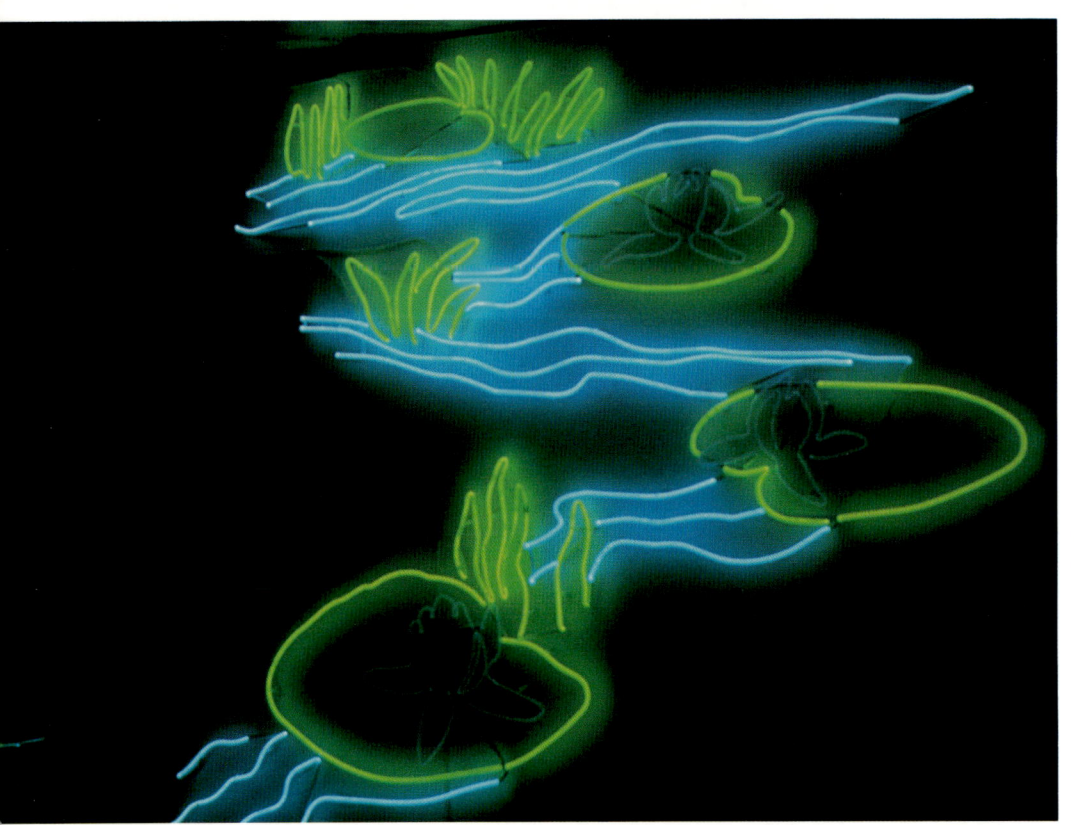

WATER LILIES BY RONALD SILVIO POMPEI
Dimensions: 10' high x 15' wide
Client: The Fish Market Restaurant, Philadelphia, PA
Fabrication: Dunn Signs, Philadelphia, PA
Full Size Cartoon: Carol Palarmo
Installation: R.S.Pompei
Photo: Ronald Silvio Pompei

"This wall sculpture rests in a two story space open to upper and lower restaurant dining rooms. The light levels of the piece are designed to compliment a quiet atmosphere as well as the lyric quality of the drawing," says its creator.

"TINA"
Designer: Gary Bane, 1989
Dimensions: 60" high x 48" wide
Created in collaboration with Neon East
Client: Erasmos Laundry, First Avenue and 11th Street, New York, N.Y.
Photo: Till Bartels

The designer comments, "Her name is Tina. The client wanted a modern woman doing old-fashioned laundry, so I based her on the Tina Turner cover of 'Rolling Stone' magazine."

SIGNAL COMMUNICATIONS LOGO
London
Dimensions: 141 mm high x 1005 mm wide
Designer: Arthur Ward for Signal Communications
Fabricator: Argon (Neon) Ltd.
Director: Frances F. Basham
Photo: Phillipa Bruckshaw
Courtesy Argon (Neon) Ltd., P.J. Mason and D.T. Caleno

BUCKEROO
Los Angeles, CA
Designer: Andy Janson, 1977
Neon fabrication: Charles DiBona, Custom Neon Inc., Los Angeles
Dimensions: 4' high x 7' wide
Materials: painted sheet metal and neon
Client: Jim Edwards
Photo: Charles DiBona

WINGED VICTORY
Hess's Hamilton Place Mall, Chattanooga, Tenn.
Designer: Norwood Oliver Design Associates Inc., New York, N.Y.
Photo: Stanley Kao
Photo courtesy Toni Frances Oliver, Noda, Inc.

KOOL KAT CLUB: HARLEM SHUFFLE
12 mm Veep Green and Fluorescent Blue pumped neon
Designer: Wolf Kroeger
Neon fabrication and installation: Mercury Neon Sign Corporation and Gallery, New York, N.Y.
Client: Bakshi/Verges Productions for Promotone B.V.
Photo courtesy Mercury Neon Sign Corporation

This set was made for the Rolling Stones video, "Harlem Shuffle." It won "*Billboard*'s" Music Video's Best Scenic Design Award.

NEON HAIR CASCADE SHOPS
Carnaby Street, London
Dimensions: 2 m high x 4 m wide
Designer: M. Jordan, Partyline Lighting Ltd.
Photo: Paul King
Photo courtesy Partyline Lighting Ltd. and Masonlite, D.T. Caleno

PALNEON, TEL-AVIV, ISRAEL

MARDI GRAS
Artist: Lili Lakich, c.1989
Dimensions: 24′ w x 4′ h x 2′ d
Fabrication: aluminum, copper, brass, glass tubing with neon, argon and mercury and helium gases.
Collection: Unity Savings, Brentwood, California
Photo: Jeff Atherton

Mounted on an interior wall facing San Vincente Boulevard, "Mardi Gras" is a rhythmic, two-part composition visible from the street and adjoining courtyard. Using the reflective surfaces of honeycomb aluminum, copper and brass as well as the wall on which the sculpture is mounted, Lakich achieves an impressionistic quality of light and mood, and layers the neon on several planes to create a dense texture of multi-hued light. The aluminum is hand-finished to catch light so that it seems to emanate from the metal itself. "Mardi Gras" is Lakich's second commissioned neon sculpture for Unity Savings.

OPEN NETWORKS
Advertising campaign for Siemens
Photo: Jan Keetman, courtesy Siemens AG
Costume and Set Design: Brigitte Pannen
Creative director: Brigitte Hitzinger, Siemens AG Europe
Fabrication: neon tubes up to 15′ long were suspended from the ceiling with thin nylon line painted black.
Neon: Chris Taylor

"I'm probably the only neon designer in Europe who is a professional advertising photographer and airbrush illustrator at the same time, so I specialize in neon decoration for film and photo sets, trade fairs, etc." says Chris Taylor.

BUD LIGHT SIGN
Electriglas™: Wordenglass: Kalamazoo, Michigan
Photo: Courtesy: Wordenglass

"Channels are etched into the surface of a flat piece of glass according to a design; when the design is complete, a second piece of glass is laid across and bonded to the first piece, forming a glass sandwich; later, gas is injected into the channels and electrical connections are made on the back side of the sign; when electricity is allowed to flow into the sign, the gas illuminates, creating a flat neon display. The resulting sign is called Electriglas™ and is about one-half inch thick. The product weighs about three and one-half pounds per square foot."
          Peter Farner, President of Wordenglass & Electricity,
            Kalamazoo, Michigan
          From P/O/P Times, Ted Isaacman, March/April 1989.

A very interesting new development in neon has been brought to the market by this product and process. The Company has found excellent response in all areas of point-of-purchase advertising. The Company feels that this is a "reaffirmation of their belief" is neon signage and not meant as a replacement of the traditional methods of production.

COFFEE CUP
New York, N.Y.
Designers: Nils Eklund and Rudi Stern,
 Let There Be Neon Studio, 1988
Dimensions: 4′ vertical. Cut out shape
 on casters.
Prototype for outdoor signage.
Photo: Rudi Stern

ISLAND VIEW: DESIGN DEPARTMENT: NATIONAL NEON SIGNS Pty. Ltd.
1989
7 m High × 1.800 m Wide (23′ High × 6′ Wide)
Client: Laurie and Marie O'Kane
Fabrication and installation: National Neon Signs Pty. Ltd.,
 Mitchell, A.C.T.
Photo: Jeff Schultz Photographics
Photo courtesy Verity de Fontenay (Wayne West, Managing Dir.)

"The past decade has seen an enormous re-awakening or re-discovery of neon signage in Australia.

The big difference between the past and the present is the quantum leap in sophistication of style and design. Whereas in the past neon signage was bland and strictly functional, today it is used as an integral part of the architecture adding a decorative as well as functional dimension.

Advances in technology have helped, with manufacturers being able to design signage of far greater complexity with the help of computers and more advanced manufacturing techniques.

Neon signage as an art form has also gone through a renaissance as more architects and designers discover the possibilities of neon. It can be found in large office and hotel interiors, clubs, discos and even art galleries in most of the major cities throughout Australia.

There's a very healthy future for neon in Australia due to the enormous marketing potential of this vibrant medium."

DRUM MAJORETTE
Marketplace at the Grove, San Diego, CA
Dimensions: 49′ vertical
Owner: William J. Stone & Associates, San Diego, CA
Architectural design: SGPA/Architecture and Planning, San Diego, CA
Environmental graphic design: Richard Benson, SGPA and Integrated Signs, San Diego, CA
Fabrication: Integrated Signs
Photo courtesy Integrated Signs, Curt A. Bauer
Photographer: Jim Simon

From *Identity*, Summer, 1989, page 31. (Published by "Signs of the Times"): "Back in the 1940's, a San Diego State University drum majorette of generous proportions and brilliant neon first twirled her rotating baton at the Campus Drive-In. She wore a feathered headdress and strutted — some said, in dubious taste — in front of a neon representation of the university campus landmarks, lighting a huge painted mural on the back side of the movie screen... She was taken down in 1983 ... and re-installed in 1988 . . . not far from her original site..."

The landmark re-dedication of San Diego's neon majorette capitalized on the community's commitment to "Save our Neon Organization" (a grassroots preservation organization). The developer and architect played a major role in the resurrection of this popular folk icon, unique to San Diego. The majorette was featured in national magazines such as *Time* and *Life*.

STEER
California School of Neon
Dimensions: 32″ x 31″
Photo: Jason R. Tomas

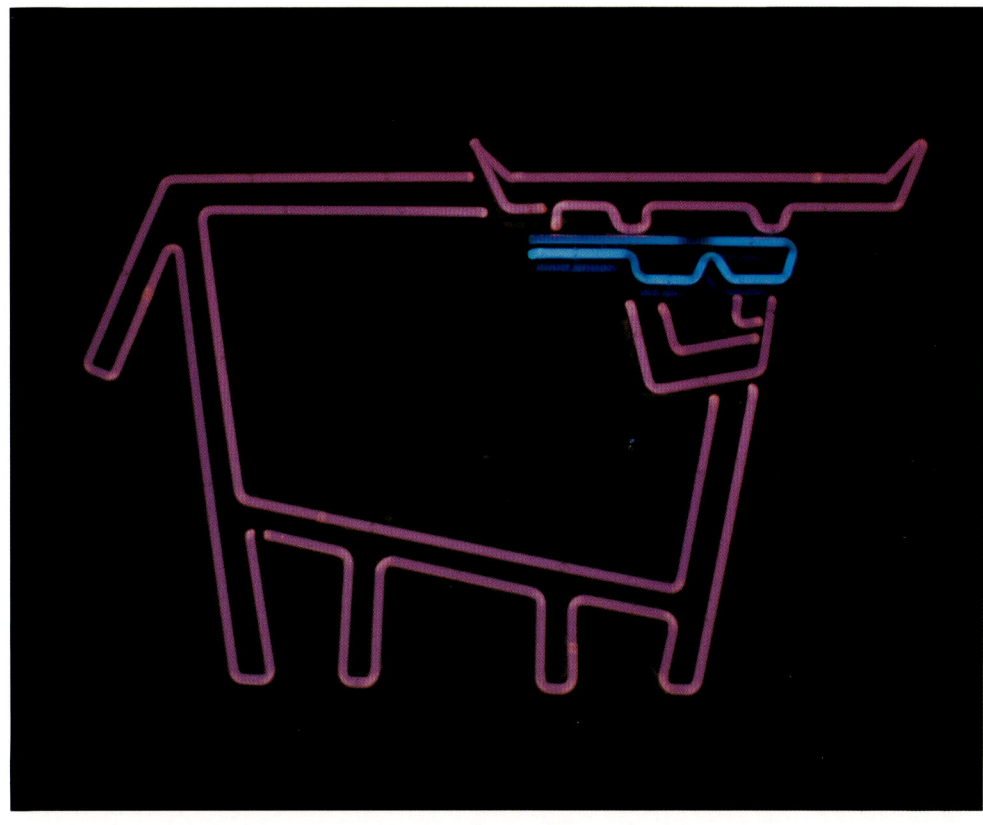

Architecture

Georges Claude, the father of neon, foresaw in 1912 the great potential of neon as an architectural light source. The early movie theaters on the Champs-Élysées made flamboyant use of neon as an Art Moderne embellishment. The delicate lines were as festively curvilinear as the Paris Metro signs and seemed as fluid as the flow of electricity itself. In retrospect, it doesn't seem accidental that neon began then. Every other material, whether plastic, iron, wood or ceramic had been stretched and pulled to satisfy the demands of spontaneous-appearing but laboriously-crafted designs. When Art Nouveau was at its purest, each individual component appeared to be immediate. This required the greatest discipline of craftsmanship because only mastery gave the impression of ease.

Media, historically, have a way of appearing when required by stylistic evolution. Neon was a fortuitous electric line with which French craftsmen highlighted and silhouetted Art Nouveau surfaces. Claude believed that this decorative application was more significant than information exchange.

Recently, architects, tired of vague hostile references to Las Vegas, have embraced neon as a normal design solution for the definition of spatial relationships. Now, as design sophistication grows, neon is taking its logical place with other accepted contract resources. The architectural uses of neon can be divided in two distinct directions. The first is neon for the definition of existing architectural and interior spaces. The second is neon as counterpoint where its use is more sculptural and three-dimensional. This latter is where neon is more sensitive to the play of forms around it. As counterpoint it creates its own presence, not dependent on its surroundings yet still adding to the overall composition. This direction tends, as one might expect, to be bolder in its applications. Sometimes, but rarely, both directions are in evidence in the same project.

Frans and Marja de Boer Lichtveld's work is purely architectural. It relates to the building forms, adds a kinetic dimension, and becomes partof the total environment. They carefully compose the movement of light in the spaces they work on. Neon is their choice for clarity and definition. Neon is the "signing."

Jan van Munster, the pioneer of neon as a public art medium in Holland, has developed an austere, rigorous linear discipline. Whether embedded in pavement or as an applied linear composition, his architectural works are distinctive and have had great influence in the field. Maryke de Goey's FNV project actually seems to pierce the building itself. Her work is known for its bold simplicity.

The Siña's with "Cascade" have used their single electrode tubes in a graceful rain-like composition which fills the vaulted space. Eric Zimmerman's "Gaylen Skylight" is a play of neon lines which amplifies and gives movement to the office below.

Paul Mathiesen and Wesley Thuro have combined cloth with indirect neon to create a rich light-painting for Harry's New York Bar in Toronto.

Michael Hayden's brilliant project for United Airlines is a good example of imaginative architectural neon. It serves to provide a moment's meditative respite in travel and works with the architecture. In a sense, the kinetic light *is* the architecture. It defines the space experientially. The careful orchestration of light and sound is an inventive concept that allows neon to make the space coherent. So, too, Hayden's New Orleans project allows neon to become a welcome architectural shape that has relevance to the rest of the space; the neon elements serve to unify the architecture.

Stephen Antonakos, one of the first sculptors to work with neon, has, in the last few years, found new inspiration with his architectural commissions. They seem to be fresher, livelier and more integrated with the spaces for which they are designed. For example, the Greektown Station in Detroit is a rich marquee of light spanning the street, connecting buildings with a luminous bridge.

Motoko Ishi is the foremost lighting designer in Japan. Her work with neon includes department store facades and atrium designs. She is represented here with several projects that attest to the diversity of her activities.

Patrick Bressette, with his "Star Chandelier," has created an interesting geometric design for an entry in a commercial building where simple and clean lines terminate in a neon fixture. Neon-Neon's arches serve to make a cafeteria more intimate without physically lowering the ceiling. Dana Burton and Dennis Dix have used a free-form ceiling line in their "Footlites" project to achieve the same results.

Paul Hartigan with his "Whipping the Wind" has created an architectural frieze which gives colorful excitement to a curved structure. Toni and Norwood Oliver's "Umbrella Ceiling" for Hess' department store uses neon to emphasize existing structure, as does the Pierre Heim Bulova Center.

Ronald Pompei, because of his unique background, is in a perfect position to use neon architecturally. His Garden State Racetrack proposal utilizes neon as an almost structural building element. In this project the medium serves numerous functions — all of them practical. The "Fantasy" project, designed by Joe Farkas, with its miles of neon seems related to a floating Las Vegas casino, which was his intention.

The "Trafikanten" Tower in Oslo is a neon landmark. Programmed light intensity and kinetic design are featured in this urban beacon. The Mars facade is a dramatic use of existing neon "fixtures" and the angled lines of light dramatize the club's presence. In Burgrov's Berlin project, neon is the event, a theatrical, temporary architectural event, integrating for a moment with the life of a city. It acts as a vibrant landmark while still a transitory and ephemeral "happening."

Carl Hillman has used the existing forms of Marley Station to create a neonized texture. The light fits with the architecture and even though it appears to follow it, the neon actually creates its own pattern quite independently. This is a good example of neon in functional, commercial applications having a life of its own while being used for specific architectural lighting requirements. Its visibility in daylight conditions is one of its appeals for the lighting designer.

The Charles Morris Mount design for McDonalds on 57th Street in New York is definitely a breakthrough in the area of fast food architectural design. The swirling ceiling lines and the soft refraction behind glass brick lend an up-scale glamour and sophistication which is revolutionary for such franchise operations. Here neon is used for specific design objectives which capitalize on its flexibility. As in his American Cafe project in Washington, Mount here proves that he understands the versatility and richness of the medium as probably few other designers.

With similarly theatrical intentions, David Rockwell designed the neon for Sushi Zen so that it creates a luminous and refined tableau. On another scale, the design of Chung Lee for the "Walkway to the Sea," in Boston, is amplified by Neo-Neon's dramatic vault treatment. There is no other medium which can be used for such effects since the lines of light must be uninterrupted for this effect. Geoffrey Hassman, the designer, and Michael Hauenstein, the neon specialist, made classic use of neon with their Wings Restaurant in New York. The curving line of pink animates and coalesces the interior space in such a perfect way that it would be hard to imagine using any other light source.

While designed for a travelling show as a modular construction, Richard Jenkins' Digital Computer neonized proscenium shows neon used as an architectural design element. The Riverchase project by Theo Kondos (as does Hillman's Marley Station) demonstrates the ability of neon to define atrium heights dramatically at night and functionally by day. Peter David's dance floor is an elaborate rendition of repeated shapes unifying a spatial design.

Neon Projects' Washington National Airport designs are crisp yet subtle highlights of existing conditions. The work of Larry Kanter and Ted Bonar is know for its discretion and attention to detail.

Leonard Davidson's I.B.M. Garage design, like that of Patrick Bressette, is a play of lines that, like a "cat's cradle," unifies the space and directs attention to specific points.

National Cathode was doing architectural installations long before neon was an accepted medium and Sy White's U.L. approved housings have provided a standard for years. Because of the smaller diameters available and the greater range of color, neon has been able to achieve more intricacy as an architectural design medium in the last ten years. While the lumen output is lower, neon offers more design potential than cold cathode.

Cork Marcheschi's "Davis's Tower" goes beyond sculpture, not because of its scale so much as because of the way it presents itself architecturally. So, too, Motoki Ishi's Seibu project with its mirrored stainless steel is a statement that integrates its surroundings in its realization. David Smotrich's Barnard College "neon tree" is functional sculpture, tying together various levels and conditions.

The next section deals with neon both as exterior facade ornamentation and as a design element creating new spatial effects. The Shinkobe Oriental City neon delineation is part of a recent revival of outlined structures. The Metro Night Club facade by Carmine Saccardo of Neo Neon is reminiscent of earlier 30's and 40's American Streamline effects.

The Financial Center rooftop project fabricated by Neon City and the Opus project realized by Brad Jirka are results of owners' desires to highlight their property in the competitive urban skyline. The Embassy Suites proposal by Bruce Fowle recalls Las Vegas but also points to new directions in neonized signatures, with its vertical fin connecting the signage below with the Bruce Goff-like forms on the tower. Had it been built, this emblematic design would have become a landmark in the Times Square area. The Wanchai office tower being proposed by Jeff Miller and the author is an attempt to create a neonized curtain wall that focuses on centralized geometry. Spandrels, see-through glass and airduct apertures are the symmetric basis of the design. This is potentially the first exterior treatment in Hong Kong of a facade with a neon pattern.

The isometric computer information about the Harborside Development project provided Ross Muir of Beyer, Blinder, Belle and myself with material to design a proposed contour silhouette as well as a giant neon clock facing the Hudson River and "front office" structures.

The Christmas decoration for *Imagination* in Covent Garden, London, is the conclusion of this chapter because it was strangely expressive of a desire to be "architectural" in its relationship with the facade. It relates, in its way, to Mundy's "Magic Garden" as pure intoxication with the medium of neon.

This survey, like the chapter on sculpture, shows the diversity of current activity. Unfortunately, the constraints on architectural projects are severe. Many levels of decision-making, the multiplicity of trades involved in a project and budget limitations combine to make this area of expression more restrained. However, with the growing sophistication of designers/artists and with the greater acceptance on the part of owners and architects, one can expect continued growth and experimentation limited in this country only by economic realities. The challenge for neon artists to work on architectural scales will remain an important and exciting one with no technical limits in sight.

Top left:
FIRE AND AMBULANCE STATION
Harlemmermeer, Netherlands, 1987
Designers: Frans and Marja de Boer Lichtveld
Materials: stainless steel, plexiglass, red and blue neon.

This 50' high octagonal form echoes the shape of the building. The neon acts as a 24 hour beacon as it reflects in the water and against the glass facade.

Top Right:
SCULPTURE DETAIL
Leiden Government Building, 1985
Designers: Frans and Marja de Boer Lichtveld
Fabrication and installation: Janse Lichtreklame, Eindhoven, Holland

Aluminum and yellow neon diagonally installed in the entry provide a glow through the glass roof, illuminating the entire space.

Left:
BAR
Amsterdam Opera House, 1986
Designers: Frans and Marja de Boer Lichtveld
Materials: stainless steel, plexiglas, mirrors and neon.
Photos: Frans and Marja de Boer Lichtveld

This abstract mirror/neon stairwell is a highlight of what has been called "the Opera of the 21st Century."

0 + -
Amro Bank Computer Center, Amstelveen, Holland
Designer: Jan van Munster
Neon consultation, fabrication, installation: Neon Weka, Amsterdam, 1989
Director: Robert Nolte
Architects: v.d. Broek en Bakema, Rotterdam, Holland
Photo: courtesy Robert Nolte, Neon Weka, Amsterdam, Holland

There is a strong tradition of public-commissioned sculpture in Holland; the "1% Rule" designates 1% of all public building budgets to art. Jan van Munster is one of the key artists in the development of neon as an accepted medium in architectural contexts.

FNV BUILDING, AMSTERDAM, 1990
FNV Building Sculpture: Maryke de Goey
Neon Consultation, fabrication, installation; Neon Weka, Amsterdam; Rob Nolte, Dir.
32.5 m. and 27 m tubes appear to go straight through the building
Photo: Victor E. Nieuwenhuijs
Courtesy: Rob Nolte, Neon Weka

Maryke de Goey is a talented sculptress who has been working with neon for many years. With the logistical help of Rob Nolte she is creating many important designs for public spaces.

These Dutch artists have been involved for many years with commissioned public sculpture and use neon as a natural artistic resource for defining form. Their work always relates directly to the architectural forms of which it becomes a part.

CASCADE
Rick's Cafe, Newton, Mass.
Designer: Alejandro and Moira Siña ©, 1988
Dimensions: 26" high x 15" wide x 1-1/2" deep
Photo: Alejandro and Moira Siña

This work consists of neon tubes suspended from the ceiling in order to create a three dimensional "light veil" in the arched wall space.

Alejandro and Moira Siña are artists from Brookline, Massachusetts who feel that their main distinction is in having developed tubes without electrodes, which gives their work an ethereal look.

GAYLEN SKYLIGHT
Designer: Eric Zimmerman
Dimensions: 10' x 10' x 4'
Materials: aluminum, acrylic tubing, neon tubing
Fabrication and installation: Archigraphics in Los Angeles
Client: Lou and Helene Gaylen
Photo: Rick Mendoza

Utilizing 4' neon struts encased in plexiglass tubing, the interior space of this skylight takes on a new dimension. A two-way solar mirror panel creates a reflective environment which is particularly stunning at night as pictured here.

Right:
HARRY'S NEW YORK BAR
Toronto, 1989
Project designer: Wesley Thuro, Div. of Luminescence
Lighting designer: Paul Mathiesen for Entertainment Technology
Neon ceiling fabrication and installation: Neon FX
Lighting and audio systems contractor: Entertainment Technology
Producer for Entertainment Technology: Wesley Thuro
Production manager for lighting installation: Anne Lough
Light control device: Pulsar Modulator IV and Dimmer System, LDS DR-1000
Photo: John Narvali

"... inspired by a Clarice Cliff design, circa 1929. The multi-layered, indirect neon system has three basic settings: a pale, architectural setting for the early evening, a stronger, secondary-color setting for the dinner hours and a deep, primary-color setting for after-dinner dancing."
                                    Lighting Dimensions.

47

SKY'S THE LIMIT
United Airlines Terminal for Tomorrow
O'Hare Airport, Chicago
Designer: Michael Hayden, 1987 ©
Photo: Michael Grosswendt

These concourses are connected only by a tunnel, 900 feet of underground congestion. United's competitive zeal led to the commissioning of art for the tunnel to turn a boring passage into something experienced for its own sake. California artist Michael Hayden was selected to design a lighting sculpture synchronized with music and orchestrated with architecture.

Hayden's solution, Sky's the Limit, uses 466 neon tubes and extends 744 feet. As travelers are pulled through this environment on moving sidewalks, they encounter monophonic tones and flashing white light. Then abstract shapes in color crash forward at speeds matching the music's tempo. A section starts with indigo and moves through the spectrum into yellow, with a middle section in orange, red and plum.

Pure neon colors are contained within Helmut Jahn's waving, translucent pastel sides and ceiling borders. The undulation "decelerates travelers" according to Hayden. The white neons are abstractly shaped. The blue/yellow neons are shaped by the curve. The red neons with V shapes reflect on the ceiling as diamonds, and the floor's cartographic semicircles also reflect on the ceiling. A light absorbing band of black provides a backdrop for all colors of the light sculpture.

"As one looks up one sees down. We become the sky. We become the limit," said Jim Billings in "Chicago: A Luminescent Happening, Hayden Sculpture at O'Hare," in *"Public Art Review,"* published by Forecast Public Artworks: Volume 1, #2: Spring/Summer, 1989.

GREEKTOWN STATION
Detroit, Michigan
Designer: Stephen Antonakos, 1988
Client: Downtown People Mover Art Commission, Detroit
Photo: Balthazar Korab

The creator of this street-spanning walkway speaks of his philosophy: "The task of an artist is . . . to be clear and truthful to your inner vision . . . I have always wanted to work in the purest, most straightforward way possible . . . I have never doubted that we live to reveal life. I have always understood that what I can do is try to create in visual terms how we understand our existence. . . For me the basic vocabulary involves placement, color, light and the inescapable unknown."

Right:
NEON FOR EMBASSY SUITES HOTEL
San Diego, California
Designer: Stephen Antonakos, 1988
Dimensions: 18′ high x 14′ wide x 12′ deep
Client: Pacific Market Investment Company
Photo: Phillip Scholz Ritterman

"When I was picking up found objects such as umbrellas, chairs, bits of hardware and fabric from the streets of New York in the Fifties, one of the things that attracted me to them was their simple reality . . . I made paintings, collages, constructions. I love to place and attach real things one on another. The simplest geometric figures were the ones I couldn't escape from, and color, color as physical presence was necessary. The necessity has persisted," says artist Stephen Antonakos.

Below:
NEON FOR 42nd STREET
New York City
Designer: Stephen Antonakos, 1981
Dimensions: 43′ high x 105′ wide
Project: neon and metal raceways
Client: 42nd Street Redevelopment Corporation
Photo: Greg Heins

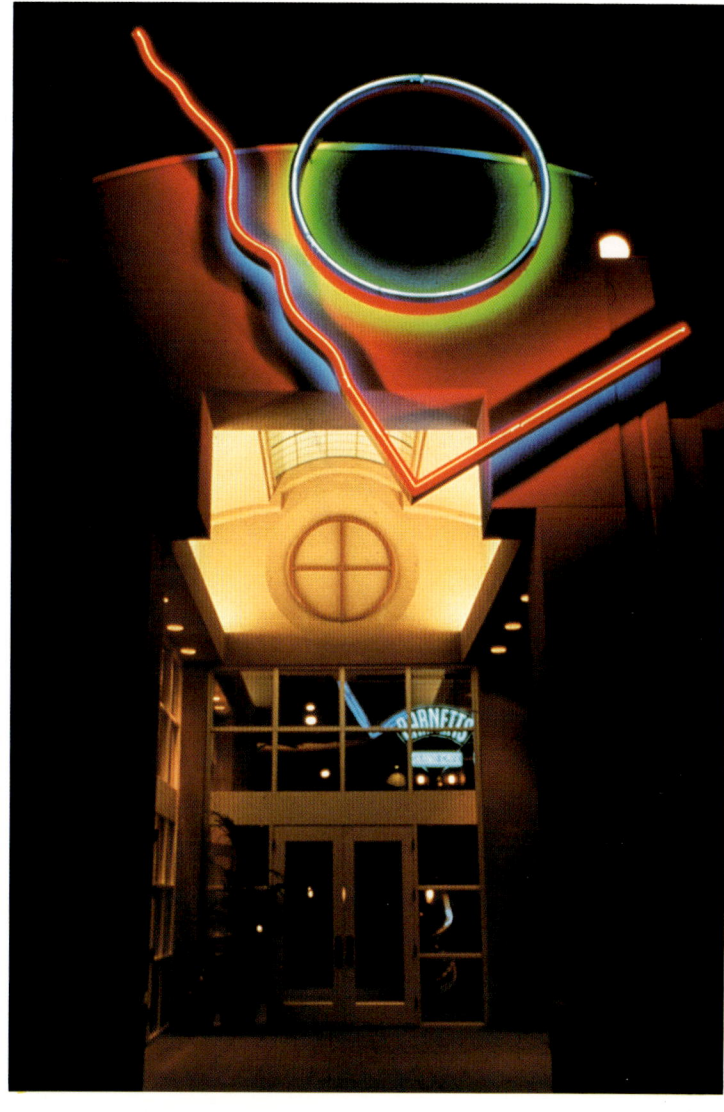

IKEBUKURO PARCO
Tokyo, 1978
Designer: Motoko Ishi Lighting Design Inc., Tokyo
Photo: Akihisa Masuda

"On the occasion of the remodeling of the building, the question of whether or not the facade could have soft lighting, rather than sparkling lighting, was posed. The uneven balconies contain halogen lamp fixtures making them look solid. In the middle there are rainbows of rhythmical neons, emanating a dynamic pattern."

STAR CHANDELIER
Designer: Patrick Bressette, 1988
Dimensions: 40" x 20' x 20'
Materials: neon and acrylic
Photo: Patrick Bressette

UNIVERSITY OFFICE PARK CAFETERIA
Waltham, Mass., 1988
Architects: Morris Nathanson Design, Providence, R.I.
Fabrication and installation: Neo Neon Inc.
Client: Vazza Associates
Photo: John Newman

FOOTLITES
1988
Artists: Dana Burton, Dennis Dix, Stephanie Gassman
Photo: City Lights Neon

"These innovative Cincinnati shoe retailers requested a decor as visually exciting as the merchandise. The sensual line of Bromo Blue coated neon tubing with neon gas lures the eye on an angled wing wall over the airy facade before piercing the center of a stainless steel canopy running the length of the store."

53

Top left:
WHIPPING THE WIND
Landcorp House, Wellington, New Zealand
Fabricator: Gone on Neon Ltd., 1988
Designer/Artist: Paul Hartigan, Auckland, New Zealand
Architect: Cockburn Millage Ltd., Wellington, New Zealand
Medium: neon and argon tubes on stainless steel
Client: National Mutual Property Group and the Wellington City Council
Photo: Paul Hartigan

Ten panels, each 3000 mm x 1200 mm, are on the second floor. Each panel is a separate circuit and the program takes about eight minutes to return to the beginning.

Above right:
CHILDREN'S WORLD
Hess's, Lehigh County, Pennsylvania
Umbrella ceiling: Toni Frances Oliver: NODA
Installation: Norwood Oliver Design Assoc., New York
Photo: courtesy Toni Frances Oliver, NODA

This sloping umbrella ablaze in colored neon rings behind Lexan is so animated that old juke boxes would hide their heads in shame.

Left:
CREO
Tsukuba Shopping Center, Japan
Lighting plan: Motoko Ishi
Photo: Motoko Ishi Lighting Design, Tokyo

Tsukuba is a unique experimental city. The Creo shopping center was planned to enrich its commercial facilities as well as to provide cultural interest and a lively human atmosphere. The pole lights at 4.5 meters add human scale; each pole has mercury and metal halide lamps as well as neon tubes.

GARDEN STATE RACETRACK
Cherry Hill, New Jersey
Proposal for a large scale light sculpture of neon and steel for the atrium
Designer: Ronald Silvio Pompei, 1986
20: full size mock up with neon behind fluted glass panels
Photo: Paul Wilson
21: rendering by Craig Slater

The designer explains: "This sculpture is conceived as a monumental ring of steel light and glass that engages the partrons of the race track. As they ascend the atrium escalator their visual connection with the sculpture changes." Mr. Pompei is a trained architect as well as a neon artist.

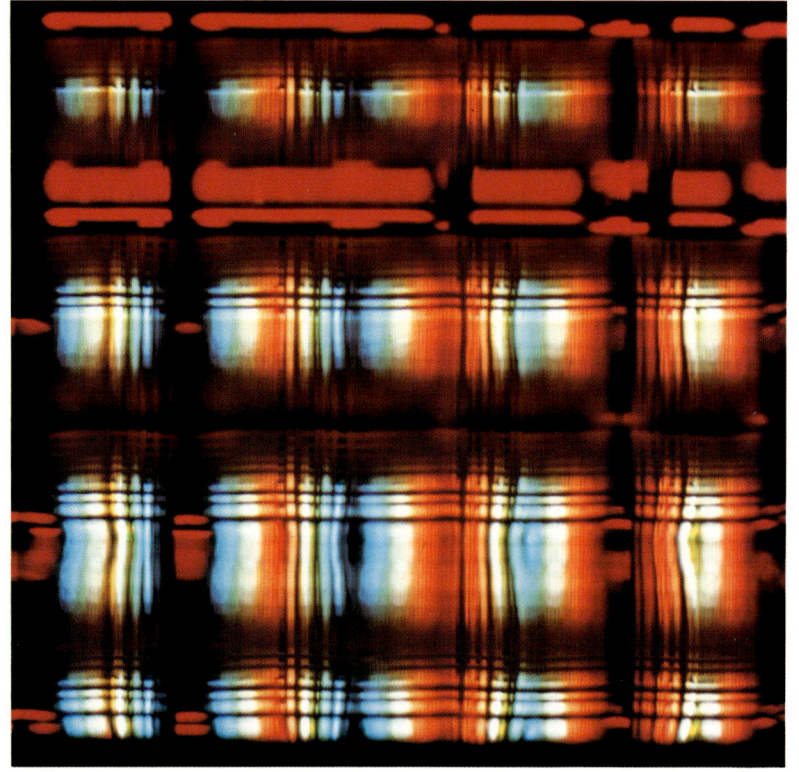

Above:
THE FANTASY
Owner: Carnival Lines, Miami, Florida
Architect: Joe Farcus
Construction: Masa-Yards, Helsinki, Finland
Neon system, design, fabrication, installation: Janse Lichtreklame
Director: David de Goede
Photo: courtesy of Janse Lichtreklame

The world's largest neon project includes 20 kilometers of neon. The after lounge alone covers 2,400 meters.

Facing page, top left
MARS
New York City
Facade design: Marc Malamud, 1989
Equipment: Universe Stage Lighting Inc.
Client: Rudolph
Photo: Tom Sobolik

This most ingenious facade was designed with a neon product known in 1987 as "Lazerstik." Self-contained units tilt at many angles making a porcupine-like texture, and wash the building in a bright orange glow.

Top right:
TRAFIKANTEN TOWER
Oslo, Norway, 1989
Designers: Graham Phoenix and Jonathan Spiers of Lighting Design Partnership, Edinburgh, Scotland
Materials: neon tubing directly mounted to steel and glass tower
Height: 35 meters
Neon footage: 585 meters
Architect of tower: Ola Mowe
Neon supplier, fabrication and installation: ElektroVakuum a.s.
Client: NSB (Norges Statsbaner) National Railway Company
Photo: Knut Valmot, ElektroVakuum a.s., Oslo, Norway

LITCHFELD STRASSE
des 17 Juni, Berlin, 1989
Below: Drawing for Project
Artist: Valerij Bugrov
Installation: Bezirksamt Tiergarten von Berlin and Aedes Galerie und Architekturforum
Technical information: 36 masts: 12 meters high; 139.7 mm diameter; 150 kg weight per unit; 1590 meters of neon tubing: 22 mm diameter: clear red; 180 transformers: 6,000 v. 40 ma.

Facing page:
WALKWAY TO THE SEA
Boston, Mass., 1986
Dimensions: 60′ high x 80′ long x 30′ wide
Materials: 12 mm 6500 white, 12 mm clear neon outlining steel trusses
Architects: WZMH Group
Designer: Chung Lee
Client: Marketplace Central
Neon fabrication and installation: Neo Neon, Inc.
Photo: Avanti Studios, Cathy McDermott

Left and below:
MARLEY STATION
Glen Burnie, Md., 1987
Owner: The Taubman Company, Bloomfield Hills, Michigan
Architect: design: Brown/McDaniel, Architects
Architect of record: Hoyem-Basso Associates, Inc.
Lighting designer: Carl Hillman Associates, Inc.
Neon fabricator: Triangle Sign and Service Co., Baltimore, Md.
Photo: Carl Hillman

Excellent examples of the integration of neon with architectural spaces. Carl Hillman used the medium of neon as a creative resource in the definition of space. It is clear from this usage that the foremost lighting designers in the U.S. recognize neon as a meaningful and valuable design component.

Facing page:
WINGS RESTAURANT
Soho, New York, 1983
Dimensions: 2″ deep x 2″ wide channel cut into the ceiling to receive the 12 mm orchid
Interior design: Geoffrey Hassman
Neon fabrication and installation: Neon New York, Michael Hauenstein and Martha Bills
Photo: Mark Ross

This project has always stood out for the clarity of its design and the integration of neon as an environmental element. Here pink neon defines and accentuates space as well as providing a compatible lighting quality.

Left:
McDONALD'S
47 West 57th St., New York, N.Y., 1988
Designer: Charles Morris Mount, New York
Neon: Neon City, Inc., New York
Photo: Norman McGrath

Below:
SUSHI ZEN RESTAURANT
New York, N.Y.
Designers: David S. Rockwell and Jay M. Haverson
Neon: Let There Be Neon, Inc., New York
Architects: Haverson/Rockwell, New York
Photo: Mark Ross

Facing page:
RIVERCHASE GALLERIA
Dallas, Texas
Dimensions: 17,000 feet of neon, 12 mm pink, white and blue
Architectural design: Hellmuth, Obata & Kassebaum, Inc.
Project designer: Bill Lacey
Lighting design: Theo Kondos Associates Inc.
Photo: William Mathis
Photo courtesy Theo Kondos Associates Inc.

Left:
DETAIL OF DIGITAL COMPUTERS CORPORATE SET, 1989
Concept design: Jim Leverton and Richard Jenkins
Dimensions of project: 150′ horizontal x 20′ vertical
Client: Digital Computer Corporation
Photo: Richard Jenkins

"An untouched area of neon is corporate theater where a vast market exists for those willing to take a risk. Normally, corporations use conservative and understated sets but when they decide to use neon it creates a dramatic statement," says designer Richard Jenkins.

Below:
NEON DANCE FLOOR
Bellevue, Washington 1989
Designer: Peter David

400 square foot floor of half inch tempered glass and plexiglas, with 21 foot wall of tempered glass infinity mirror, neon and video screens.

Facing page top:
SUMMIT BUILDING "F"
Valhalla, N.Y., 1987
Architect: T.A.C., Boston, Mass.
Engineer: Robert Parillo & Associates, New York
Cold cathode fabrication and installation: National Cathode Corporation, Jim Evanisko, President

Cold cathode was used as the general light source for each atrium corridor as well as to highlight the office building's architecture.

Right and below:
NATIONAL AIRPORT
Washington, D.C., 1987
Fabrication and installation: Neon Projects, Washington, D.C.
Architect: Kerns Group Architects, Alan L. Hansen, AIA, principal in charge
Photo: John Troha

The 1987 remodeling of this retail concourse at Washington's National Airport used materials seen throughout the original 1940 International Style project—architectural glass, aluminum, and neon lighting. Neon (cold cathode) tubes inside the glass block walls illuminate the walkway. Cobalt blue neon rings on the columns mimic airfield landing lights.

Below, left:
I.B.M. GARAGE
2005 Market Street, Philadelphia, PA
Designers: The Hillier Group, Maguire Thomas Partners & Davidson Neon
Dimensions: 32' x 16' suspended from a reflecting aluminum ceiling
Fabrication and installation: Davidson Neon, Philadelphia
Photo: Neil Benson

The neon ceiling design utilizes a geometric diamond motif that recurs throughout the IBM building. Beyond reiterating this architectural theme, the neon functions as a marker for the elevator access. This design works so effectively that it has opened up many new architectural applications of neon.

Facing page, bottom:
CRYSTAL PAVILLION
805 Third Avenue, New York, N.Y., 1983
Architect: Bromley-Jacobson, New York
Lighting consultant: Brian Thompson, New York
Cold cathode fabrication and installation: National Cathode Corporation, New York
Photo courtesy Jim Evanisko, president, National Cathode Corporation, N.Y.C.

"The use of the two colors (Filene Pink and Daylight) throughout the public areas enhances the general spaces and the artwork with a soft source of light utilizing a fiber optic dimming system," says Sy White, founder of National Cathode Corporation, and a recognized influence in the development of architectural lighting.

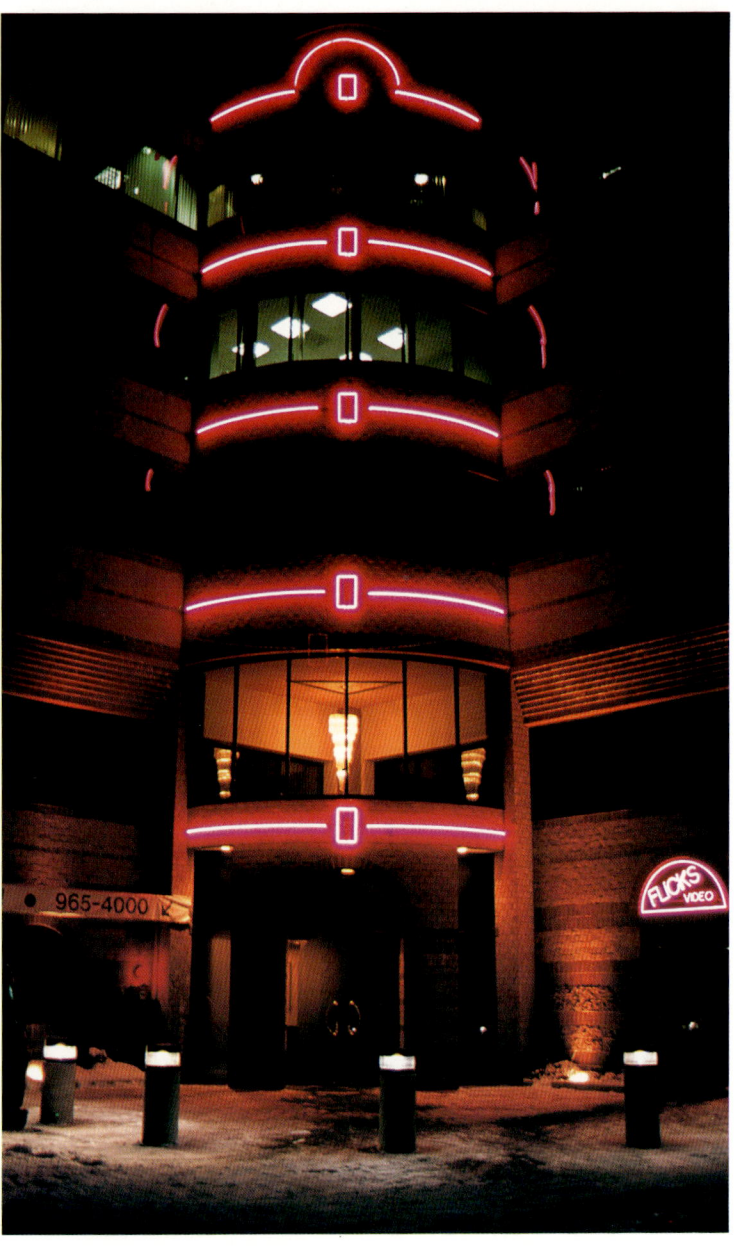

PARAGON TOWERS
Newton, Mass., 1987
Dimensions: 70′ high
Materials: 12 mm Voltarc Blue pumped with neon
Designer: Marvin Glick
Neon fabrication and installation: Neo Neon, Inc.
Photo: Carmine M. Saccardo

Right:
DAVIS TOWER
Davis, California, 1989
Creator: Cork Marcheschi
Dimensions: 32′ x 10′ x 10′
Materials: wood, steel, aluminum, plastics, neon, various transformers
Photo: Sandy Clifford

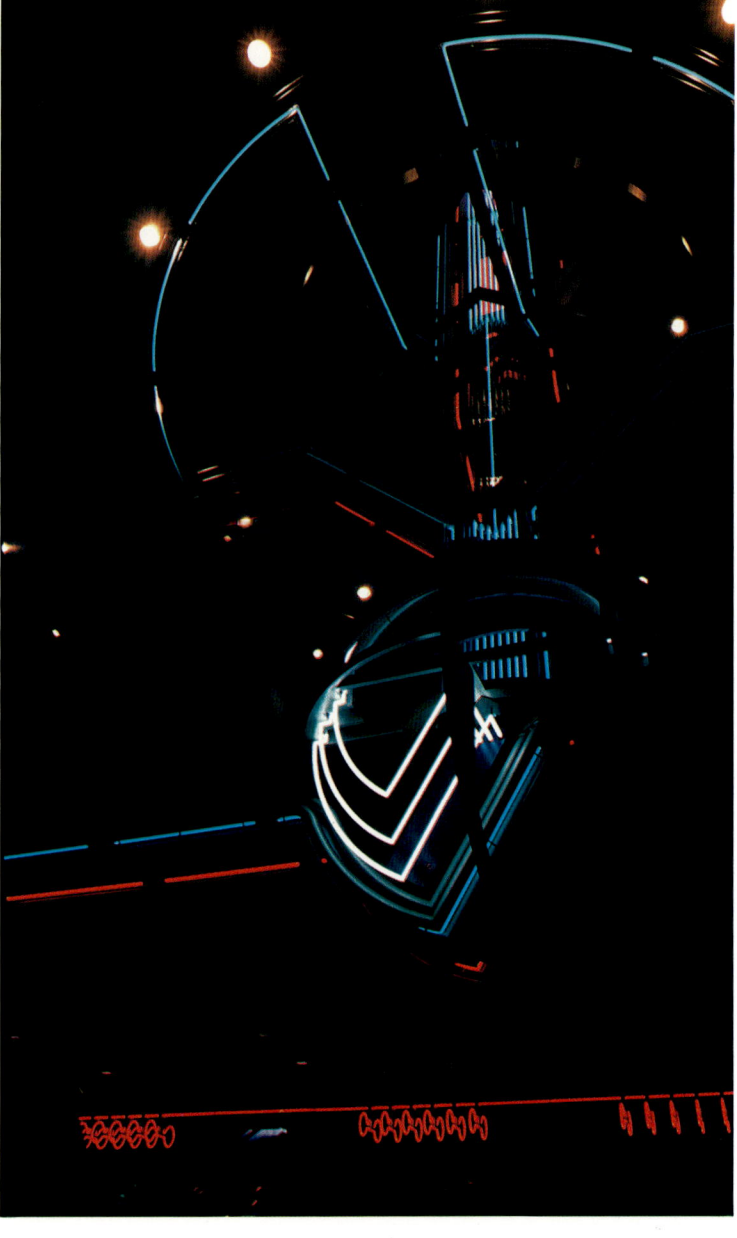

BERLIN CONGRESS HALL
Designer: Frank Oehring, 1979
Photo: Till Bartels

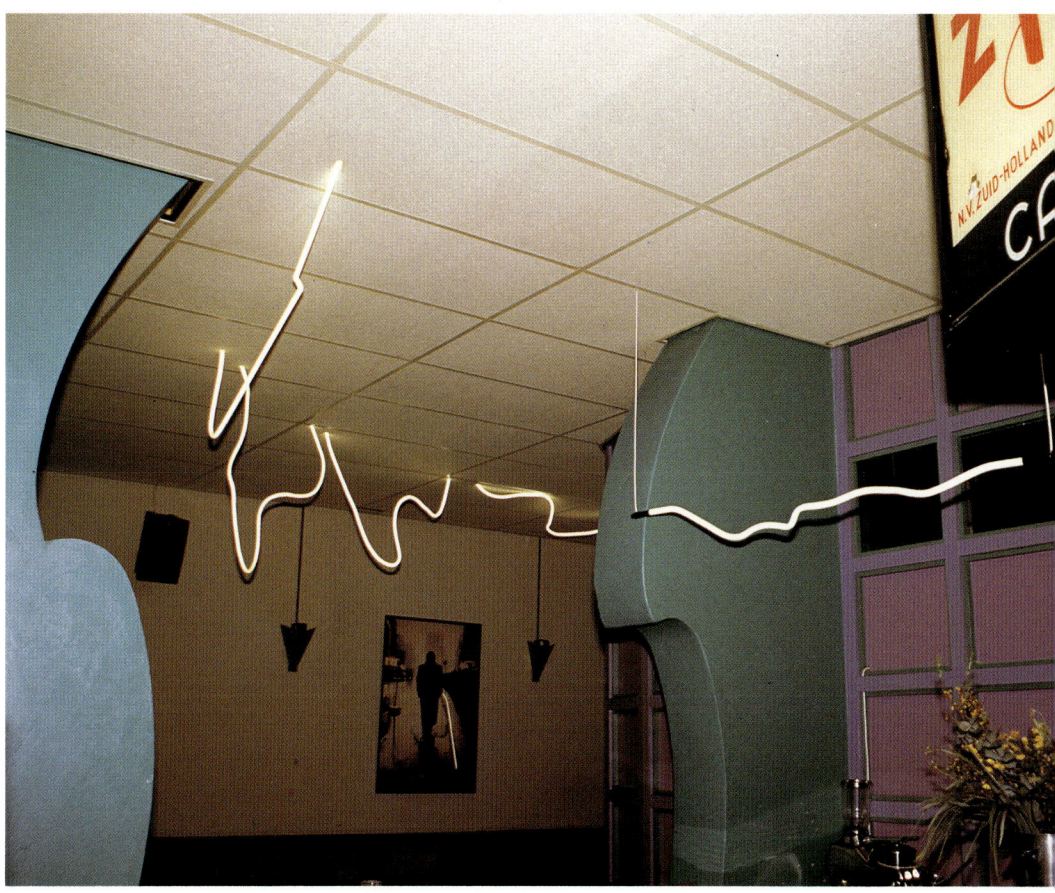

CEILING SCULPTURE
Groningen, Holland, 1989
Designer: Hein van de Water
Photo: Henk Wiersema

Hein van de Water has a multi-faceted, multi-media company in Groningen called Lunacy UN, Ltd. The neon was made by SiO2 in Groningen.

Top left:
AMS - SEIBU DEPARTMENT STORE
Sendai, Japan
Fabrication and installation: Motoki Ishi
Photo: Akihisa Masuda
Photo courtesy Motoki Ishi Lighting Design, Tokyo

Located opposite Sendai Station is the newly opened AMS Seibu Department Store. With three sides of the building facing onto streets, the department store offers seven entrances in all. Lighting for the first floor entrances is designed to be bright and attractive, while the second floor entrance offers a quieter atmosphere. The photo above shows the first floor entrance. A mirror effect creates a visual illusion of squares of neon tubes in the ceiling.

Below left:
WEND
Canal Place 2000, New Orleans, 1985 ©
Designer: Michael Hayden
Dimensions and materials: 140′ long, 96 neon elements. It is made up of 32 units each comprised of 4 light elements separated from each other by 4 1/2′.
Photo: Michael Grosswendt

Overleaf, top left:
BIG SPLASH
1987
Dimensions: 96″ x 96″ x 4″
Designer: Michael Young
Materials: neon, brushed aluminum, lucite, perforated steel
Photo: Michael Young

"This piece evolved from a practical need. The people who commissioned me wanted a sort of room divider to give them privacy from the view into the house through a large picture window. The piece adds drama from the outside and creates an interesting aquatic-like environment inside," says the designer.

Top right:
EIGHTH STREET PLAYHOUSE
New York, N.Y., 1980
Neonized design: Michael Hauenstein
Neon fabrication and installation: Neon New York
Photo: Michael Hauenstein

Two identical designs — one for each side of the projection screen. 3 channel sound animated wall sculpture. Modular units for easy maintenance which was a significant factor because the theater was home of the midnight Rocky Horror Show every weekend.

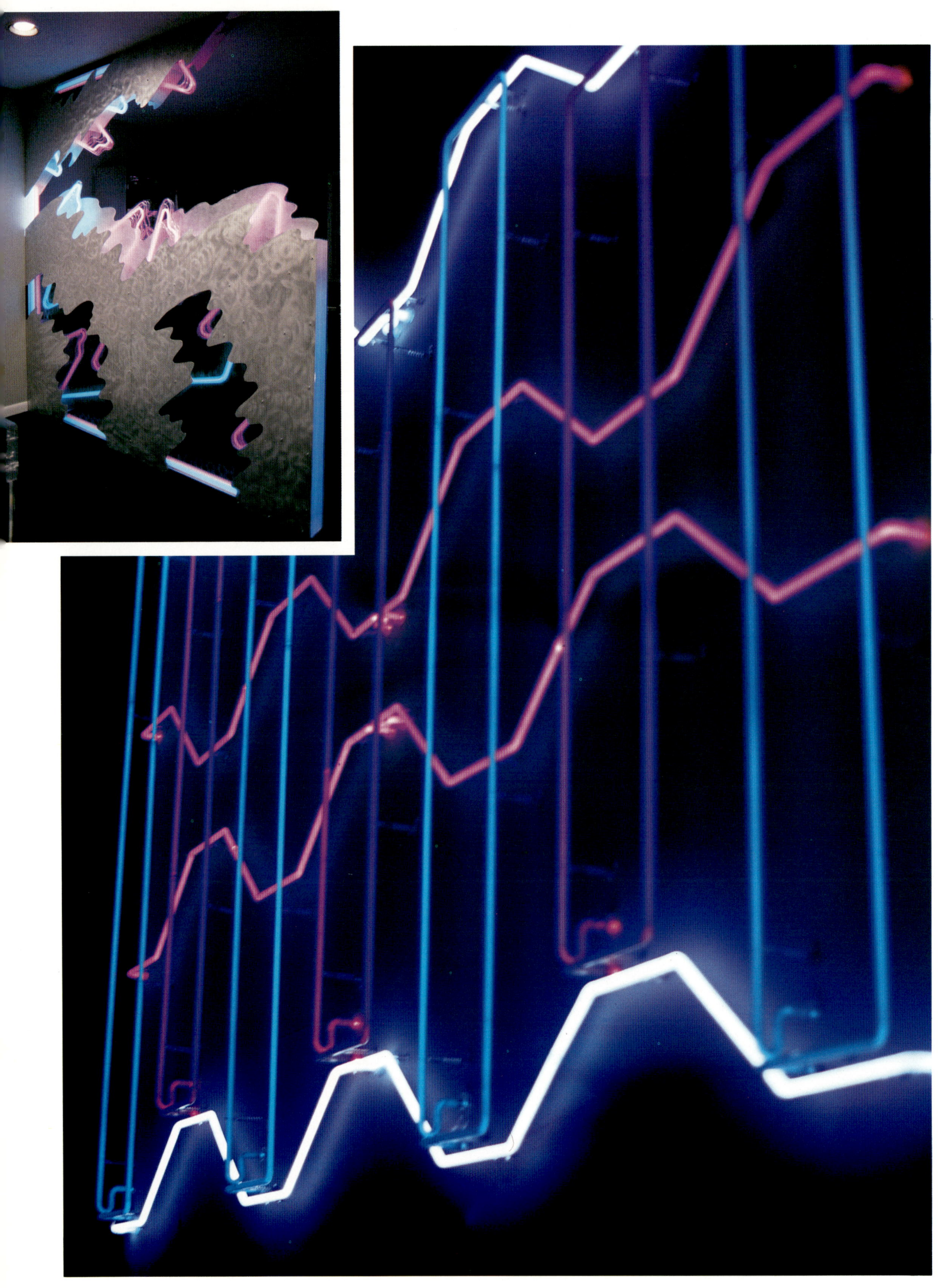

MCINTOSH STUDENT CENTER
Barnard College, New York, N.Y., 1988

Neon fabrication and installation: Manhattan Neon, Inc., Pat & Marilyn Tomasso
Architecture/interior design: David Smotrich & Partners, Architects/Planners
Design team: David I. Smotrich (partner-in-charge), Richard D. Saravay, Nancy McCoy
Electrical contractors: Gunzer Electric (lighting)
Special consultants, lighting: Theo Kondos Associates Inc.
Photo: Norman McGrath

"Interiors": December, 1988, Billboard Publications, Inc.: "To establish an immediate visual enticement, the designers created a neon 'tree' (with branchlike extensions on the upper level ceiling) in the center of the spiral stair which connects the two levels. The neon acts as a powerful visual lure on the above grade level, and spreads out, on the lower level ceiling, in three loose curvilinear lines informally linking the three areas of the lower level." Justin Henerson

Above:
THE SILVER DINER
Rockville, Maryland
Designer: Charles Morris Mount, Mount and Company, Inc.
Neon: R.J.P. Signs, Div of ADCORP
Photo: Doug Brown, Washington, D.C.

This project is the culmination of two years of research. The Silver Diner is a synthesis of many design ideas that express the classic American diner, a restaurant that pays homage to the past, yet turns itself towards the future. The strongest statement is the 26 foot glass block tower lit from within by an incandescent pendant light. Crowning this illuminated tower is a six foot clock outlined in exposed red and blue neon with the diner logo emblazoned on its face with the tag line "It's time to dine."

BULOVA NEW YORK RESTAURANT
New York, N.Y., 1989
Architect: Jean-Pierre Heim
Developer: Edward Blumenfeld
Coordination: Design Connection International, Tyrone Roper, Susan Blumenfeld
Neon installation: Let There Be Neon, New York
Photo: Serge Hambourg

COFFEE TABLE WITH UNDERGROUND PARKING
Dimensions: 16″ high x 48″ x 36″
Materials: wood, glass and neon
Artist: Steven Tatman
Photo: Steve Tatman

"It is both furniture and sculpture. I've always been a mad scientist at heart. As a kid I would hang out at the local college chemistry building buying chemicals for experiments that usually had something to do with pyrotechnics or making some sort of glowing potion. I remember the building had a lot of glass pipes throughout the basement and there would always be vivid and unusual colored liquids flowing through them as different chemicals washed down the drain from the sinks above. I've always found the convolutions of subterranean architecture compelling and mysterious. This is what I've tried to capture in 'Coffee Table with Underground Parking'." Steven Tatman

SOUND SPECTRUM
Vancouver, B.C.
Architects and designers: Stephen Emmerson, Perkins & Cheung Ltd., 1989
Dimensions: 42′ high x 34′ wide
Fabrication: steel, aluminum, neon
Sign fabrication and installation: Imperial Sign Corporation, Port Coquitlam, B.C.
Art director: Ted Baker
Photo: Ted Baker, Imperial Sign Corporation

This interesting and bold signage is an up-date on the visibility requirements of swing signs. The solution becomes, because of the strength of the graphic design, architectural. The art director describes it as "flying wedge of tubular steel utlizing 1,000′ of aqua and ruby red neon made in five pieces and assembled on site."

Right:
FAIRMONT HOTEL
Old Miami Beach, Fla. Historical Deco Area, 1989
Designer: Debra Lee Rose
Fabrication and installation: Abaca Neon Signs, North Miami Beach, Florida
Tube bender: Ron Zapata
Photo courtesy Abaca Neon Signs

The sign is designed and engineered using four colors of 1/8th inch acrylic; illumination is Voltarc turquoise coated glass pumped with neon and argon. All is mounted on plywood and metal for strength. The revival of Miami Deco has provided an opportunity for neonized architectural embellishments.

METRO NIGHT CLUB
Boston, Mass., 1988
Materials: 12 mm purple neon for outline. Sign, blue mirrored plexi, 12 mm Neo-Blue pumped with neon imbedded in acrylic stock. Lettering: 12 mm turquoise.
Neon fabrication and installation: Neo Neon, Inc., Boston, Mass.
Client: That's Entertainment
Photo: John Newman

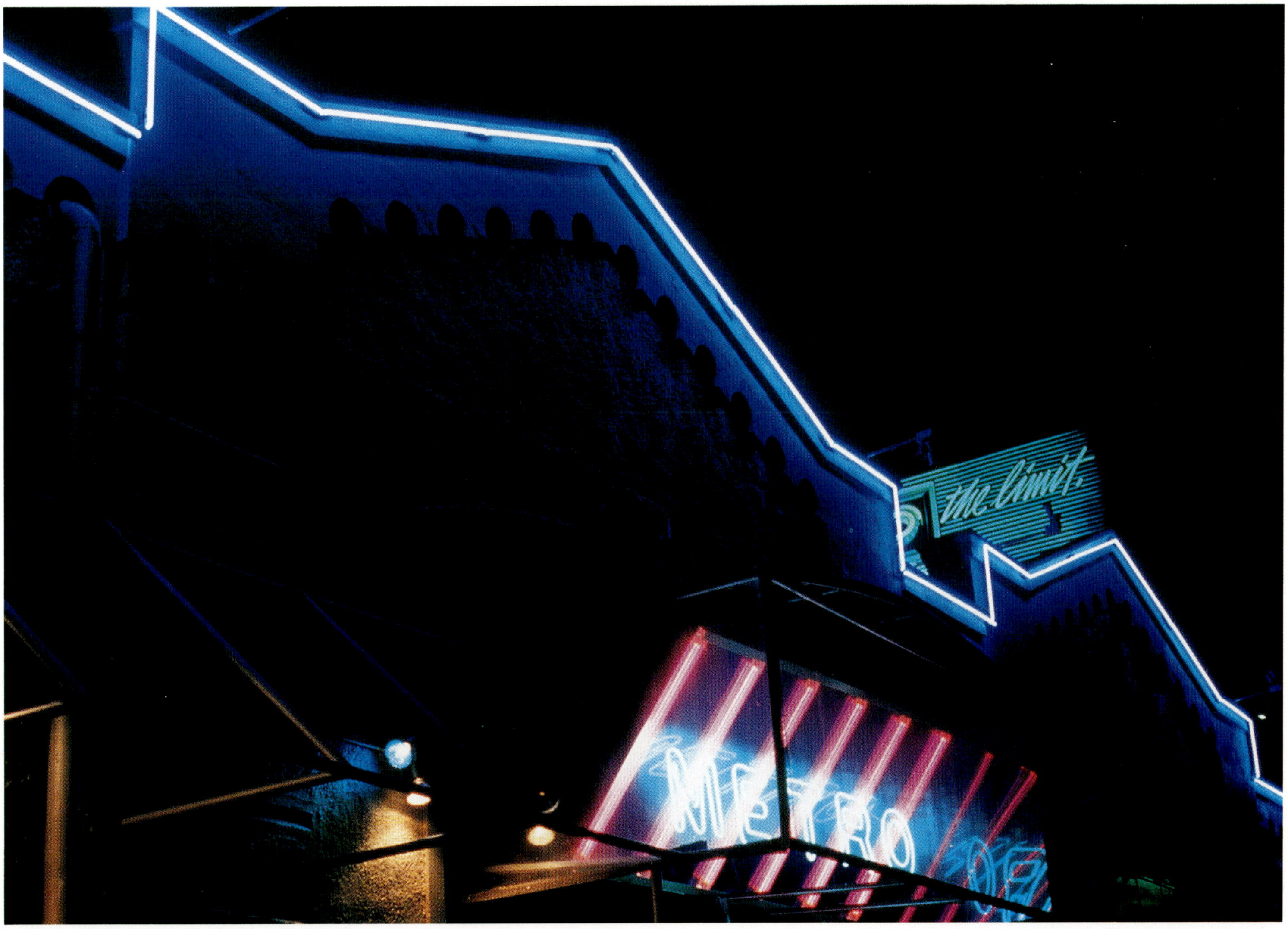

SHINKOBE ORIENTAL CITY
c3 Kobe: 1-1 Kitano-Cho, Chuo-Ku Kobe-Shi, Hyogo
Photo: Takashi Kamagata
Courtesy Nobuyuki Sasaki, Sun Neon, Tokyo

FINANCIAL SQUARE
Financial Center, New York, 1989
Design: Cosentini Associates, New York, N.Y.
Realization: Neon City, Inc., New York, N.Y.
Project manager: Harley Fine/Neon City, Inc.
Neon fabrication and installation:
 Neon City, Inc.
Photo: Abe Rezny

OFFICE BUILDING

under construction at Wanchai, Hong Kong
Size: 72 stories
Owner/developer: Sino Land Company Limited and Sun Hung Kai Properties Limited
Architect: Ng Chun Man & Associates
Renderer: Paul Rook
Neon facade and spire lighting: Lightsource Incorporated/Rudi Stern
Presentation: Jeff Miller, Lightsource/Rudi Stern

A proposal for a neonized facade in Hong Kong. In the Colony, there is almost no use of neon which is not related to outdoor signage, suspended swing signs in particular. We are looking forward to seeing this from the airport which is in the middle of the city.

OPUS TOWER ROOF
Minneapolis, 1988
Concept: Cain-Ouse Lighting Design
Material: 1,200′ FMS aqua
Consultation and fabrication: St. Elmo's, Brad Jirka
Photo: M. Corky Taylor

Brad Jirka with his company St. Elmo's and his American School of Neon in Minneapolis has been a respected neon practicioner for many years. He studied the craft with Cork Marcheschi and they founded the School, which is directed by Katherine Jones. The employment rate of graduates is higher than 90%.

RENDERING OF EMBASSY SUITES HOTEL
Times Square, New York, N.Y., 1989
Architect: Bruce S. Fowle, FAIA, Fox & Fowle Architects, P.C., New York, N.Y.
Project: marquee, building fin, roof top sign
Dimensions: marquee: 3′ high x 162′ wide; fin: 360′ high x 4′ wide; roof top sign: 24′ high x 80′ wide
Client: Silverstein Properties
Materials: painted aluminum and neon
Fabrication and installation: Artkraft-Straus
Rendering courtesy Fox & Fowle Architects, P.C., New York, N.Y.

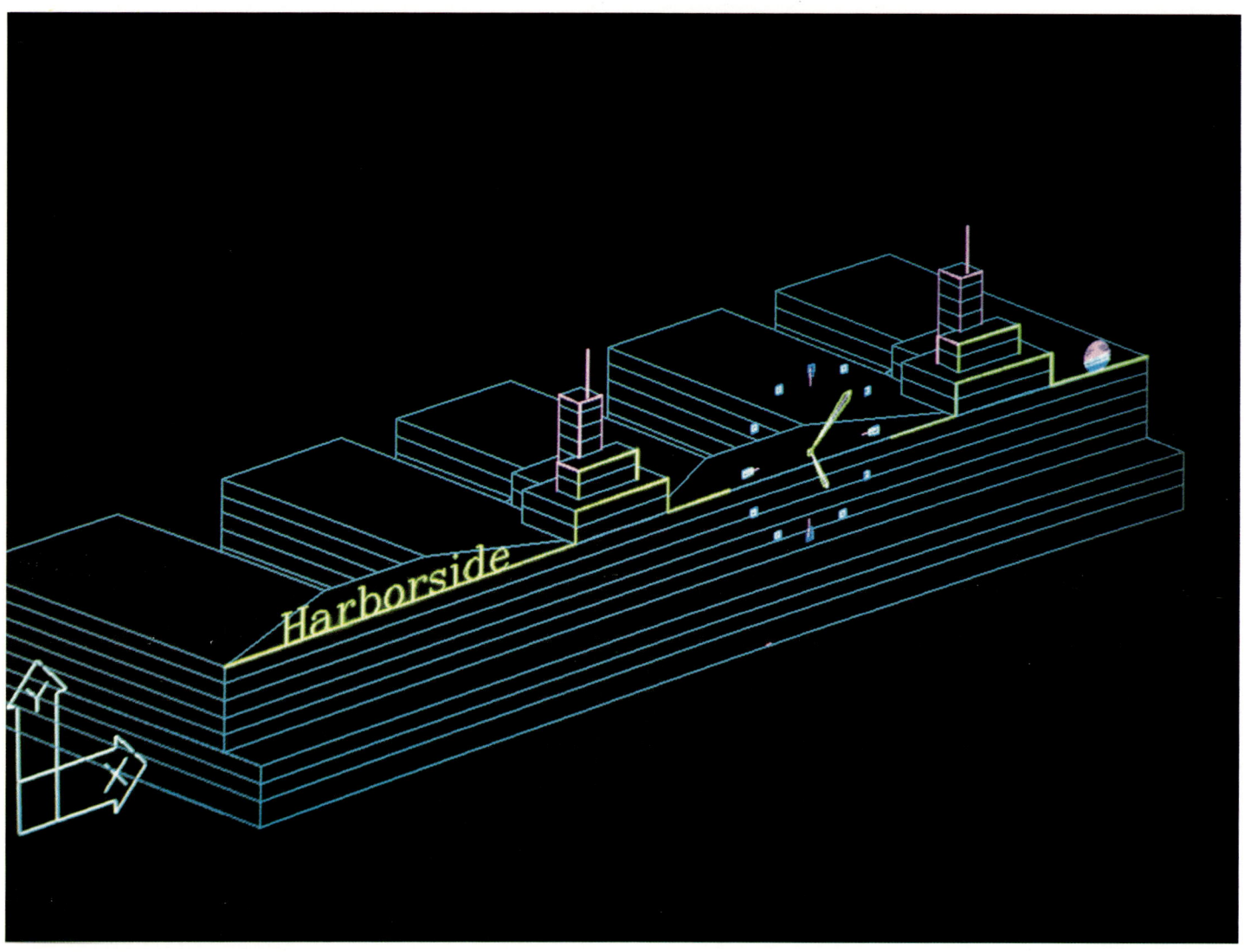

HARBORSIDE DEVELOPMENT
Hudson River, New Jersey, 1989
Proposal for a Facade Lighting Project
Architect: Beyer, Blinder, Belle, New York, N.Y.
Designers: Rudi Stern and Ross Muir
Photo: Ross Muir
CADCAM project to present neon facade ornamentation. On the right is proposal for a neon clock.

"As an architect I have seen CAD revolutionize our profession and introduce many breathtaking possibilities. CAD is organized largely by using color to distinguish different layers of information. The presentation to the client of the CAD generated design provides more variety and realism than any other neon presentation technique. For a neon designer it is incredibly satisfying to see one's imagination so thoroughly and easily brought to life," says Ross Muir.

CHRISTMAS DECORATION FOR "IMAGINATION"
Covent Garden, London, 1987
Dimension: 90' horizontal x 30' vertical
Designer: Gary Withers of Imagination
Architect and fabricator: Syrett Neon International, Kent, Great Britain
Photo: Imagination
Photo courtesy P.J. Mason, Dave Caleno

This project uses 80 transformers and took 6 days to install. It was difficult to choose the right chapter for this. At times it seemed clearly "sculptural" (for its sense of play with the medium, it connected with Mundy's "Magic Garden"); at other moments it was clearly "graphic" and at still others it was "architectural." It is an unusual work reminiscent of sculpted English garden shrubbery — fanciful, a bit eccentric and primarily an intellectual concept, an elaborate and witty conceit.

Products

Neon products are finally becoming a reality. In 1928, at the beginning of neon's history in this country, the need for point-of-purchase advertising display was already established and neon was a welcome novelty. With the end of Prohibition in 1932, beer signs were immediately in great demand. Neon beer signs became a genre and a tradition that continues today with greater and greater quantities involved. (A small order might consist of 20,000 units.) There are five principal manufacturers in this country, with Everbrite the largest. Their seven plants in and around Milwaukee are back-logged with orders from breweries. Unfortunately just as price structures have been set by competitive tradition so, too, have the aesthetics. There has been little or no innovation in terms of the graphic design and "look" of these signs. However, because of television, the public's visual sophistication has developed and more and more creative impact will be necessary to capture consumers' attention. Also, the field of point-of-purchase display is reaching out to other clients, often with products that will require different kinds of graphic and kinetic reference points. As competition for customers increases the field of signage and display will continue to grow and neon's place in this expansion is assured.

Clocks have been the only other traditional mass-produced neon product. The man responsible for this was Sam Kamin from Lima, Ohio. His sense of graphic design and production methods have made his clocks "collectibles." By allowing the local sign shop to be the final distributor, he insured a wide proliferation in retail businesses. Brand name American products were closely identified with this form of advertising. Most of the new-wave neon people cherish these clocks and the tradition they represent. It was only natural for them to want to make a "house clock" if simply to celebrate the history of their own craft.

There have been numerous "neon-look" products but because none of them involve actual neon but rather other light sources they will not be included here. Since the noun "neon" has been marketed for clothing, it has come to represent a "look" with all the vague connotations that one might expect. The word "neon" has come to mean "exciting," "now," "electric," "bright" and "colorful." What this means to us who are involved with the medium is that products which actually use neon are showing signs of life and real potential.

Because of the advent of halogen sources, the potential for ambient lighting combined with decorative effects is at hand. Lighting fixtures and architectural lighting designs are utilizing neon for specific and functional purposes. Yet the process of developing lighting fixtures is a rigorous one; the market is treacherous and far from supportive of innovation. Good design historically has a smaller market than bad design; good neon design has even a smaller potential in terms of functional product. Despite these pressures new areas of product design are opening for the creative use of neon as a viable component. This chapter will show some of the activity in this area but, as with any new development, it will raise more questions than it will provide conclusions.

Some of these products are romantic and nostalgic in their use of the medium. Others are naive in their view of marketability. All of them express a love of the craft and a need to live with it. These are more than just neon objects, they are examples of neon that has a function.

KISMET
Cincinnati, Ohio, c 1986
Designers: Dennis Dix and Dana Burton of City Lights Neon
Size: 16" diameter
Photo: Erik Owen

Kismet is a wall clock utilizing direct and indirect lighting technique. An elegant sculptural statement, this exemplifies the creative abilities of these two artists/designers.

HEXAGON CLOCK
New York, N.Y., 1984
Size: 19" high
Design and manufacture: Let There be Neon, Inc., New York, N.Y.
Photo: Let There be Neon, Inc., New York, N.Y.

A re-creation of a favorite Sam Kamin classic clock.

CHASING RAINBOWS
1983
Size: 22-1/2" diameter
Materials: vacuum formed plastic with silk screened drum and neon ring
Creator: Jay Simmons
Distributors: The Museum of Neon Art, Los Angeles, California
Photo: Rudi Stern

One of the prettiest of the "spinners," this clock is influenced by the Wurlitzer look but has its own electric charm. 650 have been produced as an after-work hobby.

NEON CITY CLOCK
New York, N.Y.
Size: 21" diameter
Designers: Jeff Friedman and Liz Matcovich
Maker: Neon City, Inc.
Photo: Aaron Rezny, N.Y.C.

Inspired by American Streamline, this wall clock with spun aluminum case has its own distinctive graphics.

WHISTLING OYSTER CLOCK
North Hollywood, California
Size: 26" diameter
Courtesy Shane Blake

Shane Blake is a collector of nostalgic American outdoor signage. He distributes his spun steel clock chassis with or without neon — leaving the options of customization.

JACKIE
Design and manufacture: Cicena
Photo courtesy Cicena

This mantle piece/table clock is powered by an AA-sized battery and comes in different neon colors, a combination of neon and acrylic that is both functional and contemporary.

DIANA
Size: 10" diameter
Design and manufacture: Cicena
Photo courtesy Cicena

This neon wall clock is operated on one AA-sized battery and comes in six different versions, each powered by an AC/DC adaptor.

NEON CLOCK
Huntington Valley, PA, 1989
Designer: Robert Levitt
Dimensions: pedestal, 9" x 3"; total height, 16"
Weight: 1-1/2 lbs.
Exclusive marketers: Diamond/Marcus
Photo: Horowitz Studios of Philadelphia
Courtesy Barrie Levitt, Diamond/Marcus

STEP NEON CLOCK
1986
Size: 7.5" high x 10.5" wide x 4.25" deep
Materials: vacuum formed ABS plastic and neon
Weight: 6 lbs.
Designer: Eve Kahn
Photo: Obata Design, Inc. (Scott Smith)

"I wanted to buy a neon clock and discovered there weren't any available, so I designed and produced one. Three others soon followed. I love lighting design; I see it as sculpture with light," says Ms. Kahn

FLOAT
1982
Dimensions: 24" x 24" x 24"
Designer: Tom Anthony with Chuck McClain
Photo: Lockwood Hoehl

This lacquer and neon is a prototype for a line of lacquered tables. The concept: to create a table where the top would appear to float on a field of colored light.

ADA (AMBIENT DECORATIVE ACCENT)
Manufacturer: Lightolier/West

The subtle and intriguing effects of neon light can be used for mood, atmosphere, directional or purely decorative lighting.

Right and bottom:
SE'LUX TUBULAR LIGHTING SYSTEM (TLS)
Berlin
Designers: Bansbach Brothers and Helmut Senkel
Photo courtesy Helmut Senkel, Se'lux, Semperlux GmbH, Berlin

Developed by an old Berlin lighting fixture company, the engineering is immaculate. The option of including directional signage as part of the lighting system was encouraged by this book's author in the early 1980's. Unfortunately, economics make its marketability questionable. Unlike the Lightolier product there are no appreciable gaps in the "line of light" and this product sought to make neon a functional component in commercial lighting.

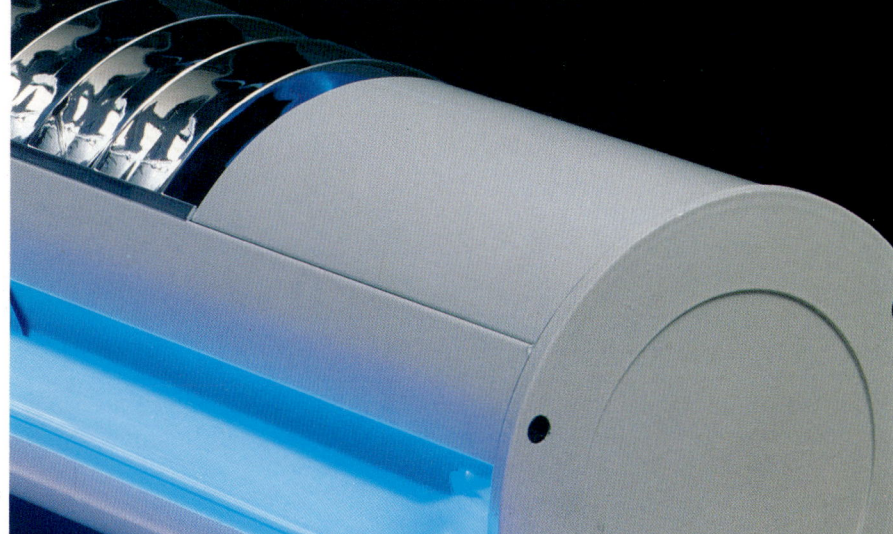

Facing page left:
SE'LUX TUBULAR LIGHTING SYSTEM (TLS)
Berlin
Designers: Bansbach Brothers and Helmut Senkel
Photo courtesy Helmut Senkel, Se'lux, Semperlux GmbH, Berlin

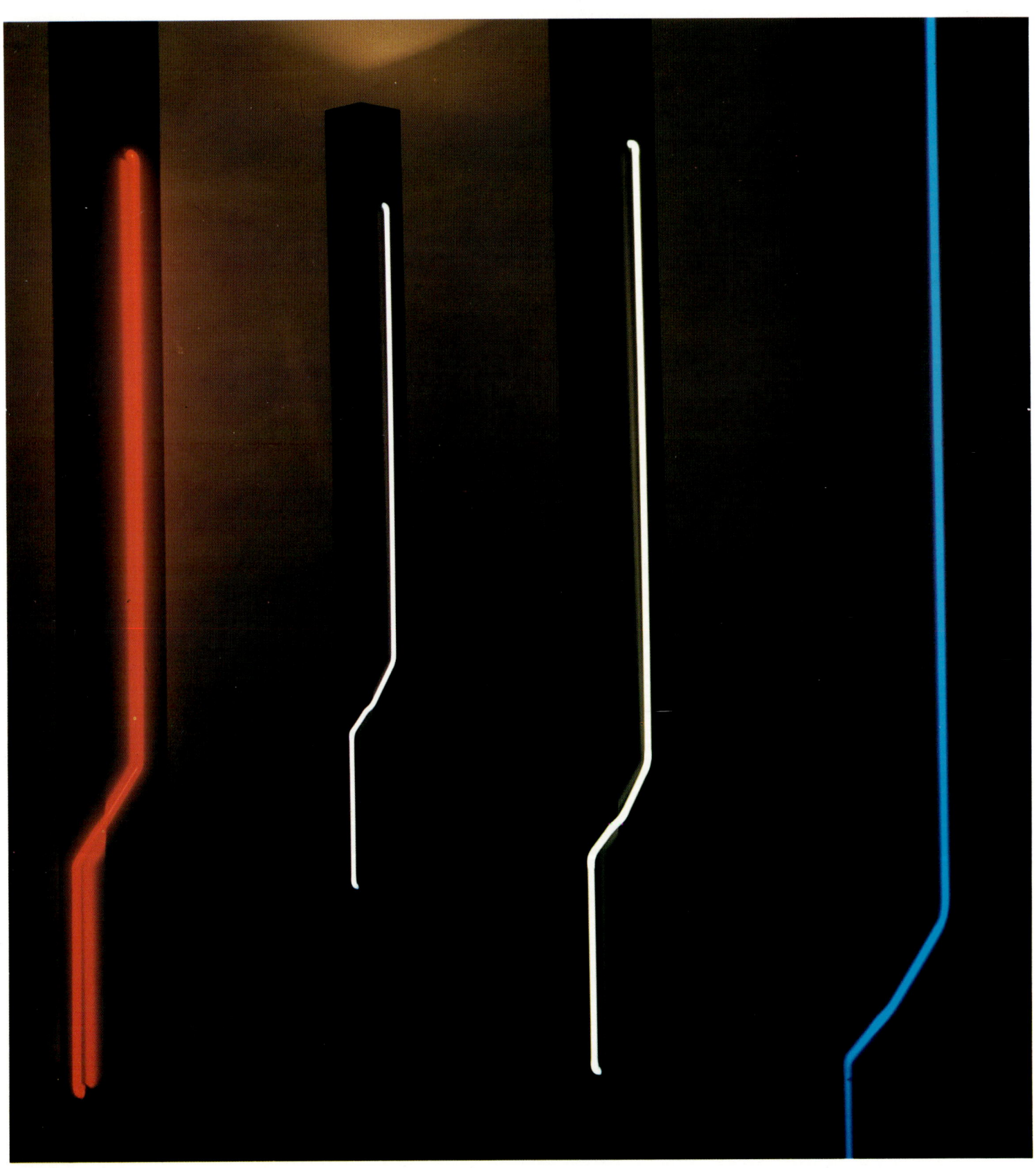

LN 1
1985
Designer: Dan Chelsea of Let There be Neon, Inc.
Manufacture and distribution: George Kovacs, Inc.
Photo courtesy Heidi Kurz of George Kovacs Lighting, Inc.

This torchiere combines halogen for ambient lighting with neon wrapping the exterior for decorative effect. It was the first in a series of lighting fixtures designed by Let There Be Neon for George Kovacs and has proved to be the most popular.

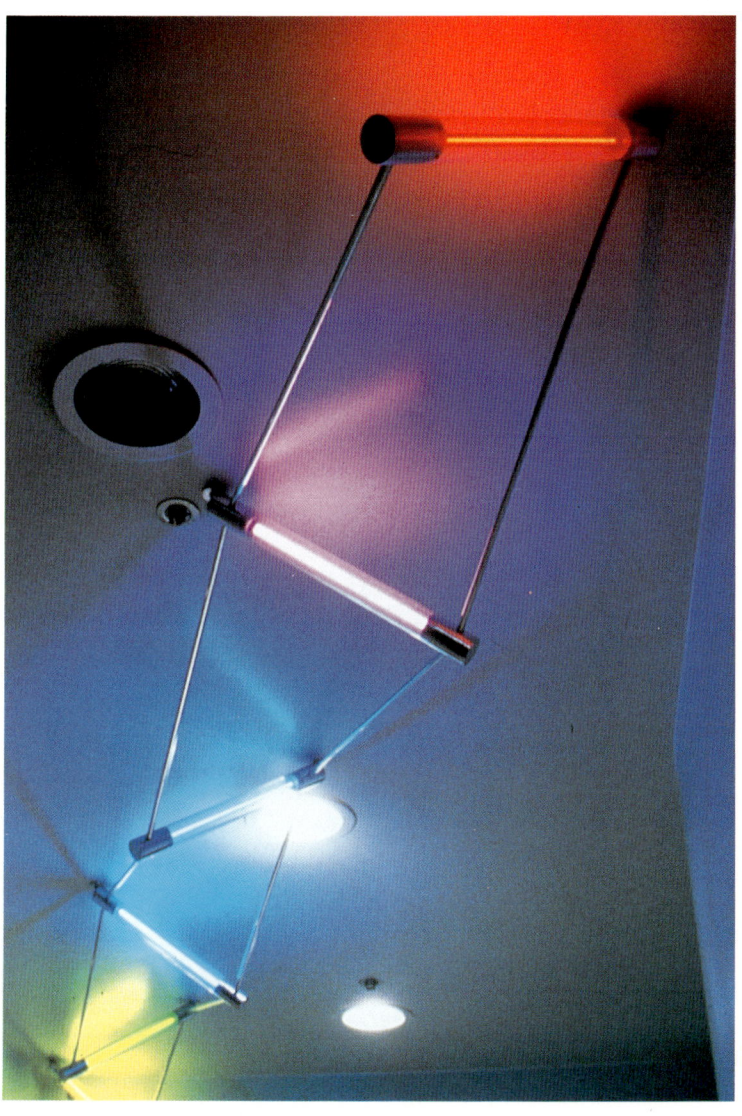

STRUTS
Los Angeles, California, 1986
Designer: Eric Zimmerman
Dimensions: 3′ high x 4″ wide
Materials: neon, aluminum conduit and caps, and acrylic tubing
Fabrication and installation: Archigraphics, Los Angeles
Client: Leo Perilstein for Keye, Donna, Perilstein Advertising Agency
Photo: Rick Mendoza

These unique neon "struts" were designed by Eric Zimmerman for use in his sculptures. The highly polished aluminum caps are precision machined by Archigraphics, an installation company owned by the artist. The actual sculpture is in the elevator lobby of the ad agency's Los Angeles offices.

BE-BOP
New York, N.Y.
Design: Nils Eklund and Rudi Stern
Technical design assistance: Michael Rocco Pinciotti
Manufacture and distribution: George Kovacs Lighting, Inc.
Dimensions: 70-1/2″ high, cone 14″ diameter
Photo courtesy Heidi Kurz of George Kovacs Lighting, Inc.

Combines halogen uplight with decorative neon circles.

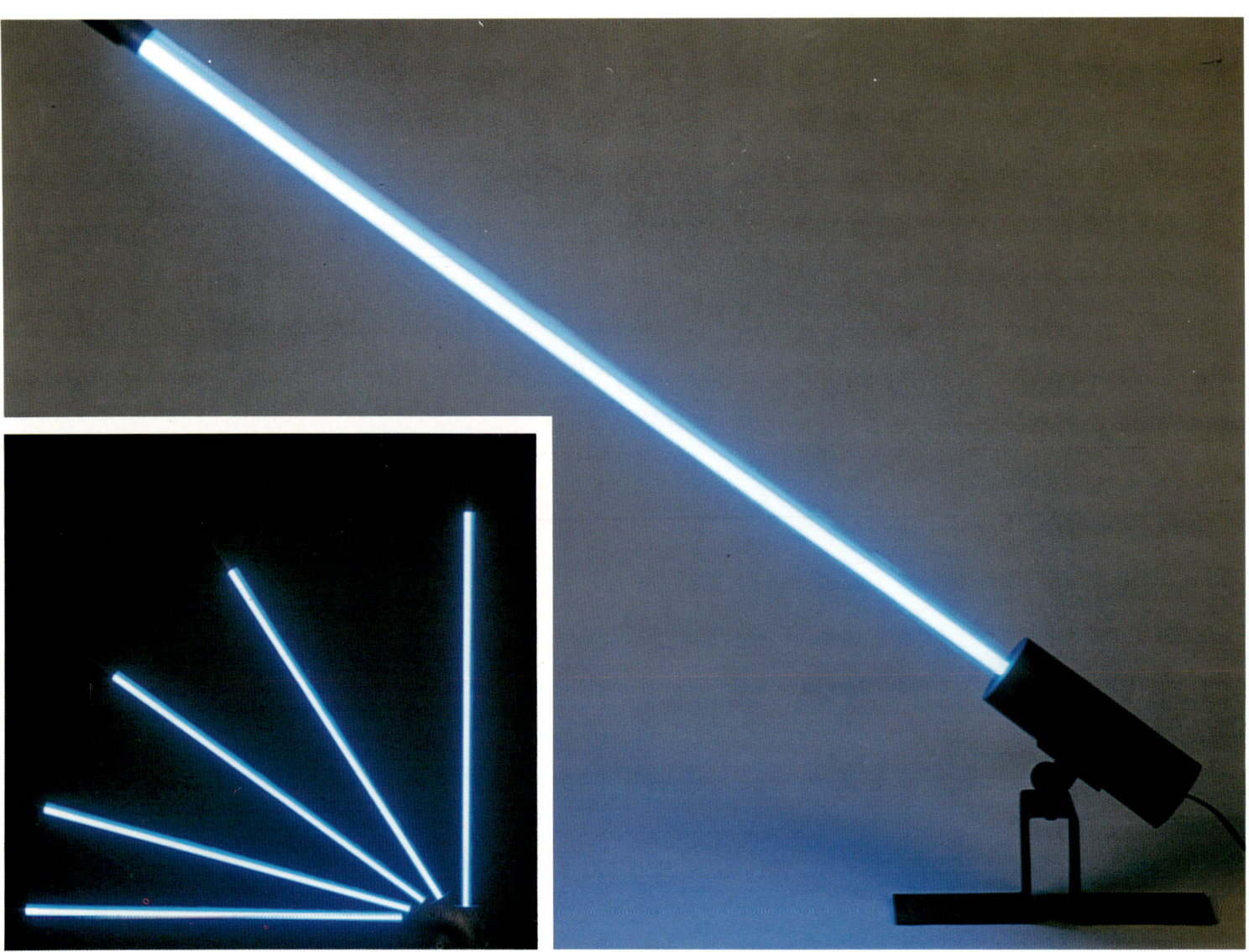

NEON STROKES ™
1989
Designer: Robert Levitt
Exclusive marketing: Diamond/Marcus
Size: 47" in length
Weight: 3.5 lbs.
Materials: neon and molded plastic
Photo: Horowitz Studios of Philalephia

PHAETON WALL SCONCE
Designer: Ian Macartney
Dimensions: 30" vertical x 15" horizontal
Materials: stainless steel, incandescent and neon light
Photo courtesy Ian Macartney

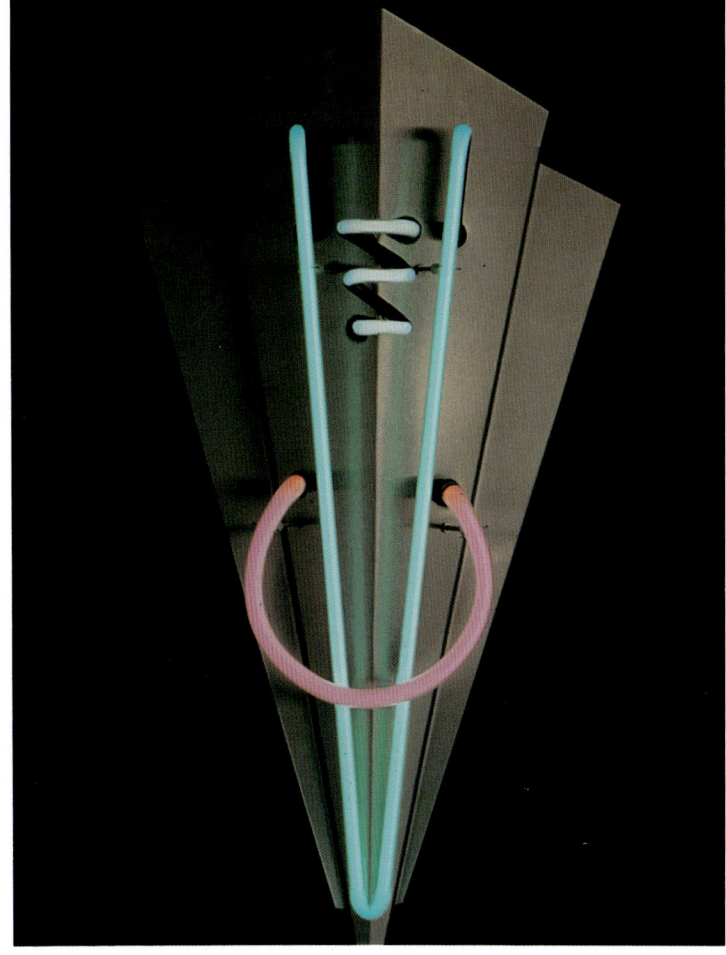

NEON MULTIPLES
Designer: Eric Zimmerman of Aerographics, Los Angeles
Photo courtesy Aerographics

Neon lamps are developed and marketed by this innovative West Coast group which ships components as a package to be assembled by the buyer.

MARILYN
Design and manufacture: Cicena
Photo courtesy Cicena

"Marilyn" is an AM/FM radio set which contains blue and pink neon tubes that flash in response to music. The tubes can be constantly lit or switched off. "Marilyn" also flashes in response to music from a cassette or CD player.

CLEO
Design and manufacture: Cicena
Photo courtesy Cicena

This two-way speaker system has built-in neon tubes that flash on and off in response to music.

ROXANNE
Introduced in 1988
Design and manufacture: Cicena
Photo courtesy Cicena

This telephone operates on energy efficient low voltage. The intensity of the neon can be adjusted from very dim to very bright and the neon tube flashes when receiving incoming calls. This is the big winner in the neon product lottery.

Far right:
BACKGAMMON TABLE
Designer: Kyle Gaffney
Photo: Kyle Gaffney

"The table is made of red oak with transformers housed in insulated metal boxes. Playing pieces are stained glass in complimentary colors. Having never before worked with neon, I consulted a local sign company and had them bend the glass for me. Dark smoked glass panels diffuse the brightness of the neon making it a functional game table," says the designer.

DINER
Design and manufacture: Verry Berta
Dimensions: 19″ × 10″ × 10″
Materials: ceramic with metallic lusters and neon
Photo: Phil Schaafsma, represented by the Zenith Gallery, Washington, D.C.; Margery Goldberg

MAMBA BEER SIGN
1989
Designers: Rudi Stern and Sharon Bachure, Let There Be Neon, New York, N.Y.
Dimensions: 30″ x 30″
Client: Manny Sanchez
Photo: Rudi Stern

This attempt to make beer signs out of the traditional format was supported by a client who was open to new directions and who had the masks from the Ivory Coast where the beer is brewed. This point-of-purchase display is now being tested in Texas.

Sculpture

These remarks are meant to be read not as formal art criticism but as a sort of surveyor's of contemporary neon sculpture. The healthy development of this creative energy needs only time and freedom, not critiques — at least not from me. All of these artists have individual creative directions. I would rather not attempt to compare their work while it is in such a state of formative vitality. I prefer to simply present the multiplicity of ideas, approaches and visions which the body of this art signifies. I am happy that neon sculpture, with few exceptions, has been free and dynamic enough to be unnoticed by the art world. Most of these artists have not broken the barriers of formal acceptance. On a local level some certainly draw enthusiastic response but on the level of blue-chip, international-auction art most are not yet considered to be commodities, which leaves the growth and exhuberance of the field unchecked and horizons open. It is the moment when everything is still possible, every maverick concept is still taken seriously and explored. The artists encourage each other to go further out into new territory of creative expression. This is a fertile and exciting time for neon art.

I consider it a blessing that almost all of these artists are free from the manipulations and machinations of the art world. Their experimentation is free from market pressure because their market values have not yet been established. Many of these sculptors teach, and because the field is so young and lively their teaching has been inspiring; they have imparted the excitement of the medium.

Cork Marcheschi, Fred Tschida, Brad Jirka, Joe Augusta and Chris Freeman have helped to stimulate a new generation of talented young artists. The bias of the gallery establishment and museum circuit, with some noteworthy exceptions, has relegated this art form to a "side show." For a long time any art which requires an electrical cutlet has, with marketable exceptions, been automatically considered less than high art. Regardless of the artistry, content or skill of execution, technological art of any medium has been kept from the general art public and its system of values. By and large neon art is not, as a body of work, considered to be serious. I am sure this will change but I don't regret this incubation period that has served to stimulate the form. It was because of this dichotomy that I asked a number of artists to comment, hoping that their statements would provide a clearer view of this interesting moment in development.

The world of art glass itself has, until recently, been quite isolated from the art establishment and the art commodity market. But now that its pricing structures have been established there is, in turn, a conservative and rather snobbish attitude toward an art form that is also glass — and spectacularly self-illuminated glass at that. One would have hoped for a more receptive attitude on the part of art glass collectors towards this unique direction. While shown, and while collected on a modest scale, neon sculpture is treated condescendingly — as a novelty. Public enthusiasm for the work is construed I think as proof of superficial theatricality. Neon is treated as a "show" of a less than "serious" kind. The lack of elitism in the development of the craft has served to isolate it from the mainstream art world. Response to its messages does not require a subscription to an art journal or being partial to a movement.

The Corning Museum, the citidel of art glass, has rarely, if ever, shown its Paul Seide sculpture and has never to my knowledge given serious consideration to neon art. With the exception of a few chosen artists established and promoted by Leo Castelli in the 1960's and 70's, there has been an absence of major gallery support for artists working with this medium. In retrospect, it almost seems that the critical attention paid to artists like Chryssa, Sonnier, Kosuth and Antonakos was related only to the shock value of the medium, so that later artists don't get similar exposure. It is as if the doors closed behind them.

I have tried in this survey to draw an electric map line through the numerous stylistic approaches in order to organize this rich material. Of course, my own subjectivity is entirely responsible for the sequencing of this work of more than 100 artists.

I begin with the work that seems closest to the process itself — the very raw materials of the medium. Brian Coleman, Mundy Hepburn and Paul Seide shape and mold light itself. They are dealing with the intrinsic properties of neon. Their sculpture deals with the workings of the noble (inert) gases, the fluorescent coatings, the molten glass and ionization. These artists are carving light out of the glass. They render pure light.

Bill Parker's card reads "Artist/Scientist" and his work reflects the congruity which he has synthesized. His widely distributed plasma globes served as a neon product to stimulate public curiosity about the medium. Whether as the initial "signed edition" selling for $2,400 and distributed by Circle Gallery and the Sharper Image catalog, or in its final plagerized $120 version, his plasma globe with its participatory options became a popular kinetic neon toy. It helped to make the public aware of neon as a process. David Svenson is also involved with shaping light but his figurative designs are playful sculptures. His work has reference to the Boardwalk lamp glass artisans of the 1940's and 50's.

Peter David's dreamlife is actualized in neonized narratives of grace and delicacy. He plays in many worlds and his curiosity leads to some rewarding discoveries. Fortunately for us his knowledge and skill keep up with his imaginings.

Alejandro and Moira Siña are serious kinetic artists with specific agendas and achievements. They seem focused on precisely organized research activities. Christian Schiess is an inventor with a wide range of interests and information. His explorations become fascinating kinetic discoveries.

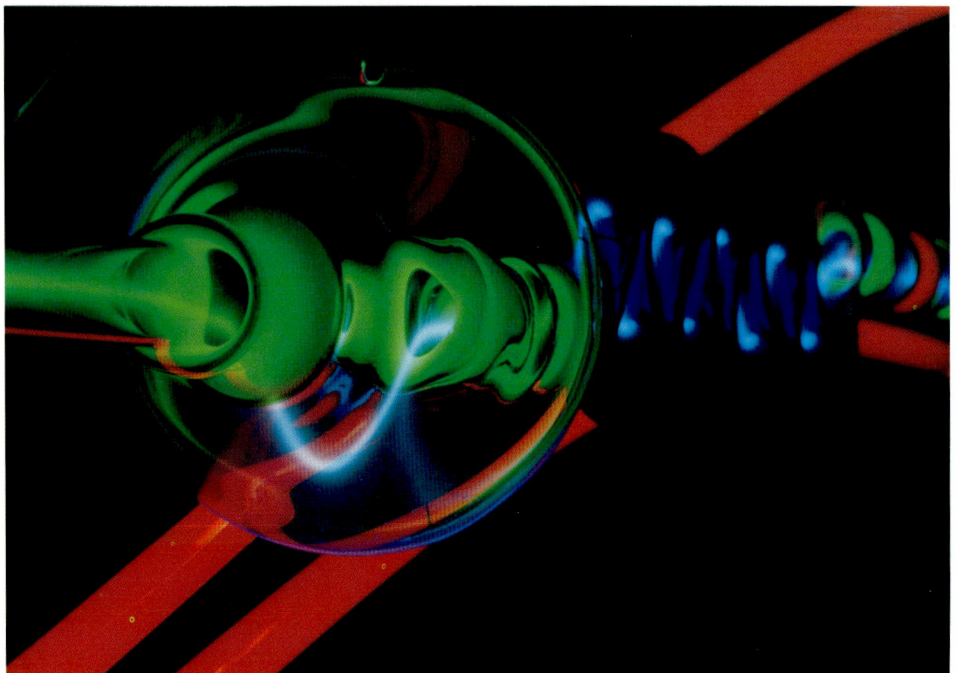

SEVERAL FISH
Brian Coleman, 1989
Dimensions: 2' high x 3' wide
Materials: argon and krypton

TWIST AND SHOUT
Brian Coleman, 1989
Dimensions: 3' high x 18' wide
Materials: xenon, krypton and helium

Patrick Bresette leads us to natural settings for poetic works in neon. Strangely at home on hilltops and in lakes, neon outdoors seems to fit in as naturally as the gas itself in the oxygen we breathe. Bresette's "Gazebo" against a painted sky in central Texas is electric poetry. The "Fire/Water" series by Chritian Schiess provides theatrically kinetic moments suspended in time. It makes perfect sense for him to actually fabricate the glass on site because he seems so in touch with the moment that to return to his studio would break the connction he has established with nature. The lines actually look like an evolving part of the landscape. Jerry Noe's Artpark "Landscape" is an electric silhouette where scale becomes deceptive in the flash of light. Fred Tschida's "Light in Motion" relates for me to the 60's craziness of Ant Farm and the half buried Cadillacs. Only here the neonized car looks like Ground Zero in an explosion of light on an Antonioni set.

"Square Wave" by James Whte must have been an outstanding performance. To orchestrate, as he did for the benefit of camping cyclists, the play of blue and red at 600 miles per second around the 144 tents created an animated sea of neon. I like Chris Freeman's guerrila neon theater where ten friends "attacked the site with light . . . no permission, just art." John David Mooney's "River Installation" completes the passage through landscape with a harmony of pattern — a kind of surveyor's luminous notation.

Now from outside to inside, with Joe Augusta's very intense and almost x-ray images of expressionistic luminosity, with the light coming through from the back. Then it seems logical to move into areas where neon is used with natural materials, where itis combined in collage — sometimes hidden, at other times revealing its electric penmanship. Michael Young's work, in both large and small scale, has interesting textures. Dave Yocum is elegant with this clay works: the fusion is a compatible one. The fabric-wrapped neon of Victoria Rivers is tropically lush and poetic. She expresses a sense of wonder and delight with her investigations. Roddy Capers, Jon Miskinis and Janet Evans are into light as a natural element which excites the other media but never dominates them. Their work, as that of Lili Lakich, sems fused and coalesced by light. Maureen Havey has gathered willow branches and, with artful simplicity, bound them together with one stick of light. "Tickled Pink" by Rozinski and "Geminis III" by the Argentinian Sicardi use silhouettes that are a dance of light.

"Fire VIII" by Lori Gene Mulherin takes us out of organic matter into the urban grid of Don Jacobson's wall piece. The simple elegance of Dennis Dix and Dana Burton continues the matrix of grids on which neon seems to float. Patrick Bresette's hay bales with floating three-dimensional halos and his "Continental Drift" with asphalt bring us around again with natural substancs transposed by the light of neon. The sculptural sconces of Woloshin are brilliant sunrises of neon. They lead into Michael Furey's dramatic eclipse. Tome Scarff experiments with onyx and the surprising translucence of stone.

The "Light Pole" by Ben Livingston and the neonized lamps of Jeff Becker, with their indirect glow, take us to the soft, tactile tubing of Christ Freeman's "Woven Lights" where neon is the very thread of the fabric. Fred Tschida's "Log Jam" is like a mobile frozen by strobes, while Chris Freeman's neon time exposure puts human silhouettes against a wall of blinding neon light.

From this dramatic neon we return to neon as sculptural form in space, an object you can look at from all sides. "Vertical Eclipse" by Carmine Saccardo is a pendulum of neon reflected by surfaces of stained glass, steel and aluminum. It is compact and highly charged. Conceptually inspired diagrammatic pieces follow, with the "Pyramid Sculpture" of Josef van der Horst, the "Blue Tilt" of Jerry Noe and the "Neon Mirror" of Michael Feith. These are concept works where neon is called into play for specific design ends. The "Technicolor" sculpture of Larry Kanter is a concise dramatic statement of planes and the depth of light. Eric Zimmerman's "Y" is filled with infinity effects and seems like a neon pinball machine. Nobuyuki Sasaki's delicate sculpture has alluring semblances of dimensionality achieved with minimal means.

Beverly Reiser's sandblasted mirror designs are graceful and elegant. One can easily understand her value to interior architects seeking illuminated murals. Mooney's architectural models are well-defined sculptures that serve as armatures for the play of curvilinear neon. "Let it Roll" by Cork Marcheschi, is a simple and strong play of neon light. This leads me back to the collage sculptures of Bill Kane and Michael Pinciotti, where neon causes spatial relief and texture. Both artists return to neon as writing: electric calligraphy and graffitti.

This is followed by figurative work with neon that ranges from the tableau of Craig Craft, the arabesque of Ellen Sandor and into the suggested movement of "Don't Look Back" by Laurie Lea where neon now seems part of an after-image. Decorative potentials are explored in the neon masks of David Morrison and Tom Gaddy's animated face. Joe Augusta's expressionistic "Elvis Machine" is an illuminated painting, color defining composition — an unusual use for such a clearly linear material as neon. Margery Goldberg's figures are instant "from the model" sketches. "Electro Man" by Michael Furey is an isometric of a mannequin built by the crosshatching of clear red. The architect Rob Robinson enjoys the freedom of his electric pen with "Groucho Marx."

The next section is one of humor and wit — where neon helps to tell stories and plays with ideas. Here the medium is directed for specific effects, focused purposes of graphic intent. In Ben Livingston's piece, neon is the electric guillotine, Fred Elliott plays with perspective and illusion, Karl Hauser with repetition. Abe Rezny and I enjoyed the semblance of structure with our "Rocker." Ben Livingston's "Skyhook" seems like an illustration for children's fables. The cars of Nils Eklund and Philip Hazard use neon as allusions to motion.

Michael Pinciotti's sculptures of buildings are technically models but really mixed-media events. They are stage sets for action-tableaux in

NITE DANCER
Brian Coleman, 1989
Dimensions: 16' horizontal
Materials: colored glass, argon, kyrpton and neon
All photos: Brian Coleman

The work of Brian Coleman deals with the pure kinetics of the process itself. He sculpts the light and shapes the color. His art seems close to the very source of the magic in the medium. For him, the adventure is with the neon light itself. Through his craft discipline he has made the light tactile.

"The visual clarity of the medium," says Brian Coleman, "has always been what attracted me most. My one constant value throughout 20 years of neon art has been to keep the intensity of the light low through control of the gases, glass and phosphorescence. Because I have always done my own glass blowing the process of working the glass and experimentation has led me to a wide range of styles."

overleaf
MAGIC GARDEN
Mundy Hepburn, 1989
Dimensions: 6' wide x 3' high
Photo: Joan Levy

This sculpture of high frequency, luminous flowers is on permanent display at the Panasonic headquarters in Osaka, Japan. "It is time for neon to be recognized as a fine art medium. Because of its intense visual impact it can be wonderfully expressive of large universal ideas and aspirations. Neon used correctly speaks to the soul, ringing ancient visual chords. The sacred fire keeps me alive in the Twentieth Century," says Mundy Hepburn.

"IRISES"
Mundy Hepburn, 1989
Dimensions: 24" high
Photo: Mundy Hepburn

Mundy is an alchemist — a magician with light. By successfully breaking the rules of neon manufacture he has created a very individual form of expression. His work evolves organically out of the raw material.

LUMINOUS BOUQUET
Mundy Hepburn, 1976
Dimensions: 14" high
Materials: neon, argon, phosphors
Photo: Mundy Hepburn

The artist's vision: "Christmas ornaments mutating into glass flowers."

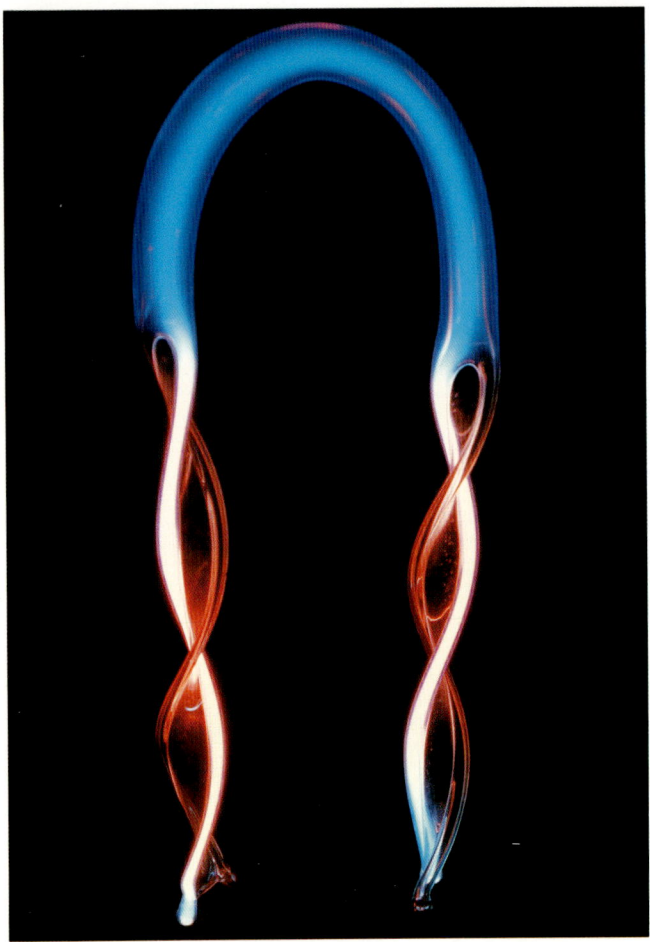

FLIP THE SWITCH
David Ablon
Dimensions: 18″ high
Materials: blown and twisted 25 mm clear lead glass tubing filled with neon gas and mercury vapor
Photo: David Ablon

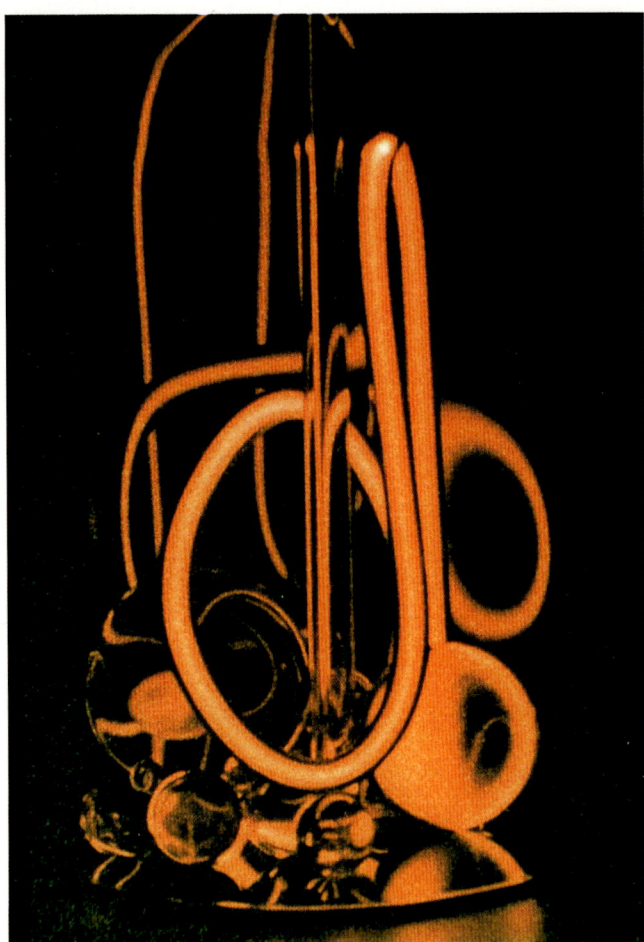

REFLECTIONS
Candice Watkins, 1987
Dimensions: 12″ x 12″ x 12″
Photo: Aubergine

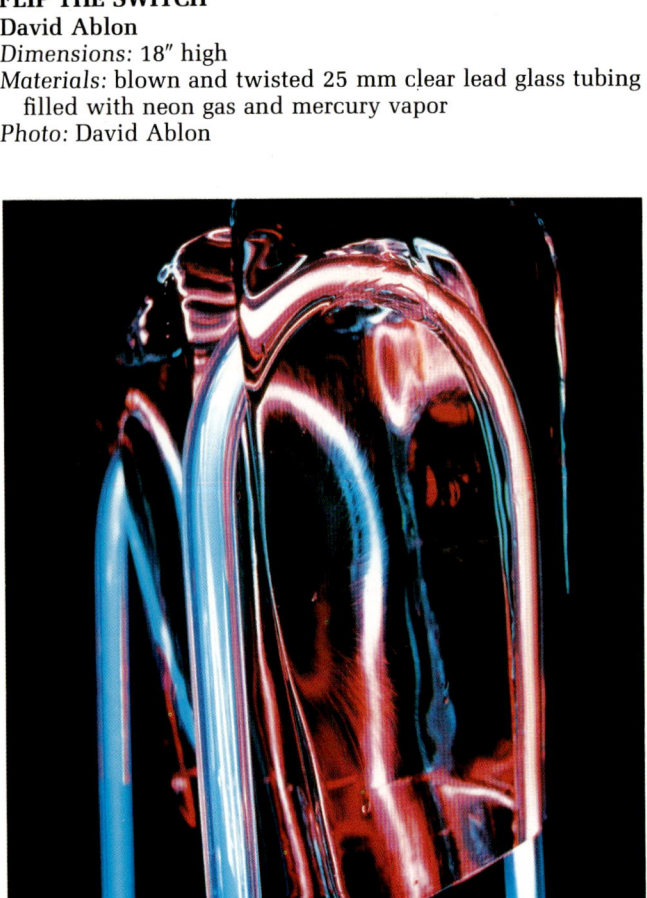

DETAIL FROM "LOADED TO THE MAX"
Steve Frerichs, 1987
Dimensions: 8′ high x 8′ wide x 1′ deep
Materials: mercury neon tubes, ice, mixed media
Neon fabrication: Cory Paisley of Paisley Neon, Phoenix, Ariz.
Photo: Jim Christy

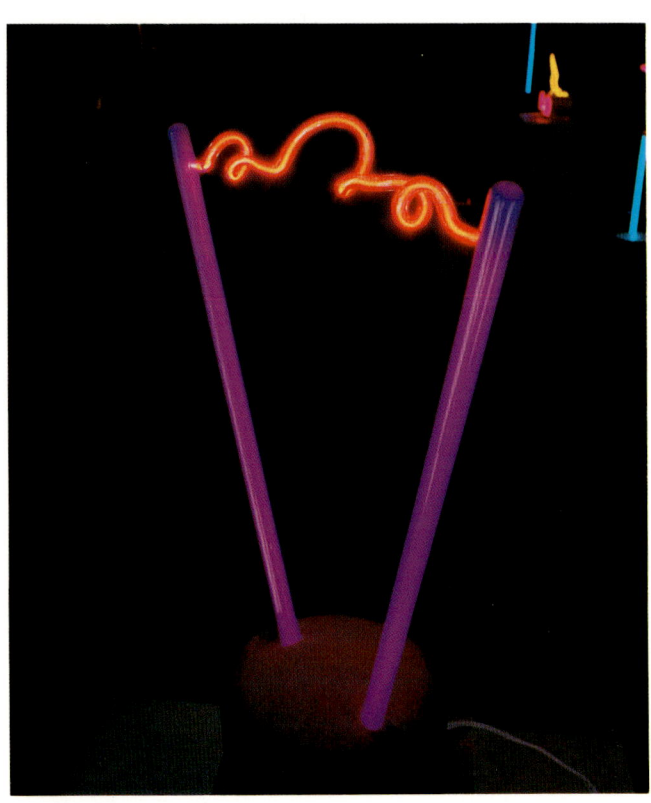

ANTENNA
Ian Macartney, 1989
Dimensions: 8″ x 18″
Fabrication: glass and neon
Photo: Ian Macartney

ARTHUR
Larry Albright, 1987
Dimensions: 18″ wide x 22″ high x 14″ deep
Materials: hardwood, old electrical hardware, plasma tube
Collection: Helen Albright
Photo: From "Art Cellar Exchange," page 25: Jeff Atherton

"Despite the limitations of thin tubing and spherical globes, Albright succeeds at recreating his timewarp memories. Albright, in the true spirit of early inventors and scientific pioneers . . . taught himself virtually everything he knows about art, although he did study photography under Ansel Adams. He also learned on his own about neon gases and plasma (a higher frequency of electricity) beginning by using found neon pieces in his work. Today he is widely known as an authority in the medium, which led to his work in films."

Larry Albright's work has appeared in many films including: Star Wars, 1976; Close Encounters of the Third Kind, 1977; Buck Rogers, 1978; Star Trek the Motion Picture Part I, 1978; One from the Heart, 1981; Bladerunner, 1981; The Man with Two Brains, 1982 and "Buckaroo Bansaii, 1983.

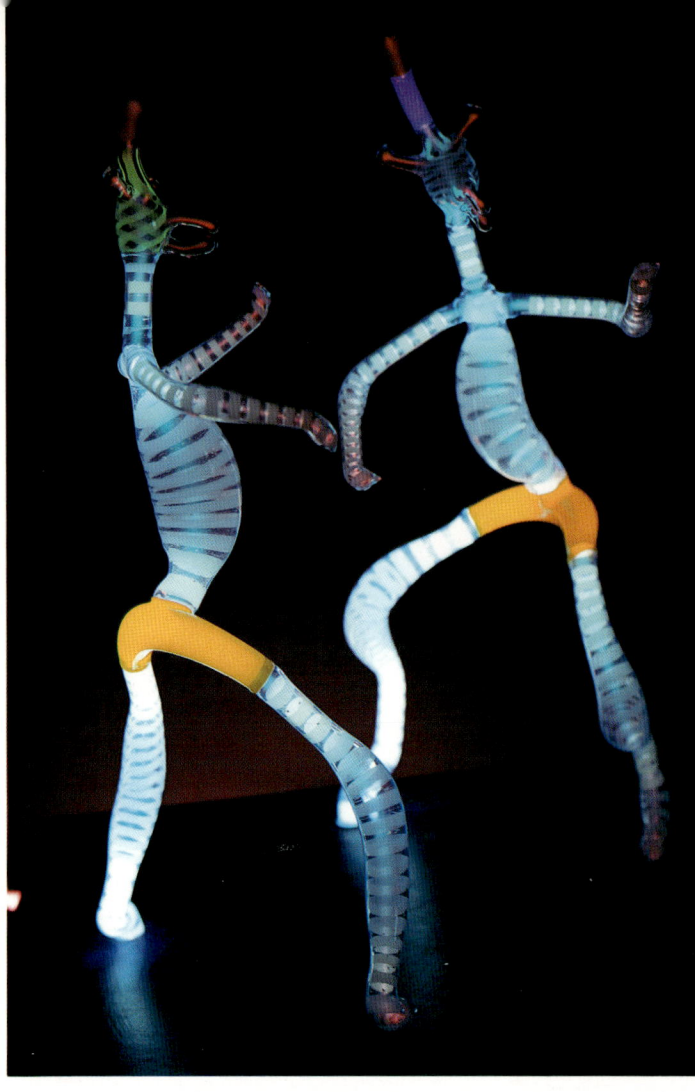

Opposite:
FLAMING BONSAI
Peter David, 1987
Dimensions: 16″ tall
Materials: ceramic base, 1/2″ black glass, neon, blown glass
Photo: Steve Wall

First place, 1987 National Electric Design Competition

"One of my Flaming Bonsai Series, the result of a 'technodream' one Saturday night. I awoke with a start, went to my studio and made the first of this searies," the artist remarks.

DANCE LEVITATION
David Svenson, 1989
Dimensions: 28″ high
Materials: Colored and phosphor coated glass construction, neon/mercury.
Photo: David Svenson

This was the poster piece for the "American Light Art" show in Tokyo, December, 1989.

"My imagery comes from personal fantasy combined with my interest in 'primitive' cultures, notably the Northwest Indians of Alaska among whom I lived and worked, carving totem poles and other art objects in their totemic traditions. These people have a close connection with the natural elements around them and I am trying to express this sensibility in relation to our own culture." David Svenson

RECLINING NUDE
David Svenson, 1989
Dimensions: 14″ long
Materials: colored glass application on clear neon/mercury
Photo: David Svenson

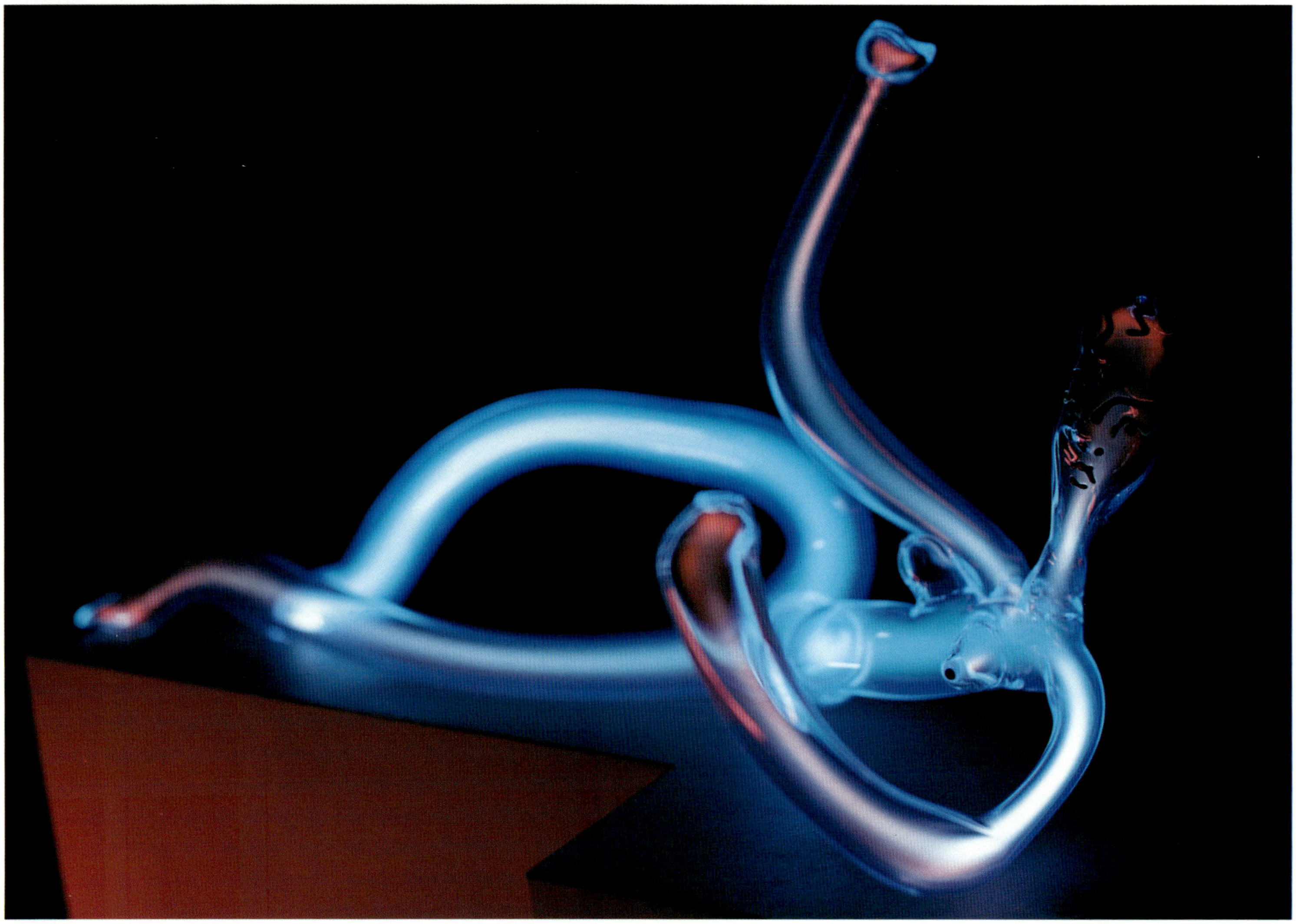

CONFETTI WALL SCONCE
Peter David, 1987
Dimensions: 20″ high
Materials: etched handblown glass and neon

"One of my one-of-a-kind wall sconces. The soft watercolor-like tones of the neon on the etched glass create a wonderful glow on the wall." Peter David.

JELLYFISH
Peter David, 1985
Dimensions: 6′ tall x 2′ wide x 18″ deep; jellyfish is 10″ x 11″
Materials: etched blown glass, neon
Photo: Peter David
Detail from "Beneath the Sea of Moons"
First place, 1988 National Electric Design Competition

"This piece is one of my 'Deep Sea Danglers,' inspired by a snorkling trip to the Tahitian Islands. The Sea of Moons is a body of water between Moorea and Tahiti," states Peter David.

MONOLITH FOREST
Peter David, 1987
Dimensions: 6' high x 2' x 2'
Materials: tinted black glass using single-ended tube technology.
Photo: Peter David

Part of a series exploring the new freedom of single-ended neon-tube technology, a forest of reflections from every angle.

Facing page top:
CRYSTAL GROUPING
Paul Seide, 1990
Materials: blown glass powered by short wave radio transmission
Photo: Tom Rose

Bottom:
BIOMORPHIC SERIES
Paul Seide, 1990
Photo: Paul Seide

"I was always interested in neon as a phenomenon as much as a visual effect. By creating these forms from glass in its molten state I am able to use colors and blends of colors that are unique. Sometimes I think of these pieces as man-made ' "Northern Lights' or stars. By manipulating the elemental forces of nature and creating light from plasma, I feel that I am in touch with the essence of creation," says Paul Seide.

Paul Seide, like Mundy Hepburn, Peter David and Brian Coleman, deals directly with light. His forms are pure glass/light art of great intensity and visual beauty. Radio frequency power sources have enabled his work to be mobile and modular. For more than 20 years, Paul Seide has refined his very disciplined approach, yet his work is still being shown within the "glass world" which has not afforded the wider recognition due him as an artist of stature.

SPINNING SHAFT
Alejandro and Moira Siña ©, 1989
Dimensions: 5 1/2′ diameter x 10′ long
Photo: Alejandro and Moira Siña

SPINNING BOX
Alejandro and Moira Siña ©, 1978
Dimensions: 8′ x 8′ x 1′
Materials: neon, motor, electronics
Photo: Alejandro and Moira Siña

A kinetic neon lightwork from a series of two and three dimensional images that are created by spinning lines of neon light.

Facing page:
CONE
Alejandro and Moira Siña ©, 1978
Dimensions: 3 1/2′ high x 2′ diameter
Photo: Alejandro and Moira Siña

A conical image is created by the rotation of neon lines of light. Patterns are created by variable pulses in an evolving light image.

IGNUS CVXXI
Christian Schiess, 1986
Dimensions: 40″ x 36″ x 20″
Materials: inflated vinyl, wire, plexiglas, aluminum and neon suspended from ceiling
Photo: Fred T. Hadlick

Fire/air inflatable light series. The light structures within the sculptures are fabricated from neon and argon luminous glass tubing, which has a life expectancy of at least 25 years. The light structure is positioned inside flexible vinyl envelopes in a variety of colors. Special flexible and insulated wire is used to suspend the inflated sculpture and electrify the light structure.

CYBER-ROSE
Christian Schiess, 1988
Dimensions: 7′ x 4′ x 4′
Materials: welded steel and aluminum, motors, wire, plexiglas and neon. Viewer inter-active and kinetic with variable speed flower petal patterns and color.
Photo: T. Hadlick

"The sculptures in this cyber flower series produce a variety of flower-like petal patterns and colors. My objective is to combine modern materials with the ancient art motif of flowers to ultimately pay homage to nature." Christian Schiess

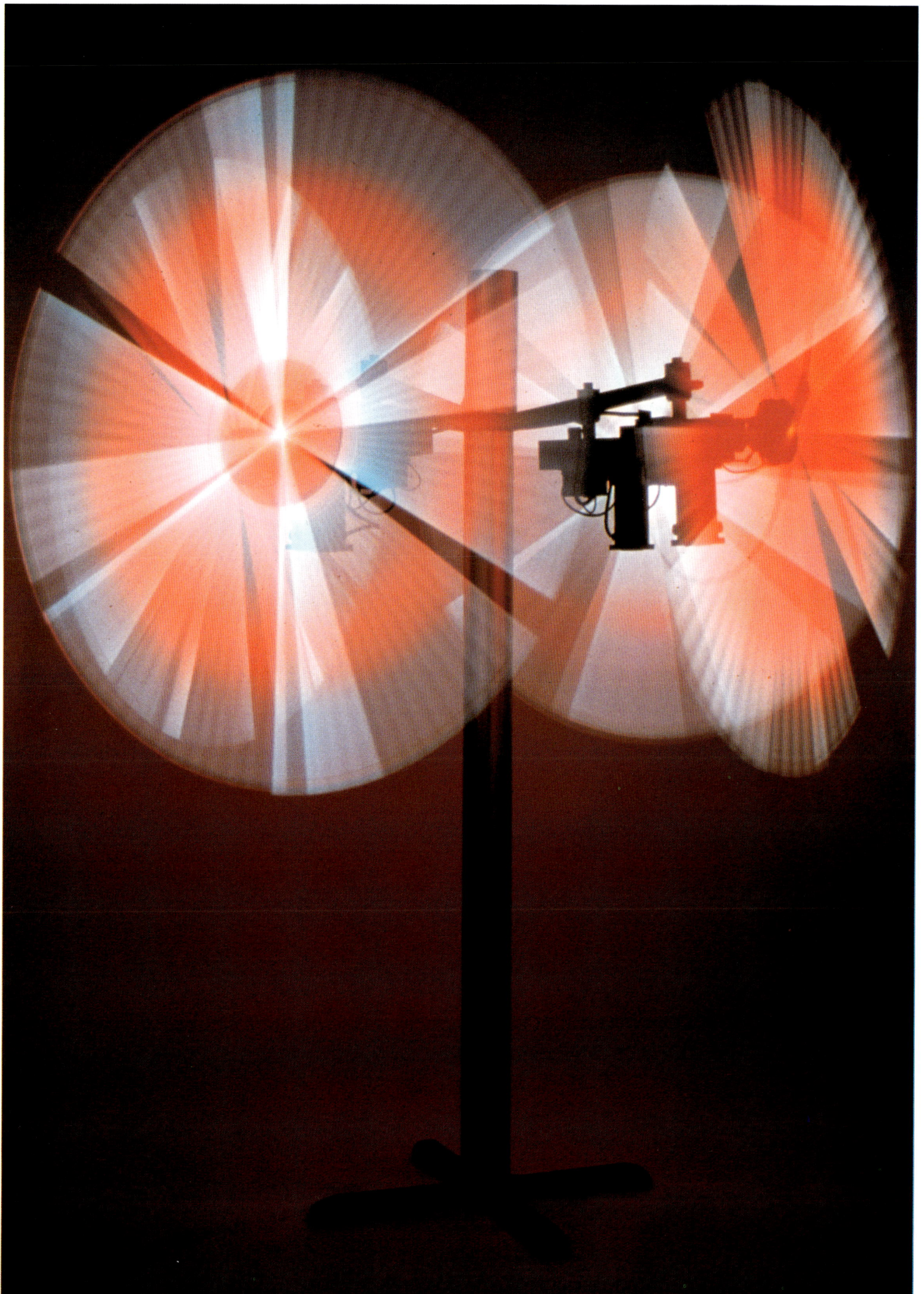

16%
Hiroki Tanaka, 1986
Dimensions: 20″ high x 16″ wide x 12.5″ deep
Mixed media: wire mesh, glass tubing, neon
Photo: Lisa Sette Gallery, Scottsdale, Arizona

HEART OF NEON
Kunio Ohashi, 1986
Dimensions: 16″ high x 10″ wide x 6″ deep
Materials: hard plaster and neon
Photo: Kunio Ohashi

Overleaf top left:
SLEEPLESS NIGHTS
Bill Parker, 1984
Dimensions: 12″ diameter globe on a 5″ high base
Materials: pyrex glass sphere with gas composition, high frequency field.
Photo: Bill Parker

"Sleepless Nights" or "La Nuit Blanche (White Night)" is a contemplative, mysterious image. It is primarily composed of a cobalt blue haze mingled with smokey black light which suffuses the inside of the glass sphere with an intense glow. At times, arms of bluish-white light radiate from the central sphere becoming fan-shaped as they near the glass. Touching the sphere draws the diffuse white forms into a single brightly defined beam that jumps to the surface.

Bottom left:
FIREFLOWER
Bill Parker, 1975
Dimensions: 12″ diameter globe on a 5″ high base
Materials: pyrex sphere with gas composition and a high frequency field
Photo: Bill Parker

"Fireflower" possesses a calm, sweet nature, with a tremendous capability for variability of image and responsiveness to touch. Gently curling tendrils of pinkish violet are tipped with diffuse spots of orange. When touched, one or two of these tendrils leap out from the suspended cluster of light forms, meeting the viewer's touch and creating an intense orange glow around the hand, leaving a skirt of wispy violet tendrils suspended in space.

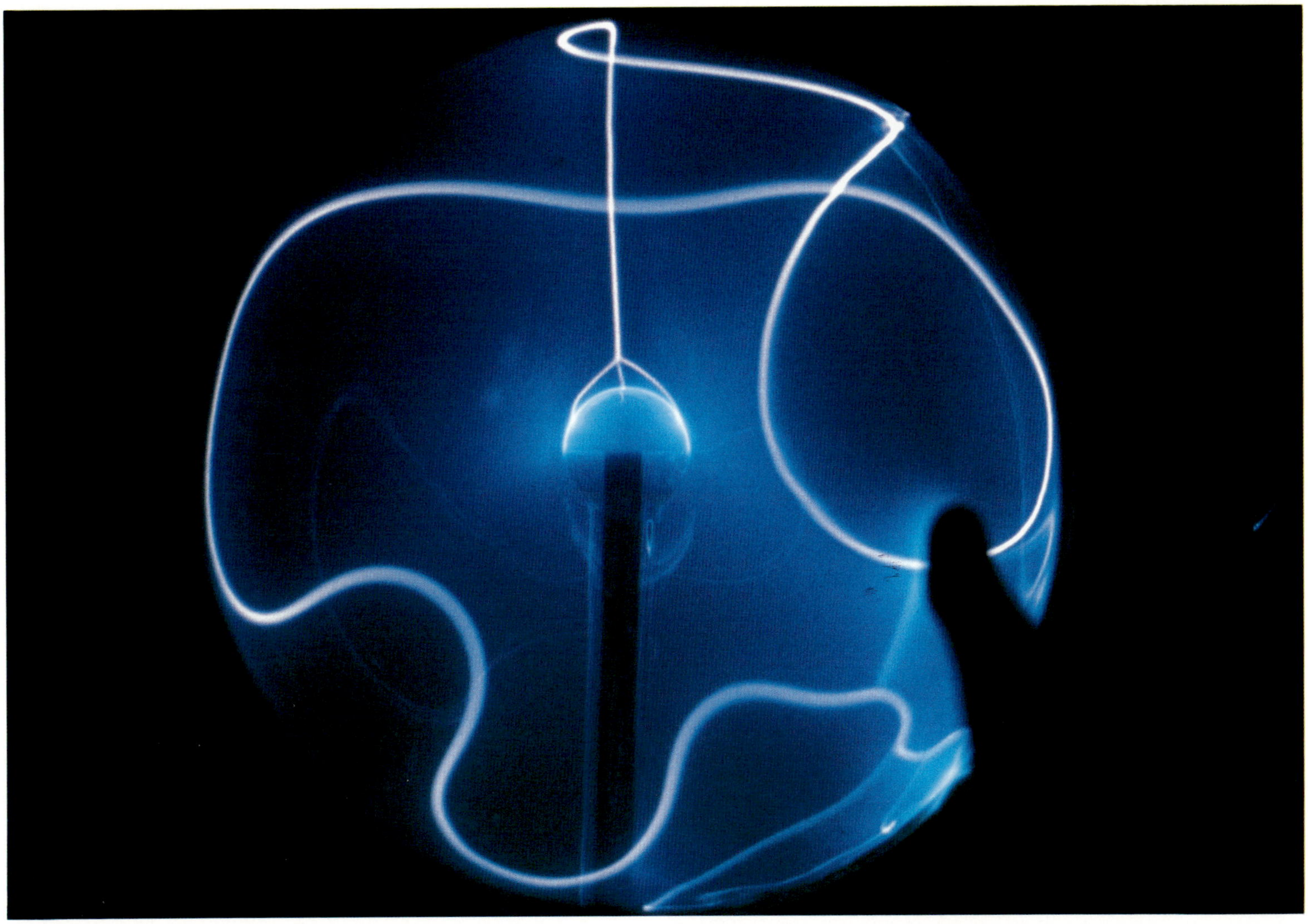

118

JEWEL OF ENLIGHTENMENT (HASHI-NO TOMA)
Bill Parker, 1989
Dimensions: 40" diameter sphere standing 5' from the floor
Materials: glass sphere, gas mixture, high voltage at high frequency
Client: Ward Group, Sydney, Australia
Created for ARTEC, 1989, in Nagoya, Japan
Photo: Alejandro and Moira Siña

"The ability to form shapes from pure naked, unconstrained light is a dream that I've had since I was a child," says Bill Parker. "My work is a combination of sculpture and choreography; my desire is to control the colors, the shapes and the range of movement of the form while freeing them to interact with the viewer."

Facing page, top:
FIRE/WATER SERIES AT SMITHVILLE FLATS
Christian Schiess, 1987
Dimensions: 95′ x 100′
Materials: submerged stainless steel, PVC, wire and neon. The marsh was flooded to a depth of 1 to 5 feet of water.

Bottom:
AT FOSTER HILL CREEK
Christian Schiess, 1987
Dimensions: 45′ x 25′
Materials: submerged aluminum, PVC, wire and neon. Submerged and partially frozen in snow and ice to a depth of 1 to 1 1/2′.
Photo: Fred T. Hadlick

Below:
GAZEBO
Patrick Bresette, 1987
Dimensions: 10′x 10′ x 16′
Materials: neon, cedar poles and saplings
Photo: Patrick Bresette

This piece was part of an outdoor neon exhibit in central Texas. There is a bench inside overlooking the fields below.

"Most of my sculpture is designed to draw the viewer into the ideas that generated its creation. Humor and the juxtaposition of neon with unlikely material help create that relationship," says Patrick Bresette.

121

FIRE/WATER #1
Christian Schiess, 1978
Dimensions: 65' of submerged plexiglas, wire and neon
To accomplish these projects, Christian Schiess developed a portable neon plant for "an artist on the move."

"My intention in developing the environmental *Fire/Water Series*," he says, "is to further my study and understanding of the four archaic elements of earth, air, fire and water. I hope to achieve a harmonious interaction between man-made light or fire and the elements of a natural environment. Man-made and natural elements can exist together when appropriately combined as complimentary opposites."

LANDSCAPE/ARTPARK
Jerry Lee Noe, 1975
Dimensions: 48′ high x 120′ wide x 60′ deep
Installation: Artpark, Lewiston, N.Y.
Fabrication: Barry Allred of C.P. Allred Neon Co.
Photo: Jerry Lee Noe

LIGHT IN MOTION
Fred Tschida, 1982
Construction: 60′ antenna mast fitted with 180′ of red neon mounted on a 1970 Chevrolet Impala custom coupe. Gasoline electric power.
Photo: Eliza Tonachel

A dramatic example of Fred Tschida's work in which a 60′ line of neon moves through an otherwise still and monochromatic rural landscape. This work, visible as a moving red line from as much as eight miles away, begins to explain what Schida describes as "neon not dependent on the gallery or the electric wall outlet."

SQUARE WAVE-AERE PERENNIUS
James White, 1989
Photos: James White

The University of Northern Iowa commissioned "Square Wave-Aere Perennius" to create a unique environment for participants in the 17th *Des Moines Register*'s Annual Great Bike Ride Across Iowa. Square wave incorporates 144 tent-like structures and neon lighting into a sculpture covering about three acres. Each structure is made of white nylon fabric, about 18' x 18'. Each unit's support pole is a 2 by 2 fiberglas panel containing red and blue neon which combine to give off purple light. The neon lights are wired to a central control panel to allow the sculpture's designer to create a colorful light show: a wave effect — first at the fast, excited rate of a heartbeat and later at the soft, pulsating pace of human breathing.

James White is a professor of sculpture at Arizona State University and director of the Center for Neon Art, a commercial gallery in Tempe. Bill Moss, a nationally known fabric sculptor from Minneapolis, acted as a consultant on the tent-like structures.

CITY FENCE
Christopher Freeman, Central Park, December 2nd, 1989
Dimensions: 4' high x 50' wide
Materials: argon, mercury and wood
Photo: Steve Hart

"Working with a team of ten friends we attacked this site with light at dusk. No permission, just art. When we left three hours later there were no traces left except memories in the eyes of the viewer and film in the camera." Chris Freeman, who is quoted above, teaches neon courses at the New York Experimental Glass Workshop, does commissioned sculpture and fabrication and installation of architectural projects with an emphasis on cold cathode.

RIVER INSTALLATION
John David Mooney, 1977
Dimensions: 100' long
Photo: John David Mooney
Commissioned by the Indiana Arts Commission

One of a series of pieces using different materials executed on the same site during the changing seasons in Indiana.

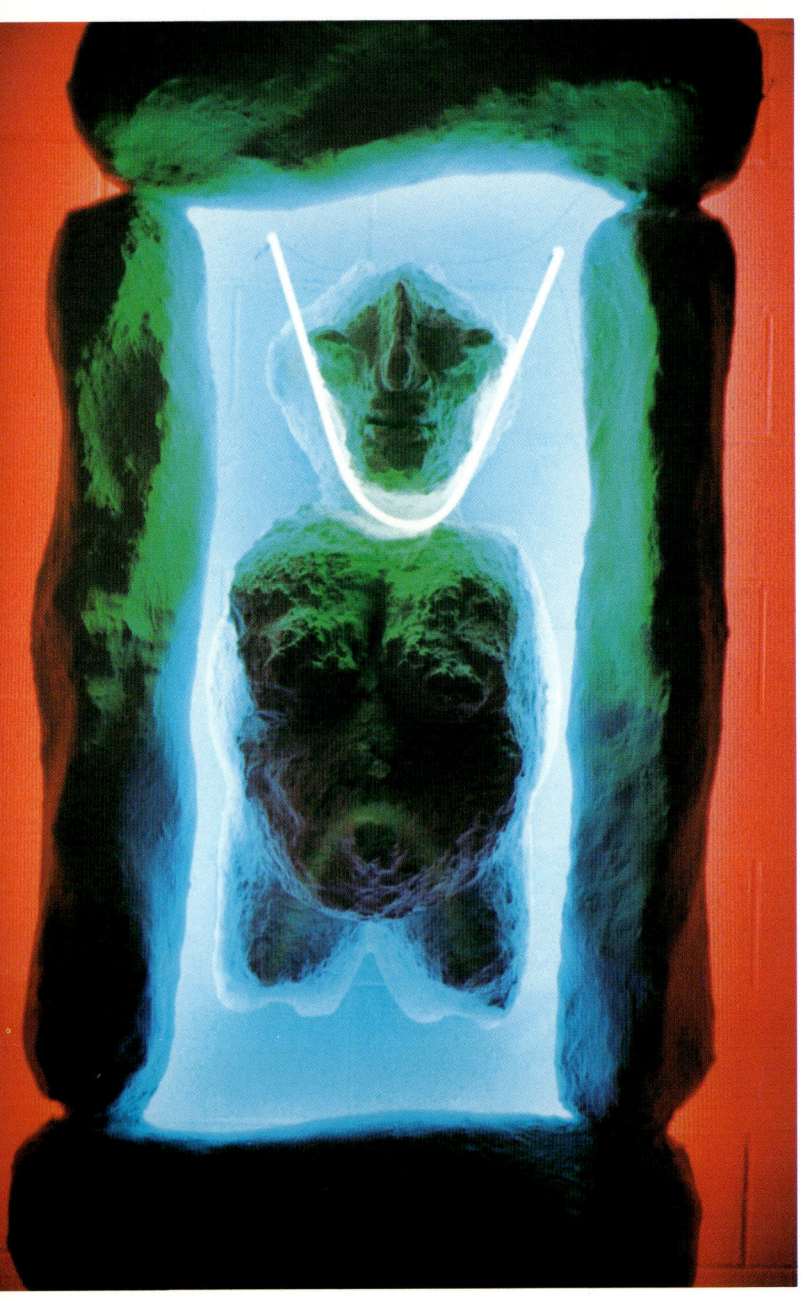

RITE OF SPRING
Joe Augusta, 1989
Dimensions: 72″ high x 34″ wide x 25″ deep
Materials: hydrocal with neon
Photo: Sheila Augusta

"This is a large female figure emerging from a frame (Spring). It's my *Venus of Willendorf,* though it began as a simple task I had set for myself: an attempt to make something round inside something square," the artist explains.

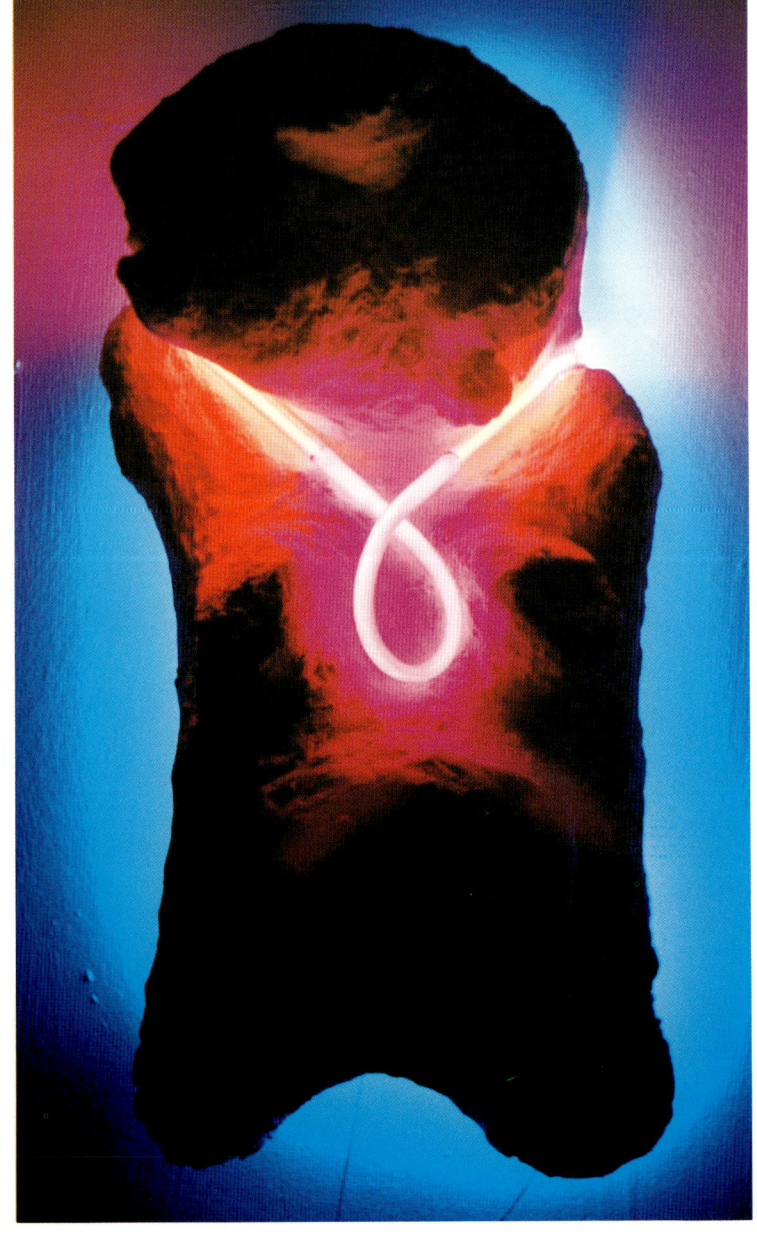

AS A LAMB IS TO A LADY
Joe Augusta, 1989
Dimensions: 30″ high x 14″ wide x 12″ deep
Materials: hydrocal with neon
Photo: Sheila Augusta

"This began as a small female figure built up in thick layers of hydrocal. It was going well until I reached the head, which became not a woman's head but the head of a lamb. I let it stand since lambs to me seem female, and gave it a necklace, or a ring to attach a rope, in neon. It is backlit in neon and floats off the wall." Joe Augusta.

TIKI
Joe Augusta, 1989
Dimensions: 20″ high x 13″ wide x 10″ deep
Materials: hydrocal with neon
Photo: Sheila Augusta

The last student of Eddy Seiss at the Egani Institute, Joe Augusta teaches at U.C.L.A. Visual Arts Department and the Otis-Parsons Art Institute. He is a prime example of a very talented neon artist who has rarely, if ever, broken the barriers of the art world. Over more than 20 years Joe Augusta has developed his very personal expressionistic neon styles, which might be compared to the force of Georges Roualt.

THE OPENING AND CLOSING OF THE EASTERN GATE
Joe Augusta, 1989
Dimensions: 45″ high x 52″ wide x 7″ deep
Materials: hydrocal with neon
Photo: Sheila Augusta

"This, though quite lush in its use of color and shape, is primarily an intellectual exercise for me, dealing with space and emptiness," says its creator.

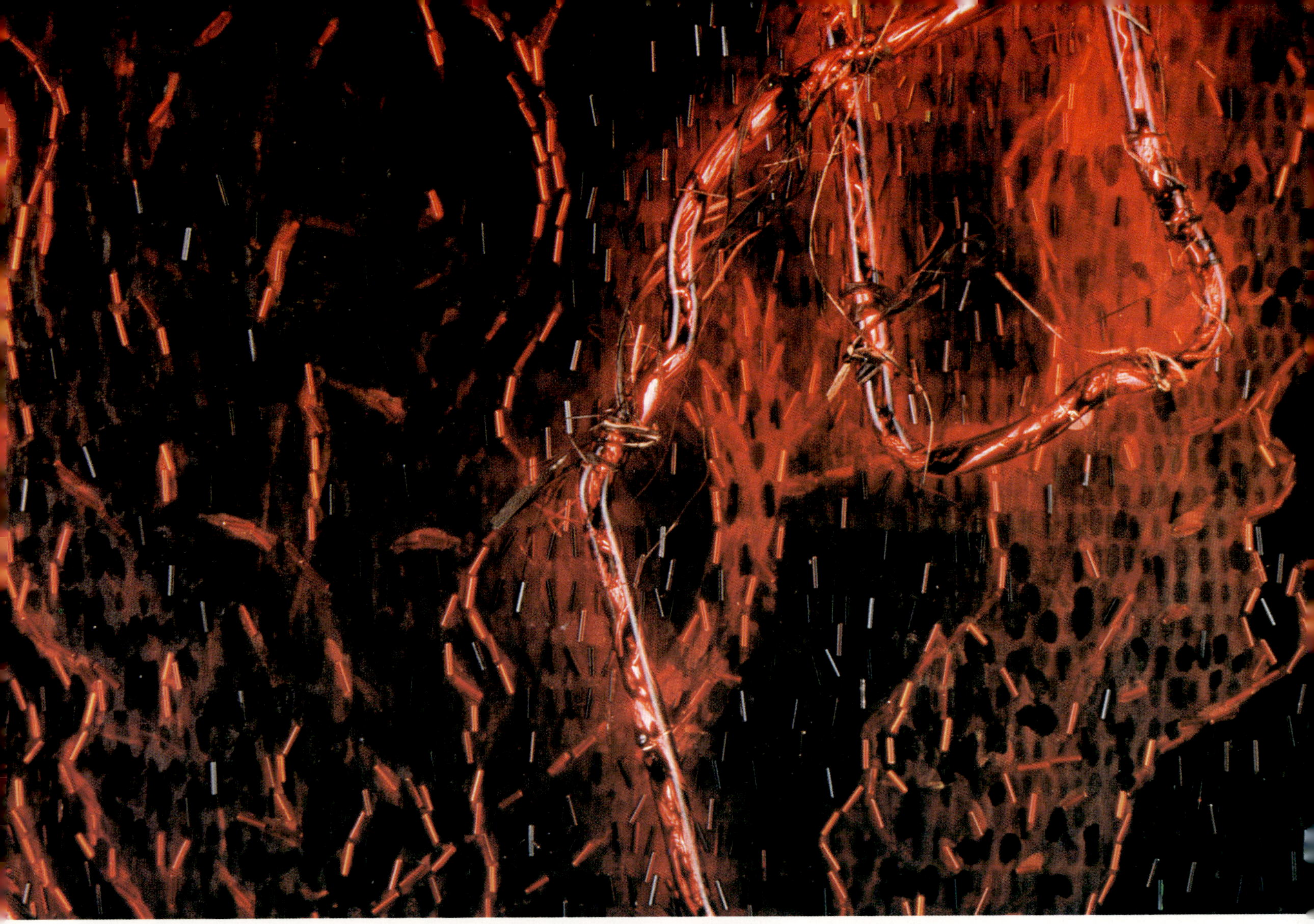

BLOODLINES
Victoria Rivers, 1989
Dimensions: 46" vertical x 39" horizontal x 4" deep
Materials: dyes, pigments on fabric, beads sewn on fabric, painted, wrapped neon
Neon fabrication: Bob Gwilliam at Advance Neon, Inc.
Frame, mounting fabrication: Christopher Liles
Photo: James Woodson

"Bloodlines is part of a series," says Victoria Rivers, "that deals with plant growth and plant energy. I am fascinated by how the tenderest, most fragile roots or tendrils can slowly and eventually go through rock or concrete and engulf entire buildings, much like ancient temples engulfed by the jungle. One of my favorite poems inspired this series: Marianne Moore's 'Nevertheless'."

> ". . . What is there like fortitude! What sap went through that little thread to make the cherry red!"

RAPTURE II
Victoria Rivers, 1983
Dimensions: 24" x 24" x 5" deep
Materials: painted fiberglas over carved styrofoam form, painted neon tubing, carved acrylic shapes.
Photo: Donald Satterlee

"I did a series of shaped, dimensional works that used forms with ambiguous and yet universal suggestions. I was trying to let a shape and the light that accompanies it express an emotion — in this case an extreme (hence the title "rapture") of jealousy or suspicion." Victoria Rivers.

DETAIL FROM PLANT DREAM
Victoria Rivers, 1988
Materials: fabrics including velveteen and silk organza,
  iridescent snakeskin, beads, raffia and other vegetable fibres,
  painted, wrapped argon and black light luminous tubing
Neon fabrication: Bob Gwilliam at Advance Neon, Inc.
Frame and mounting: Christopher Liles
Photo: Victoria Rivers

"I was inspired by a plant I have called a night blooming cereus which exhibits very eccentric growth and unusual blooming (only on a full moon at the dark of night, lasting only that one night)." Victoria Rivers.

DETAIL FROM DAGGERS
Victoria Rivers, 1983
Materials: painted dyed fabric, painted neon, fiberglas over
  carved styrofoam
Dimensions: 7′2″ high; each piece is 40″ wide x 4″ deep (a
  dyptich)
Neon: Bob Gwilliam
Fiberglas fabrication: Christopher Liles
Photo: Donald Satterlee

"This was the first piece where I enlarged the scale and was able to create without the weight and cumbersome construction of wood. I wanted to have clean lines separating the dark pink sections of the neon from the turquoise blue," says Ms. Rivers.

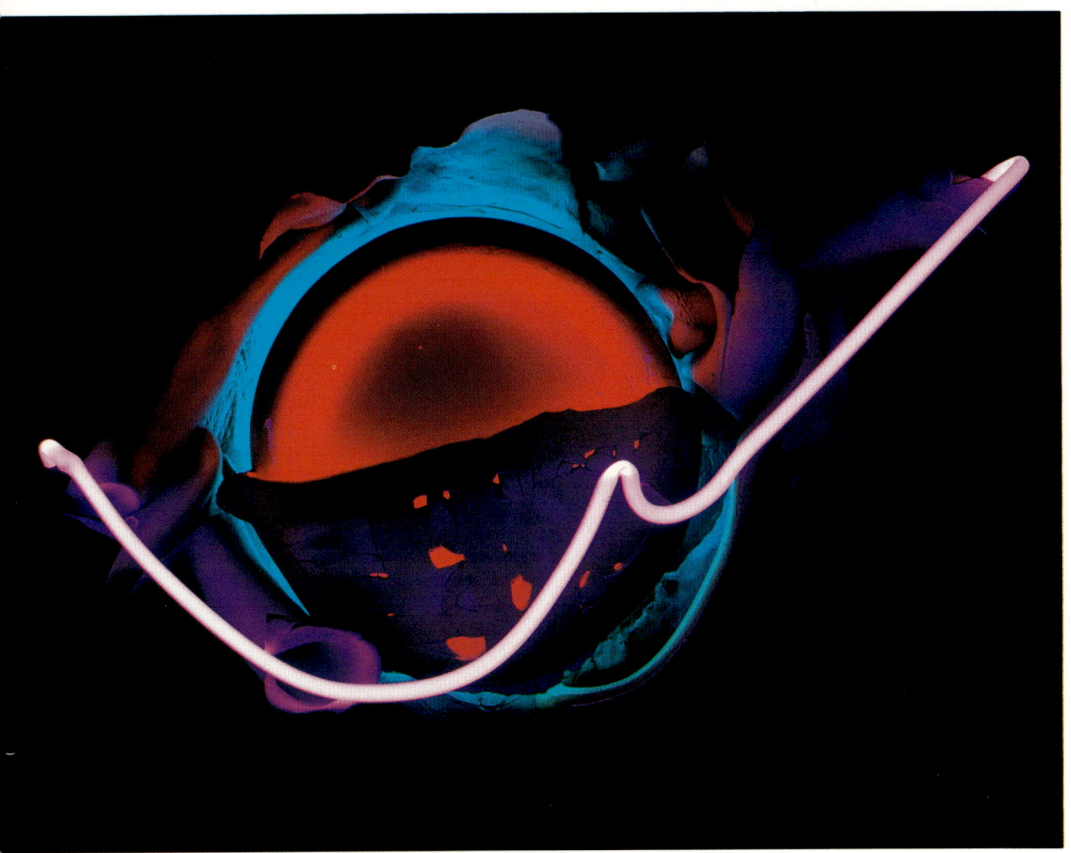

SEEDS AND SONGS
Dave Yocum, 1989
Dimensions: 22" high x 36" wide x 12" deep
Materials: clay and neon
Photo: Dave Yocum

CLOUD COVER
Michael Young, 1989
Dimensions: 42" x 24" x 3"
Materials: neon, brushed aluminum, perforated metal screen, plexiglas
Photo: Michael Young

"I like to create 'windows,' either on walls or free space, that provide views of other possible landscapes or structures in a different dimension," the artist tells us.

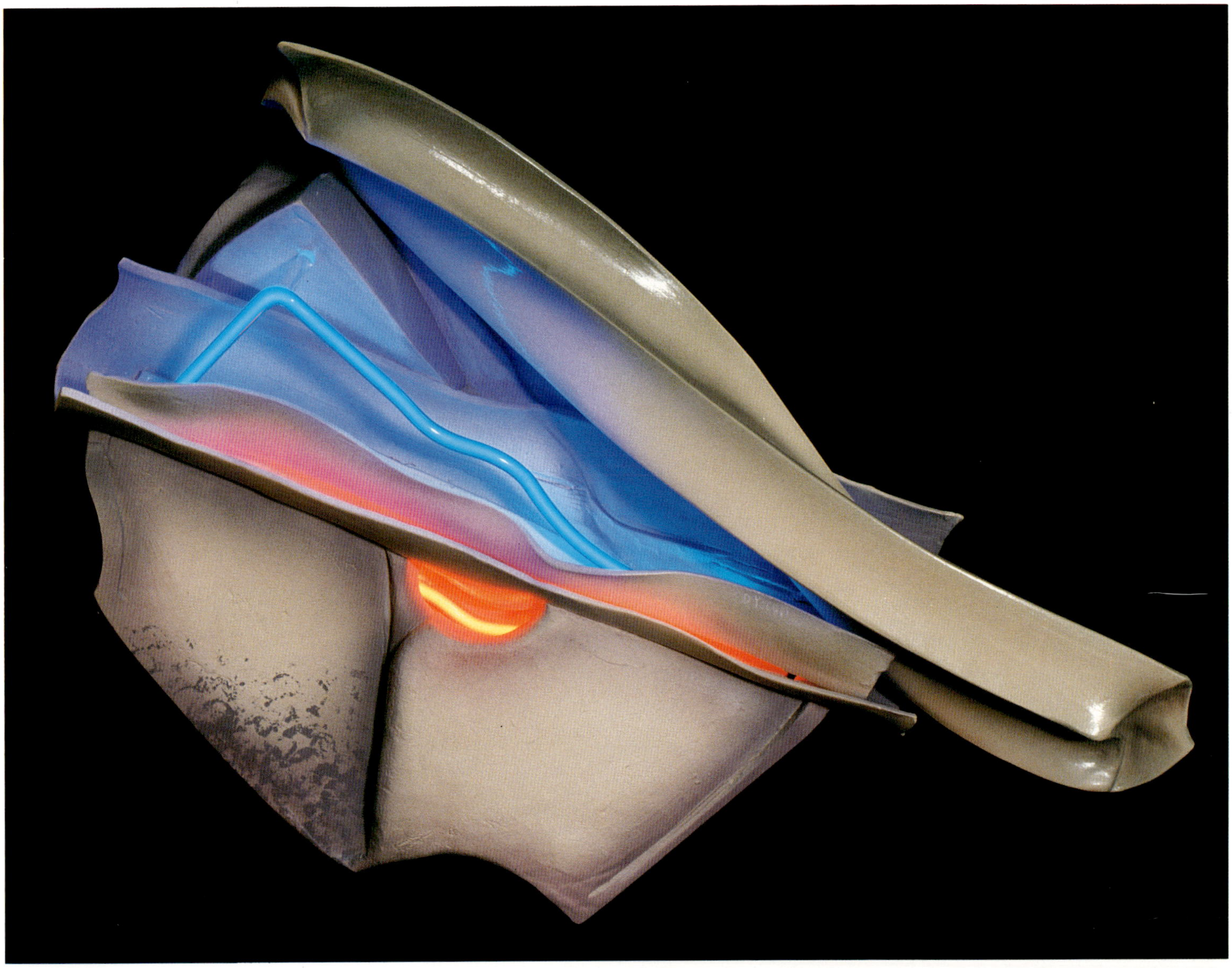

WAVE-CUT
Dave Yocum, 1988
Dimensions: 20" high x 28" wide x 8" deep
Materials: clay and neon
Neon fabrication: Brightstar Neon, Baltimore, Md.
Gallery representation: Zenith Gallery, Washington, D.C.
Photo: Dave Yocum

Dave Yocum's sculptures incorporate natural images suggesting elements of landscapes. He loves to explore the inherent properties of clay as it is twisted, folded and stretched. Neon tubing is used for contrast and high-tech shimmer. It remains a strong design feature even when not illuminated. The results suggest microscopic aerial views exploring geological forms.

Dave Yocum is an instructor at the Baltimore Clayworks.

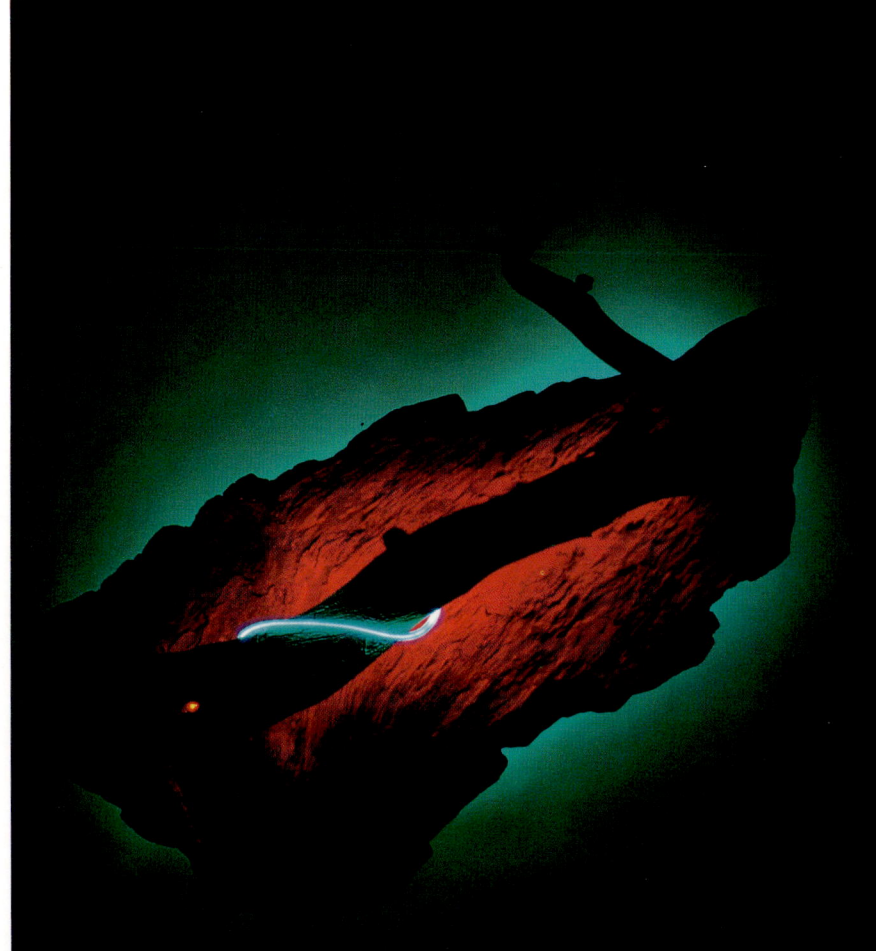

SEQUOIA
Kunio Ohashi, 1987
Dimensions: 2' high × 4' wide
Materials: wood, bark, neon
Photo: Kunio Ohashi

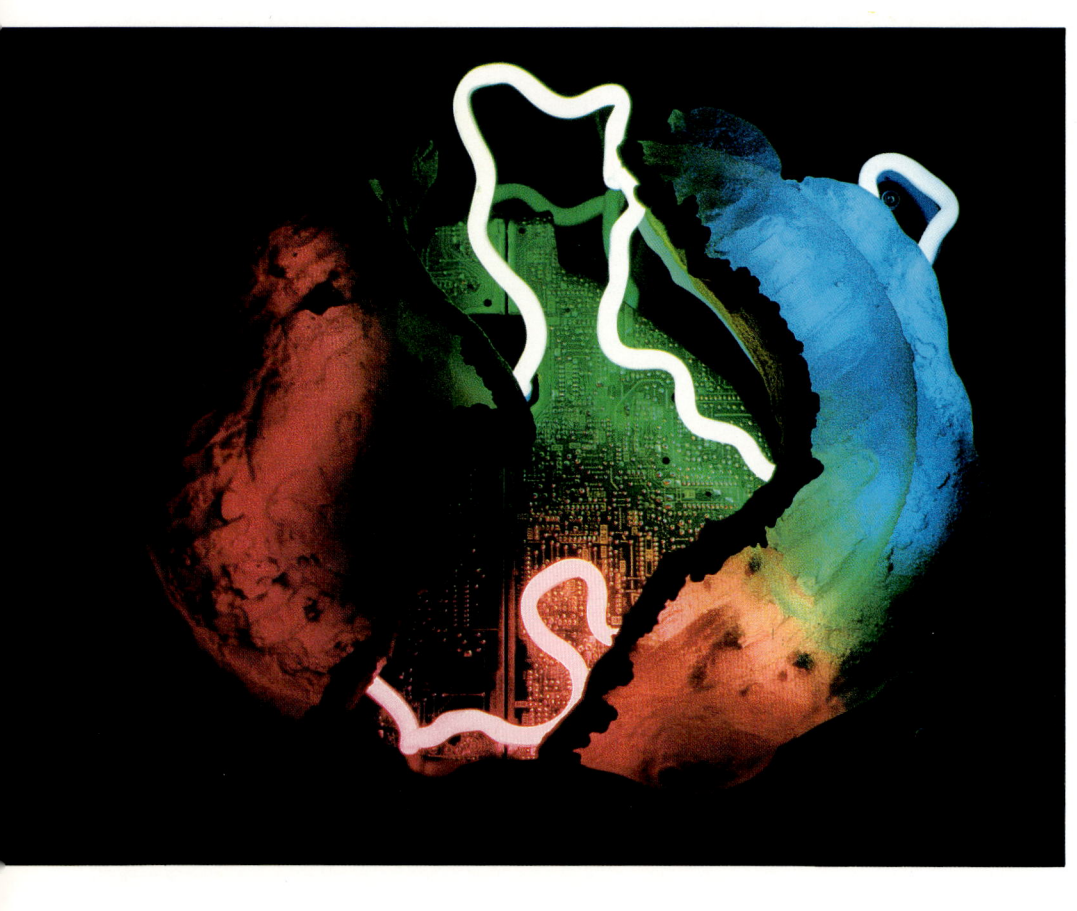

134

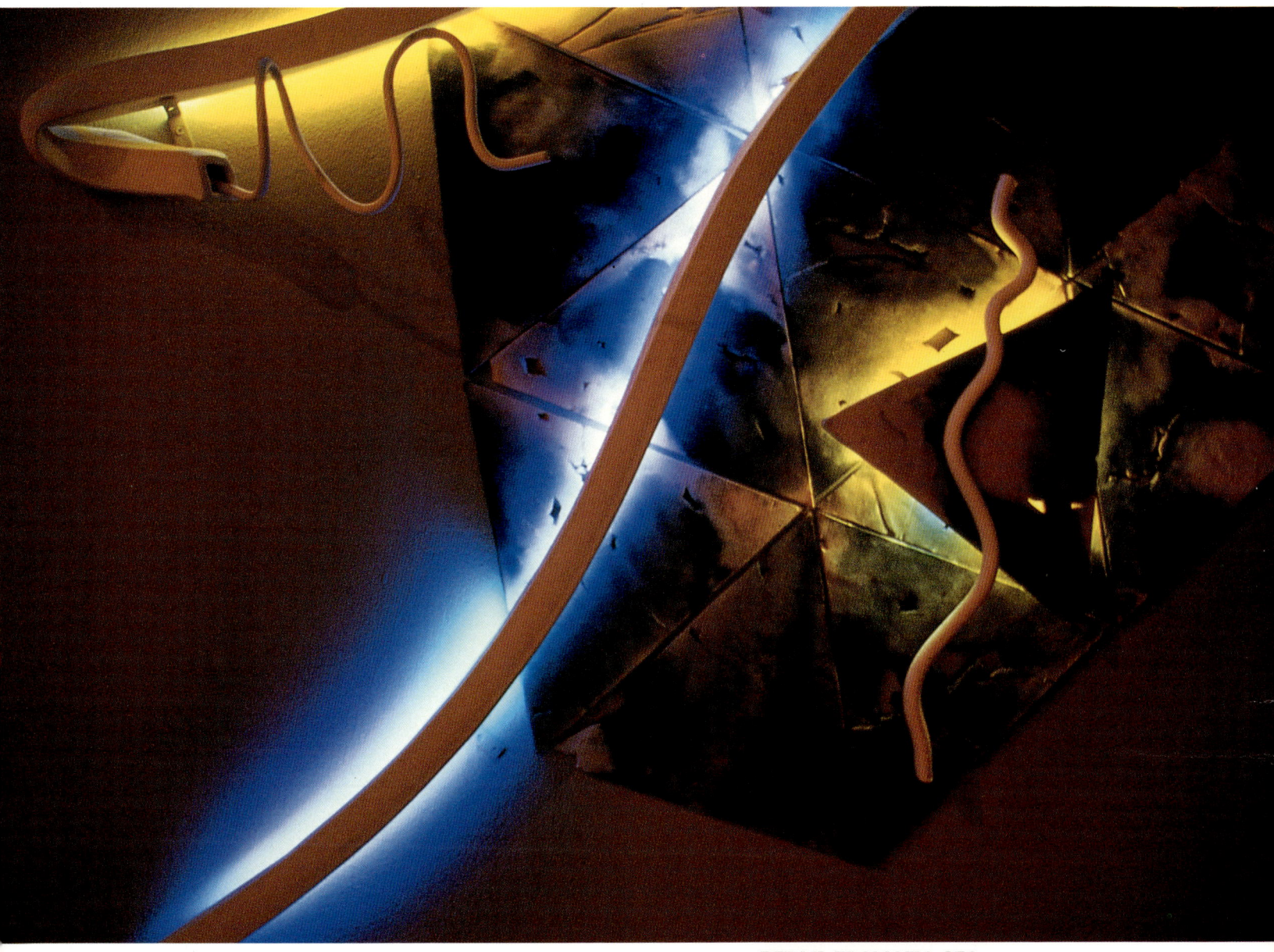

DETAIL FROM NEO-GEO
Ann Walenta and Ted Pirsig
Dimensions: 8" x 8"
Photo: Ted Pirsig

Pit-fired clay and neon wall mounted.

Top left:
EUREKA MAYBE
Roddy Capers
Dimensions: 7" high x 7" wide x 14" deep
Materials: copper plated cast glass, plexiglas, integrated circuit board, neon and brass
Neon benders: Larry Holder of Gulfport, Miss. and Gary Gray of Metairie, La.
Photo: Roddy Capers

Mr. Capers says, "I strive to integrate different media in which all materials balance out the finished piece. No one material overdominates the finished piece. I push my work in several directions with the intent of discovering new relations. Found objects are very challenging to me."

Bottom left
SUN SIGN
Jon Miskinis, 1970
Dimensions: 30" high x 48" wide
Materials: neon, vacuum formed plastics, acrylic rods, optic fiber
Photo: Jon Miskinis

"Neon light is the future, the excitement, and the dynamics of inter-stellar society," believes this artist.

FIRST PRAYER
Janet Evans, 1988
Dimensions: 15" high x 11" wide x 4" deep
Materials: mixed media on wood with acrylic paint and argon
Photo: Robert Alpert

"My work dwells on the experience of being human as one of conflict between our animalistic state and our capacity for Godliness. I work to discover and depict the sublime moment when a balanced unity is acquired. Found material from nature is mixed with layers of paint; I use neon as a strong dynamic and between this dynamic of contrasts, along with the ethereal luminosity of neon, I hope to create a metaphor of enlightenment and grace," says Janet Evans, who manages Precision Neon and Cathode, Inc.

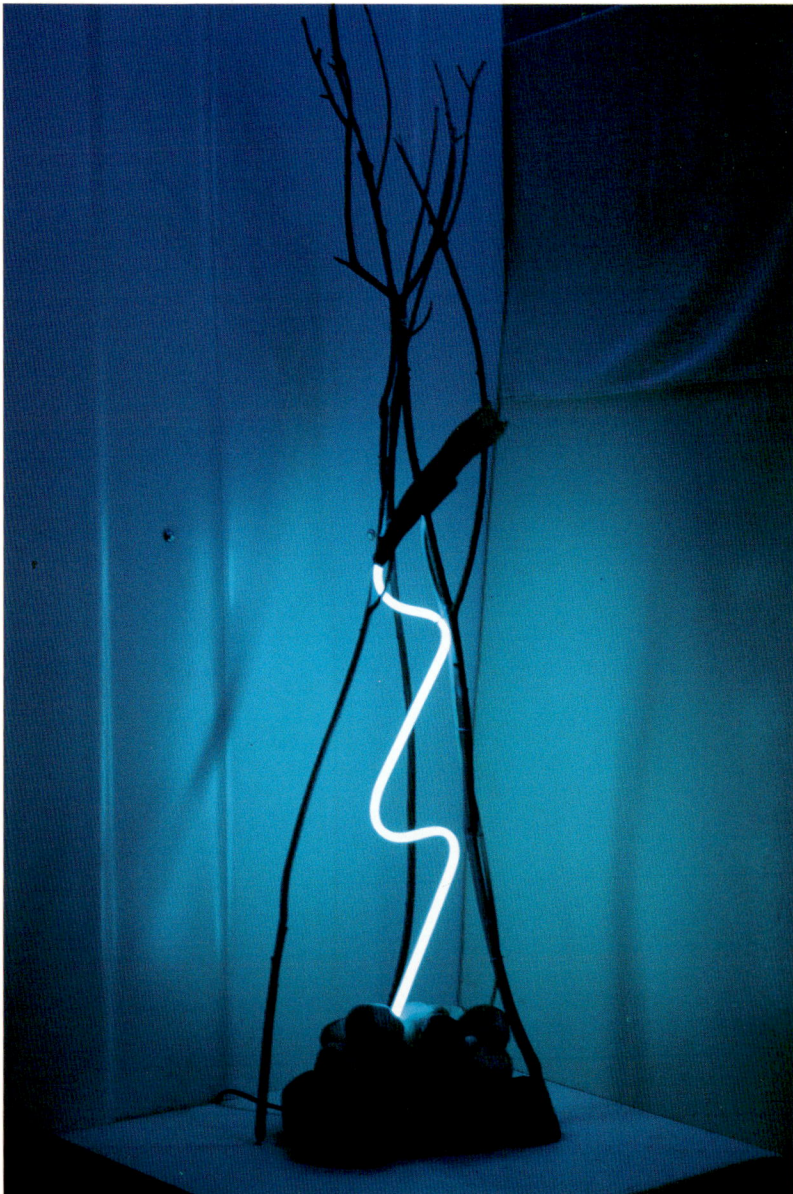

LIGHTNING STRIKE
Maureen Havoy, 1990
Dimensions: 54" high x 12" wide x 12" deep
Materials: willow, raku-fired porcelain, turquoise tubes (argon/mercury)
Fabrication: Studio One Neon
Photo: Maureen Havey

One of a series, this piece depicts the close relationship neon light has with nature, especially lightning.

POINT OF INTRODUCTION
Michael Young, 1989
Dimensions: 42″ x 96″ x 3″
Materials: neon, anodized aluminum, perforated steel, lucite
Photo: Michael Young

"Here the word introduction has two meanings. I'm introducing the visible corner of a much larger structure from a parallel dimension into the introduction area of the residence." Michael Young.

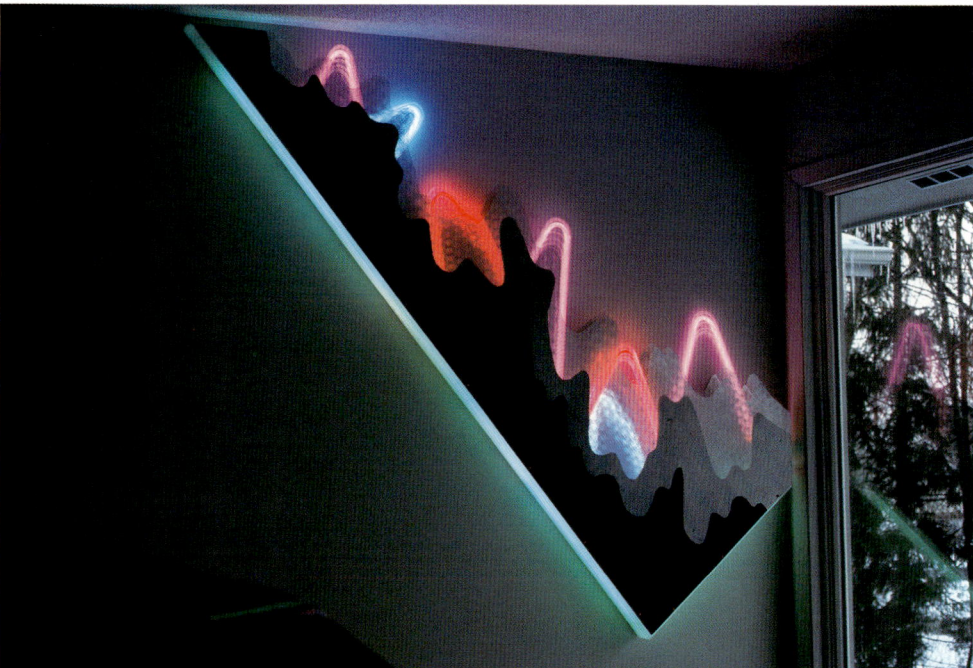

TICKLED PINK
Richard L. Rozinski, 1988
Dimensions: 48″ high x 96″ wide x 12″ deep
Fabrication: Wm. C. Paisley
Photo: Richard L. Rozinski

FIRE VIII, TRIPTYCH 31
Lori Gene Mulherin
Dimensions: 31″ high
Materials: thrown and altered stoneware, multifired, with commercially produced neon
Collection: Lawrence Nelson Hicks
Photo: J.P. Mulherin

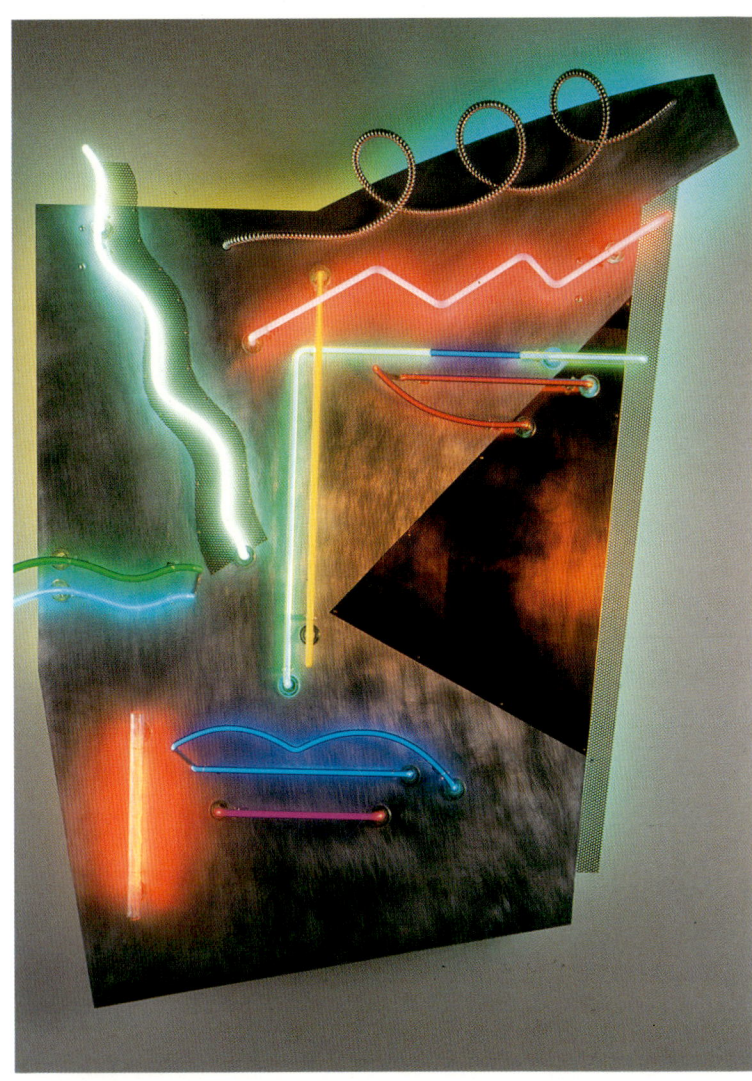

Facing page:
MAMBO
Lili Lakich, 1988
Dimensions: 72″ high x 56″ wide x 18″ deep
Materials: argon with mercury, neon, helium, aluminum, copper, brass
Photo: Jeff Atherton

The Museum of Neon Art was created by Lili Lakich in 1981. MONA is a non-profit organization which exhibits, documents, and preserves works of neon, electric and kinetic art. The Museum also offers courses in neon design and fabrication.

Left:
SAVING GRACE II
Lili Lakich, 1984
Dimensions: 60″ high x 48″ wide x 10″ deep
Materials: argon with mercury, neon, helium, aluminum, copper, brass
Photo: Jeff Atherton
Photo courtesy: The Museum of Neon Art, Los Angeles, Calif.

Lili Lakich has been working with neon for more than 20 years. She has made significant contributions to the field both as an artist and as the co-founder of The Museum of Neon Art in Los Angeles in 1981.

FIND THE FRUIT
Don Jacobson, 1985
Dimensions: 6′6″ high x 15′6″ wide x 16″ deep
Materials: neon, plastic, metal, rubber and various electro-mechanical devices
Photo: Clare Wood

"The design evolved from a study of camouflage in newspaper scribble puzzles. Because of light, the piece shows the relationship between objects hidden and revealed. My experience at the New York Experimental Glass Workshop is the foundation of my work with light as a medium." Don Jacobson

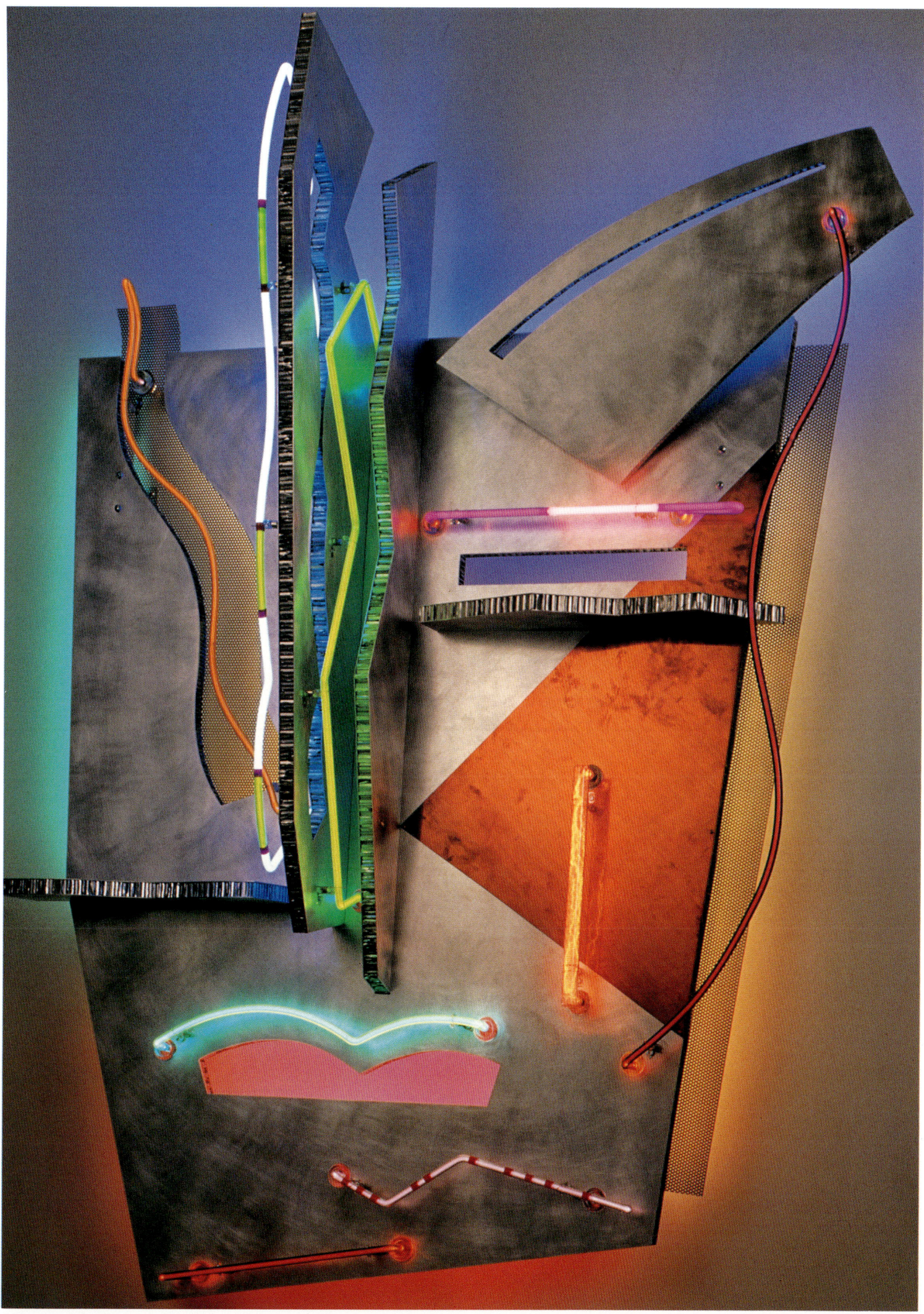

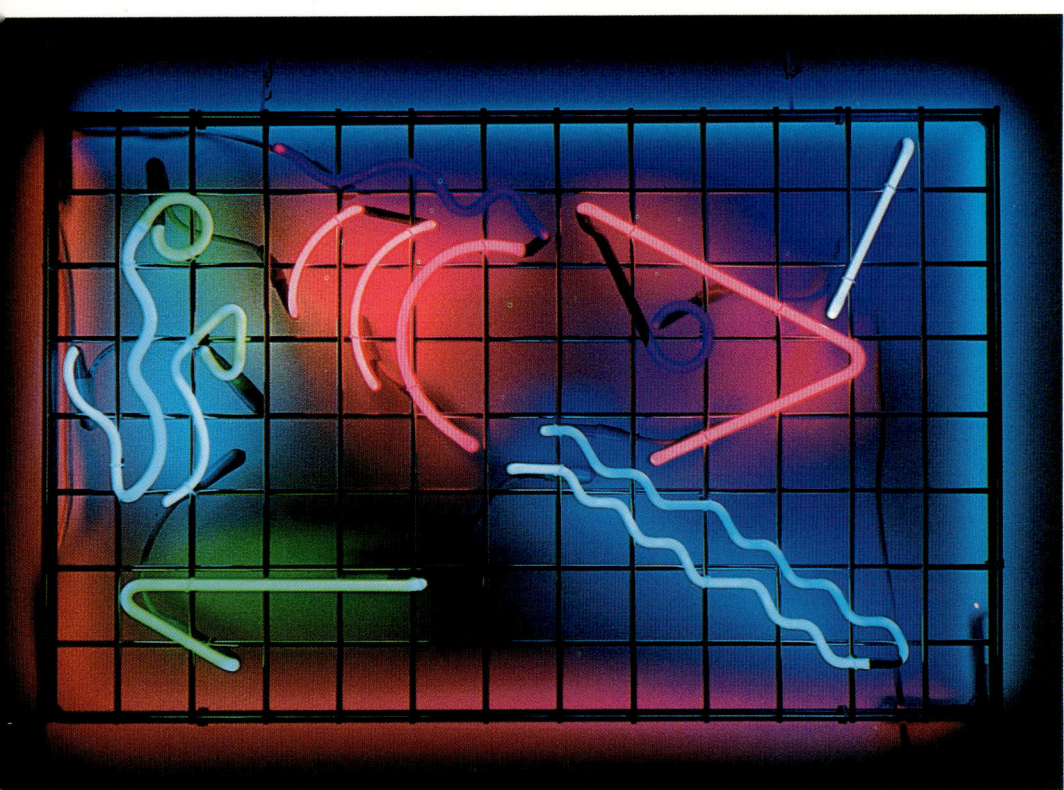

Left:
AT THE BOTTOM OF THE WATER
Dennis Dix and Dana Burton, City Lights Neon, 1988
Dimensions: 24″ high x 48″ wide
Materials: neon mounted on a chrome grid
Photo: City Lights Neon

Right:
FUTURE FARMERS OF AMERICA
Patrick Bresette, 1983
Dimensions: 2′ high x 4′ wide; overall, 14′ wide
Materials: neon and hay bales
Photo: Patrick Bresette

Below:
CONTINENTAL DRIFT
Patrick Bresette, 1987
Dimensions: 2′ high x 8′ wide x 10′ deep
Materials: neon, asphalt and mixed media
Phto: Patrick Bresette

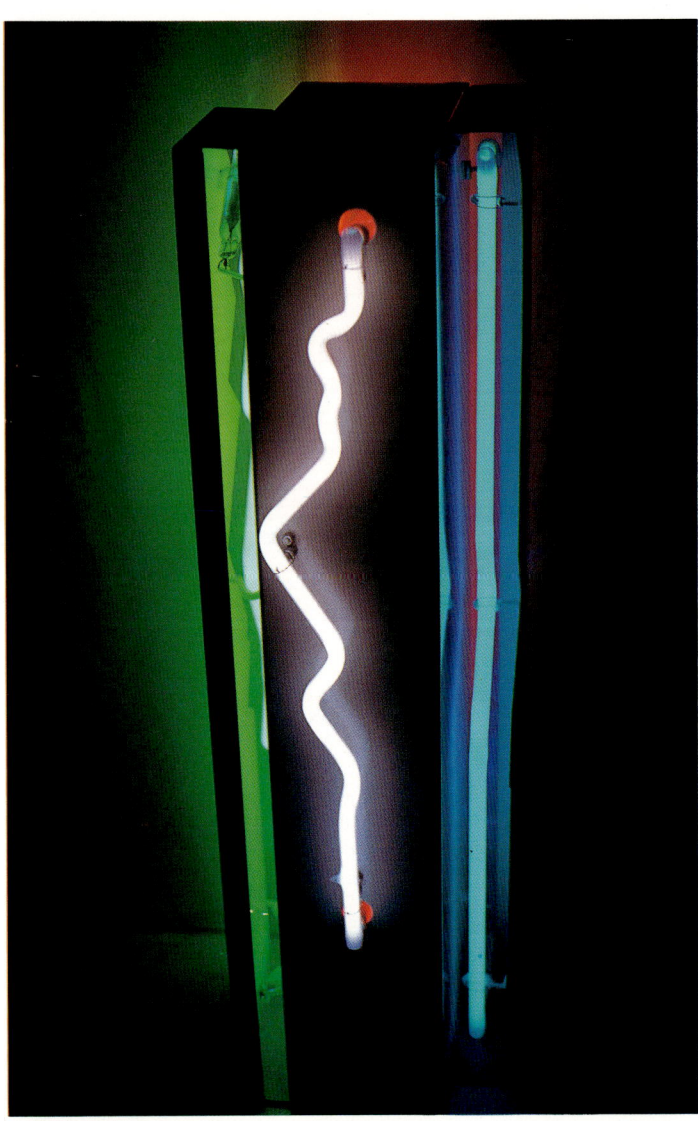

GEMINIS III
Cristina Sicardi, 1989, Buenos Aires
Dimensions: 74 cm high x 26 cm wide x 22 cm deep
Materials: argon and neon on painted metal
Photo: Maria Pita Romero

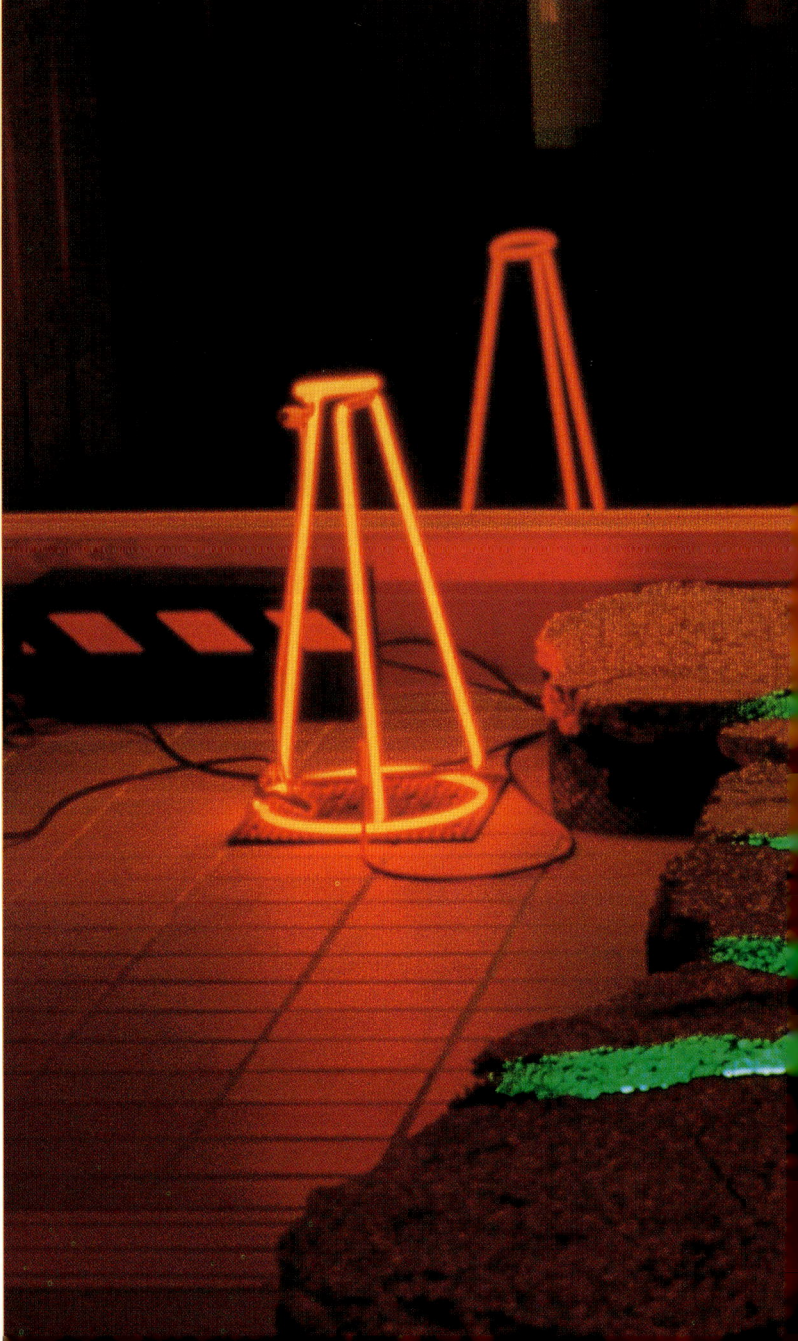

DIFFERENT DIRECTIONS
Linn Westbay Woloshin, 1985
Dimensions: 20″ high x 36″ wide
Materials: slate and neon
Photo: Linn Westbay Woloshin

ALFRED HITCHCLOCK
Michael Furey, 1988
Dimensions: 2" diameter
Materials: neon and an old clock
Client: Sam Hunan
Photo: Tom Wisherop

"Always admiring neon clocks, I decided to make one that was fun. Alfred Hitchcock's self portrait struck me as linear and graceful for this purpose. The clock is backlit so it has a three dimensional feel to it. Thus Alfred Hitchclock," explains the artist.

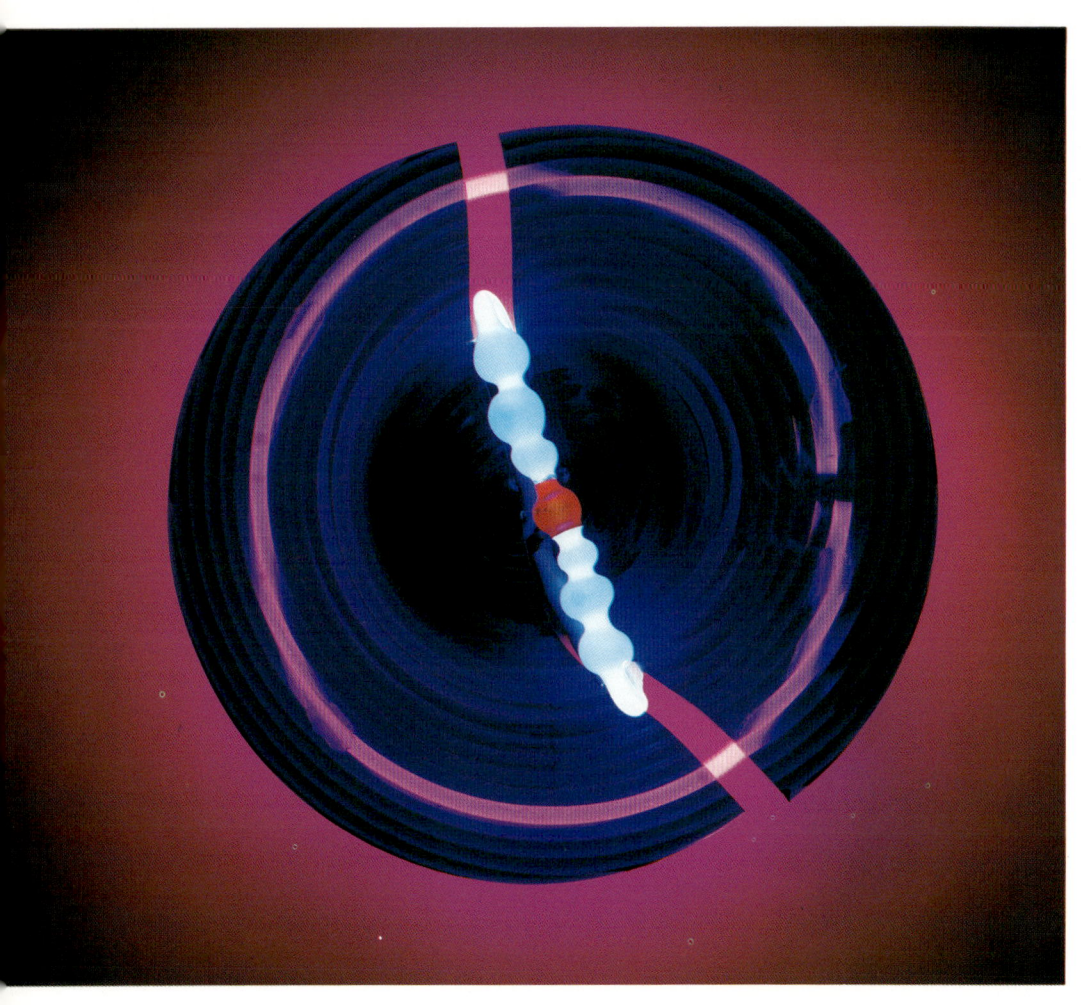

CIRCLE SERIES NUMBER 8
Kevin Stirnweis, 1989
Photo: William Artemowych

Slumped glass plate fractured, supported by casted ceramic base, which is used for wall mounting. The center neon is gathered and blown-out with ruby red and purple. The fractured plate is also illuminated from behind with hot pink neon.

Kevin Stirnweis runs Light Design Neon in Chelsea, Mass., and studied with Fred Tschida at Alfred University.

WISHBONE
Tom Scarff, 1987
Dimensions: 12" high x 16" wide
Materials: onyx, aluminum, ruby and neo-blue pumped red.
Photo: Tom Scarff

"Experiment with light and stone trying to achieve transluscence," says Tom Scarff. "Brings out the beauty and age of stone, allows you to see into stone. Neon is the only way to achieve this."

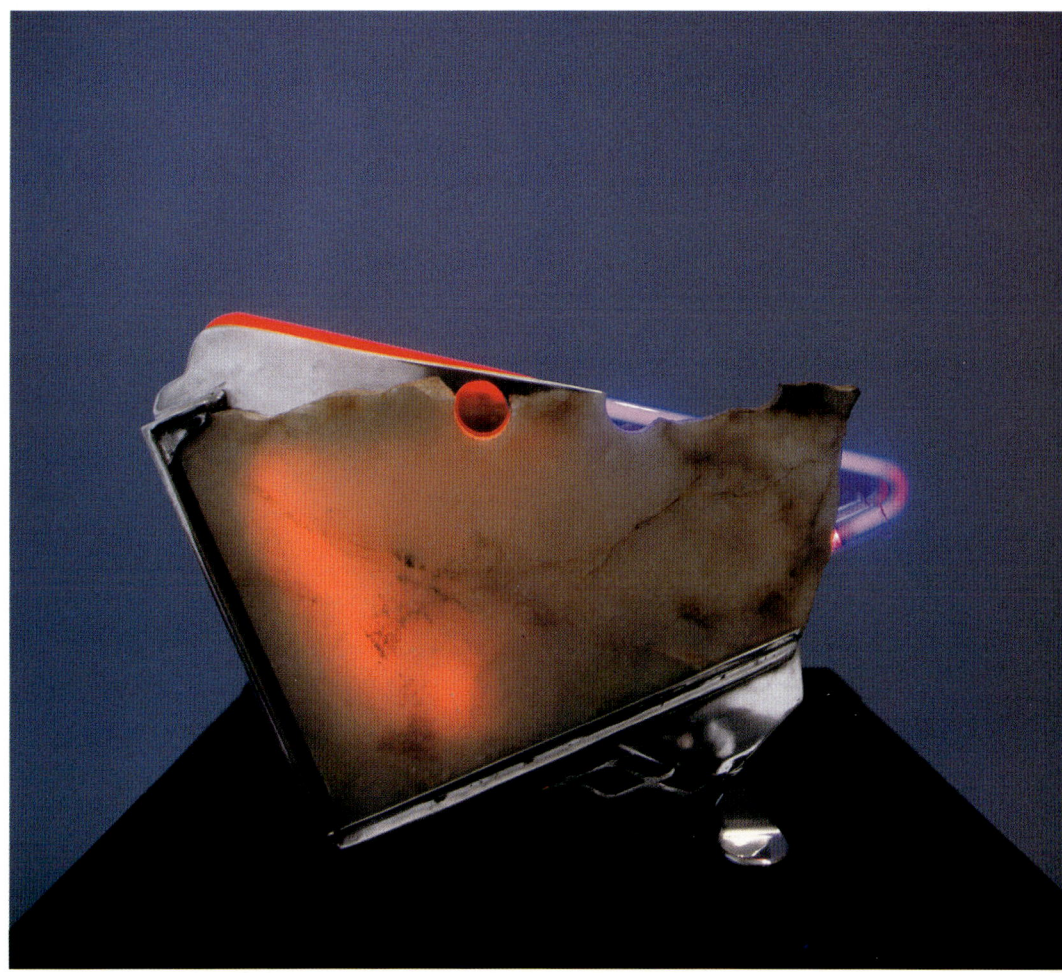

SPLIT GRID
Roddy Capers, 1988
Dimensions: 18" high x 16" wide x 7" deep
Materials: cast glass, copper plating, plexiglas, neon
Photo: Roddy Capers

A sand mold was made from an iron grating; glass was cast, sandblasted, then copper plated. Selium was used on copper areas for reddish patina. Glass was mounted on plexiglas and neon bent to glass configuration.

"Relationship of contrasts is a constant part of my work, such as contrast of materials (glass to metal, found objects to self-made objects) dark to light, internal form to external form and so on." Roddy Capers

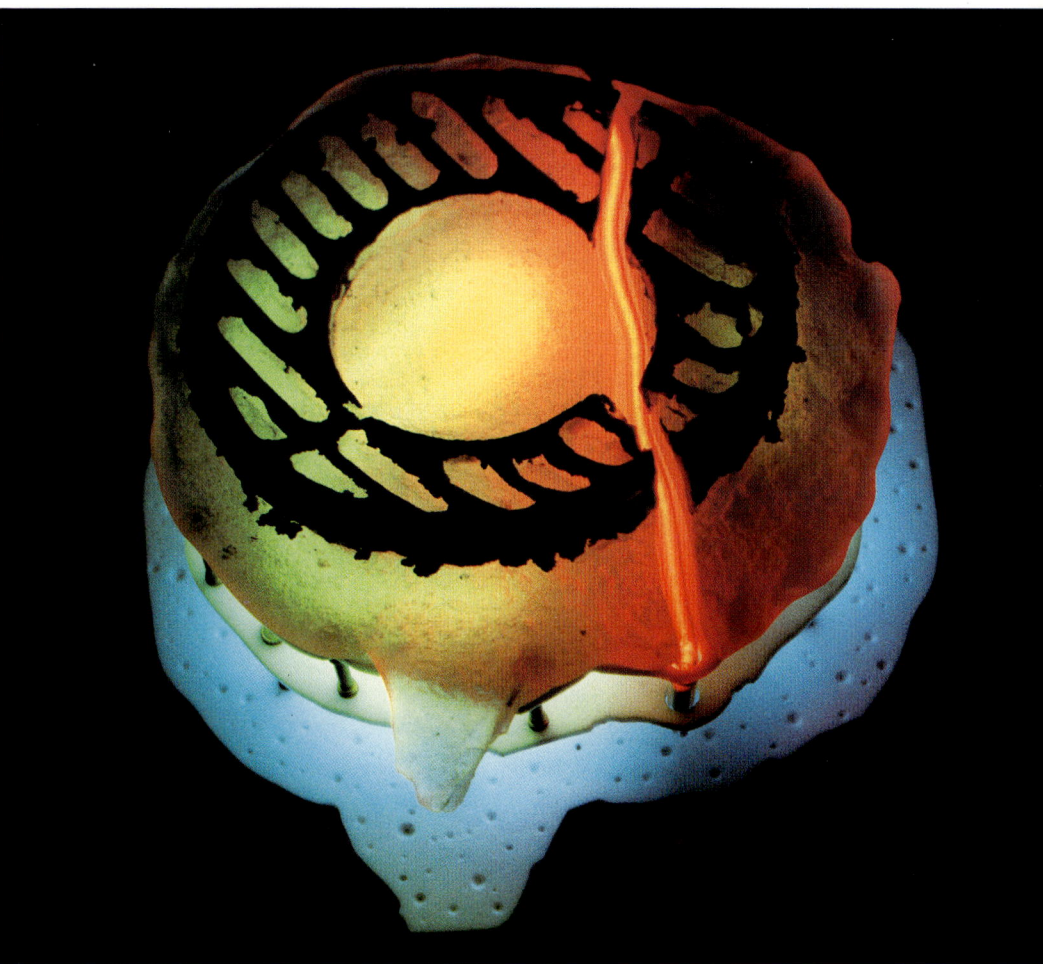

LIGHT POLE
Ben Livingston, 1987
Dimensions: 7' high and 2' wide
Materials: corrugated, galvanized spiral channel
Photo: Carrington Weems

"A study based on Paul Klee's spiral of life — a line taking a walk for itself," says Mr. Livingston.

Livingston's art is one of the more imaginative in the medium — his approach is always fresh and original.

Facing page:
DYNAMO FLOOR LAMP
Jeff Becker, 1985
Dimensions: 47" high x 28" wide
Materials: plastic and neon
Photo: Jeff Becker

This 26 year old artist has an interesting background. Currently he is working as a fine art lithographer at the American Atelier, having previously restored and repaired stained glass in the churches of Holland with the SiO2 Workshop in Groningen. He has studied and assisted in teaching at Pilchuck and, of course, with Fred Tschida at Alfred. In the fall of 1990 he will be teaching neon classes at Ohio State University.

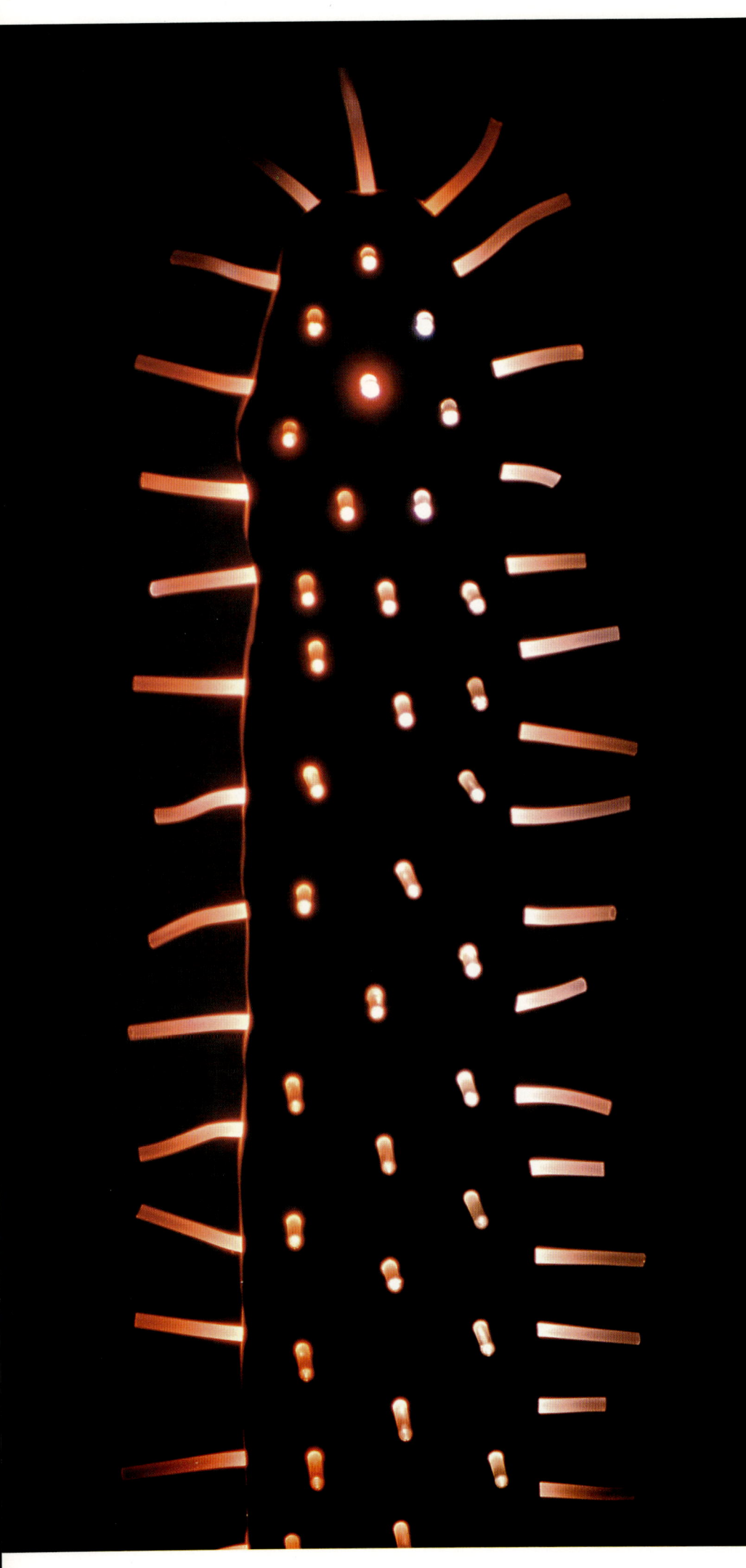

FRENCH FLOOR LAMP
Jeff Becker, 1987
Dimensions: 59" high x 24" wide
Materials: neon and wood
Photo: Jeff Becker

"Through the use of neon I illuminated a central mood in my sculpture and strive to entice the viewer with the dynamics of light." Jeff Becker

Right:
LUMETRIC POMMEL
Michael Hayden, 1980 ©
Collection: Mr. and Mrs. Rudge Allen, Houston, Tex.
Photo: Rudge Allen

"This 'Lumetric' sculpture was created expressly for the courtyard of the Allen residence and utilizes my exploration into micro processor control of a linearly aligned spectrum of gas discharge tubes. The sculpture consists of a continuous cast transparent hybrid plastic ribbon, shatterproof polycarbonate tubes inside of which are floating the 'neon' elements. These 79 tubes are made of 15 mm glass pumped with argon gas doped with mercury and powdered with 6500 angstrom phosphorous and then individually colored. The chromatic extremes meld together at the central area of the 'Lumetric' sculpture by stepping through the blues, blue violets, violets, red violets, magentas, etc. ..." Michael Hayden

LOG JAM
Fred Tschida, 1986
Dimensions: 30' x 60' x 22'
Materials: 126 polar branches hollowed out and fitted with argon/mercury tubes
Installation at the Dupree Art Center, Hope College, Holland, Michigan
Photo: Fred Tschida

This work consists of approximately one hundred and twenty six 3" to 4" in diameter poplar branches, each one hollowed out to accommodate a blue argon/mercury tube. Each branch was suspended at 7' from the 22' ceiling.

Fred Tschida is Associate Professor of Glass Design and Chairman of the Division of Three Dimensional Studies at the New York State College of Ceramics at Alfred University. He is responsible for turning on a whole wave of young artists to the mysteries and delights of neon and glass. There are active former students of his all over the country who, in turn, are now teaching, creating and exhibiting neon art.

WOVEN LIGHT
Chris Freeman, 1989
Dimensions: 9' high x 6' wide x 5' deep
Materials: argon, mercury, neon
Construction: 15 mm tubes formed into thread-like fibers create a weaving of glass fabric that is freely suspended from wall to floor
Photo: Chris Freeman

"I think of light as being plastic that I can shape and mold into any form or feeling by controlling its intensity. The raw material has endless possibilities. Light determines how we interpret our world. Our every mood is affected by light — it is because of this that I enjoy manipulating it both functionally and sculpturally." Chris Freeman

LIGHT SCULPTURE
Chris Freeman, 1984
Dimensions: 7' high x 30' wide
Materials: argon/mercury
Photo: Karen Pento

One in a series of works created solely with the movement of light recorded on film.

"My light drawings use light within an environment," says Chris Freeman, "but here the environment consists only of the light itself, and is recorded in time by the camera."

FOUNTAIN
Romano Abate, 1989, Treviso, Italy
Dimensions: 10′ high × 4′ wide
Materials: wood and neon tubes
Neon fabrication and installation: Italneon, Fontane Di Villorba (TV) Italy
Photo: courtesy Glostertube, Milan, Italy, Alberto Rizzato and Italneon SNC: Giuseppe Piovesan

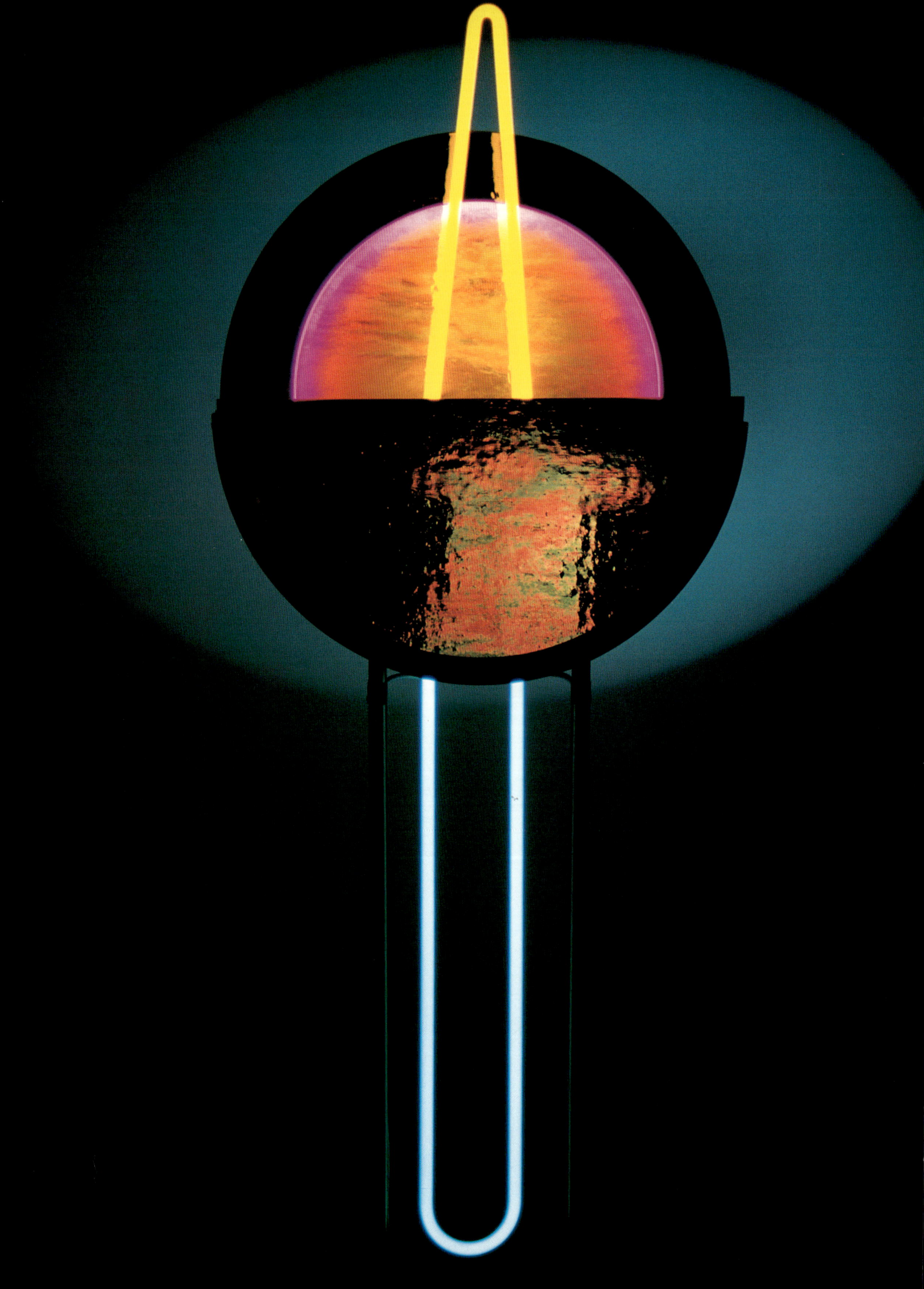

Facing page:
VERTICAL ECLIPSE
Carmine M. Saccardo, 1987
Dimensions: 72" high x 20" wide
Materials: neon, stained glass, aluminum, steel, marble base
Photo: Carmine M. Saccardo

Overleaf
JUDGEMENT DAY
Carmine M. Saccardo, 1988
Dimensions: 38" high x 26" wide
Materials: cut black glass, ruby red neon, cobalt blue
Photo: Carmine M. Saccardo

Right:
BA-O-BA
Keith Sonnier, 1972
Dimensions: 91" high x 217" wide x 12 1/2" deep
Materials: neon, glass, mirror and aluminum
Photo courtesy Castelli Gallery, New York, N.Y.

Below:
THE FIRE DANCE
Federica Marangoni, 1988
Dimensions: 270 cm diameter
Materials: neon, glass and mirror

"Neon is fire, or something which approximates it, a flame that consumes or illuminates." Vincente A. Pineda.

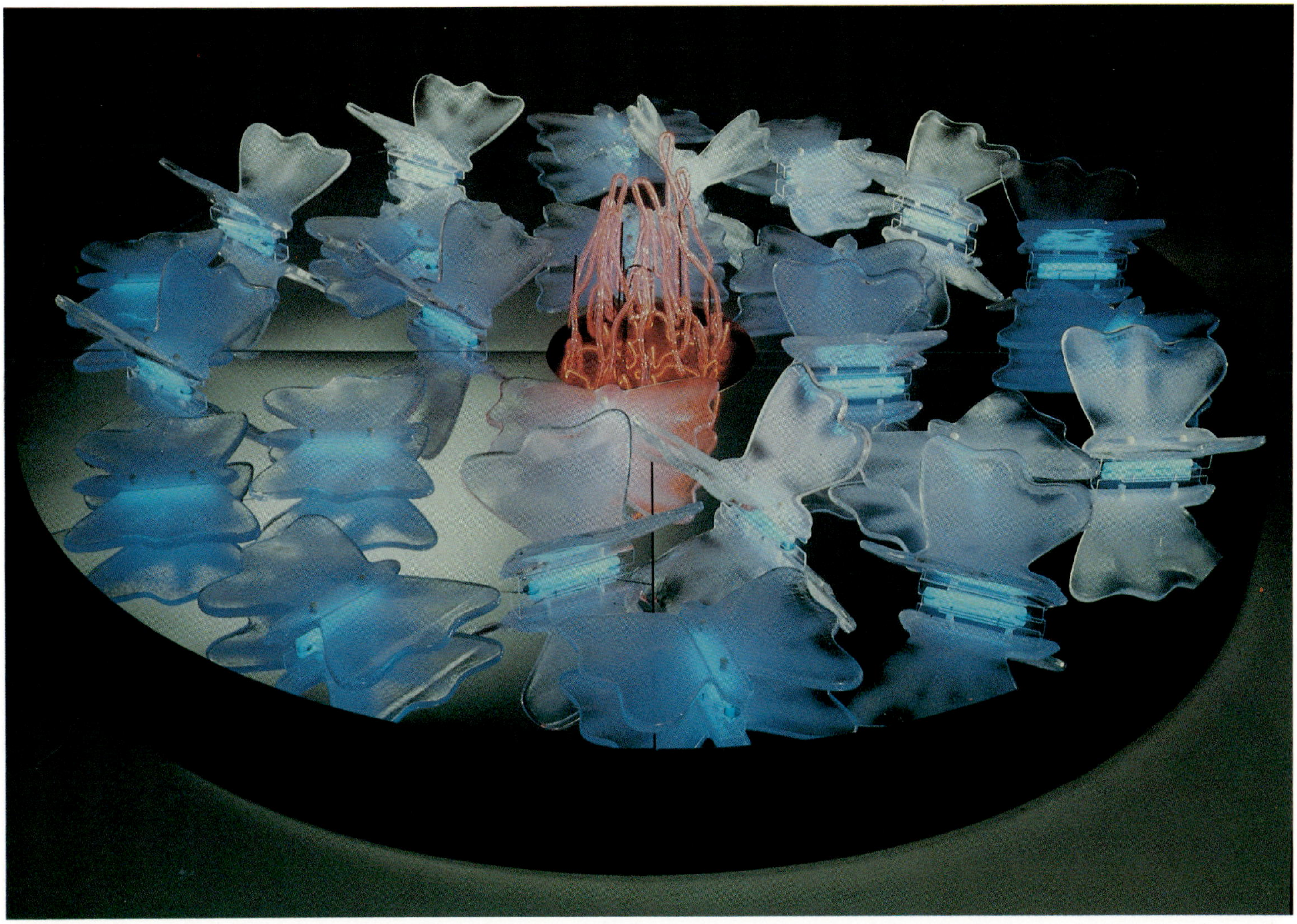

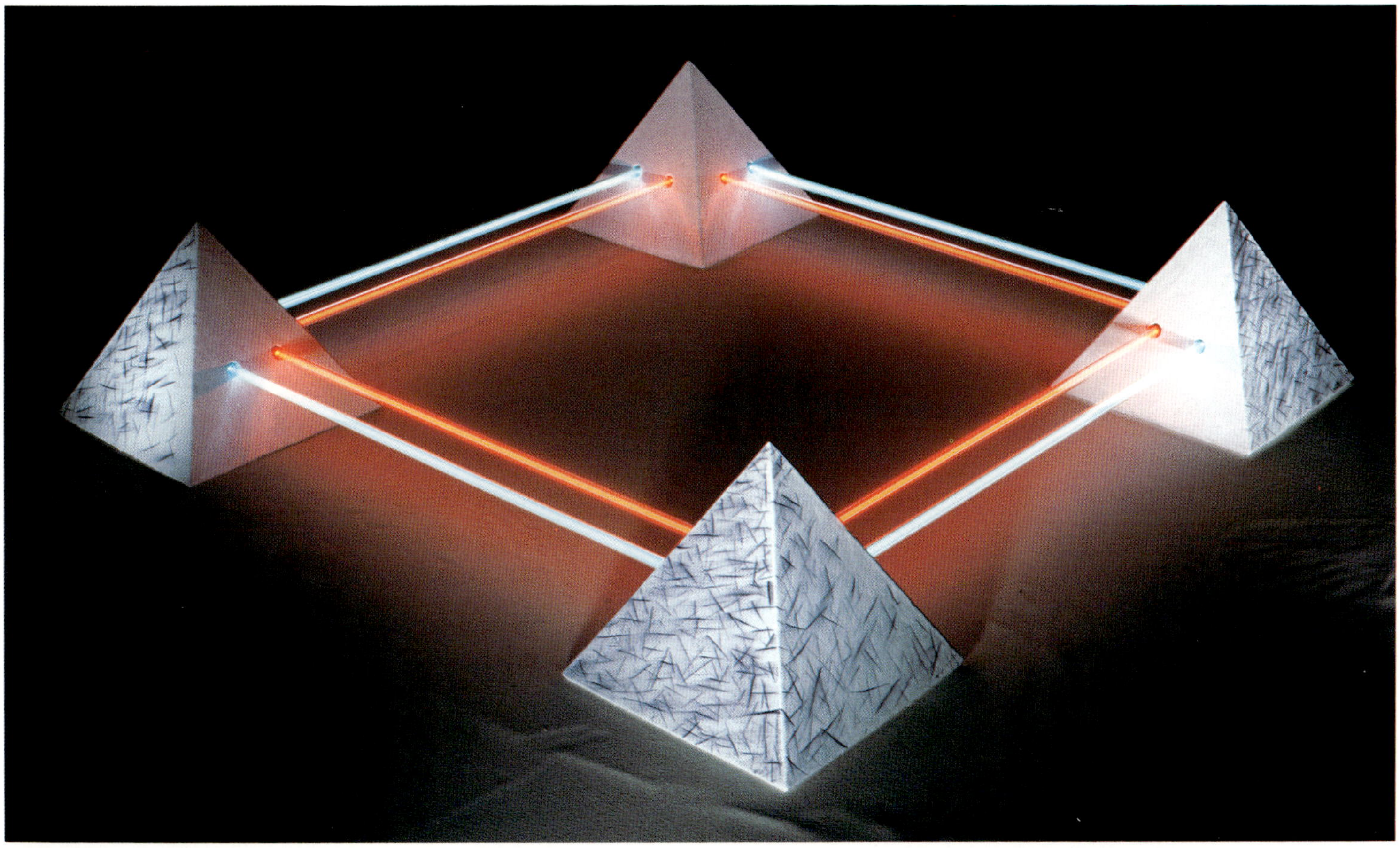

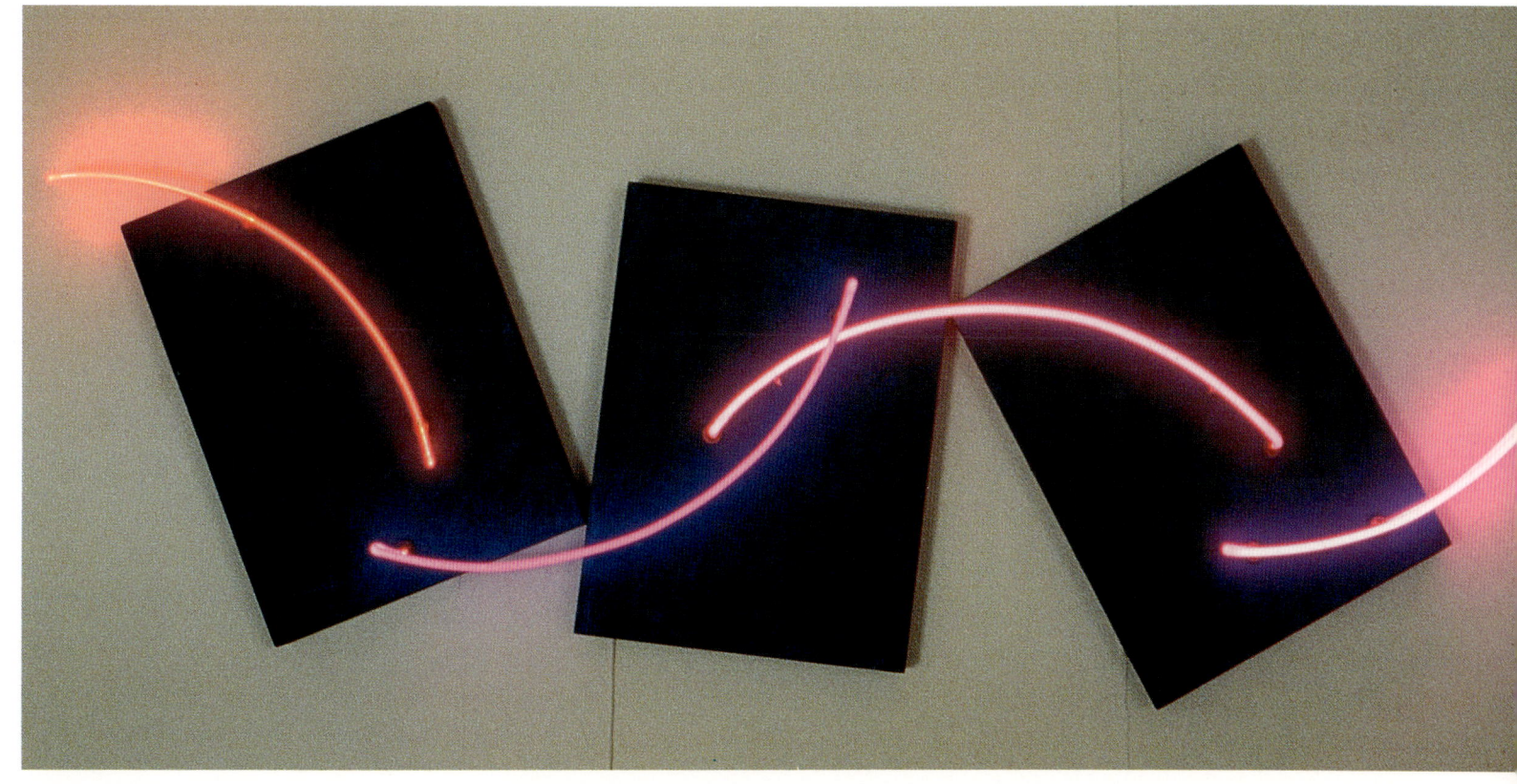

PYRAMID SCULPTURE
Jozef van der Horst, 1986, The Hague, Holland
Dimensions: 45 cm high x 2 m x 2 m
Materials: neon on sand surface
Fabrication: Gerard Leder of Neon Lewa
Photo: Fernando van Tylingen

"Neon light makes the secrets of the pyramids visible. I use neon like a painter uses his paint." Jozef van der Horst.

BLUE TILT
Jerry Lee Noe, 1989
Dimensions: 38″ high x 110″ wide x 6″ deep
Materials: neon, wood, paint
Neon fabricated by: Barry Allred, C.P., Allred Neon Co.
Photo: Jerry Lee Noe

Left:
NEON MIRROR
Michel Feith, 1979
Mobel Perdu Atelier, Hamburg
Dimensions: 110 cm high x 140 cm wide
Photo: Michel Feith

"This was the first neon 'sign' I created in the first year of my gallery 'Lux Neonlicht.'"
Michel Feith.

Below:
TECHNICOLOR
Larry Kanter, Neon Projects, Washington, D.C., 1982
Dimensions: 4' high x 5' wide
Materials: wood, acrylic lacquer, aluminum, neon
Photo: Till Bartels

This piece demonstrates the variety of colors and shades achieved when the light of neon tubes blends on a reflective surface.

Facing page:
"Y"
Eric Zimmerman, 1985
Dimensions: 46" high x 48" wide x 12" deep
Materials: neon, glass, aluminum, mirror
Fabrication: Archigraphics, Los Angeles
Collection: the artist's own
Photo: Rick Mendoza

As in many of Zimmerman's sculptures, here he uses the infinity effect of mounting neon tubing on mirror and facing the enclosure with 2 way mirror. A kinetic element is also introduced by the use of a sophisticated computerized sequencing system. This sculpture can "play" about 14,000 different sequences at a variety of speeds.

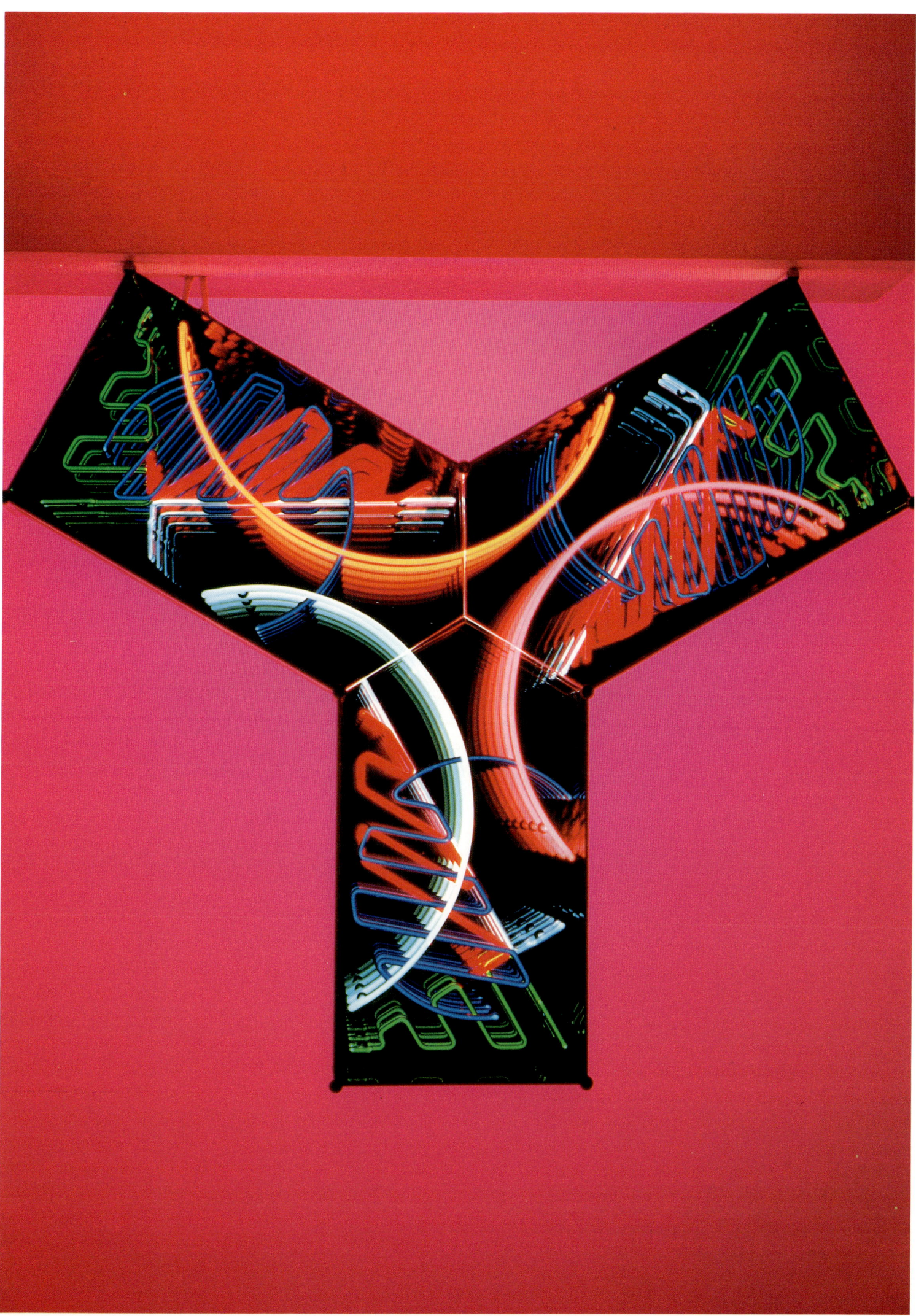

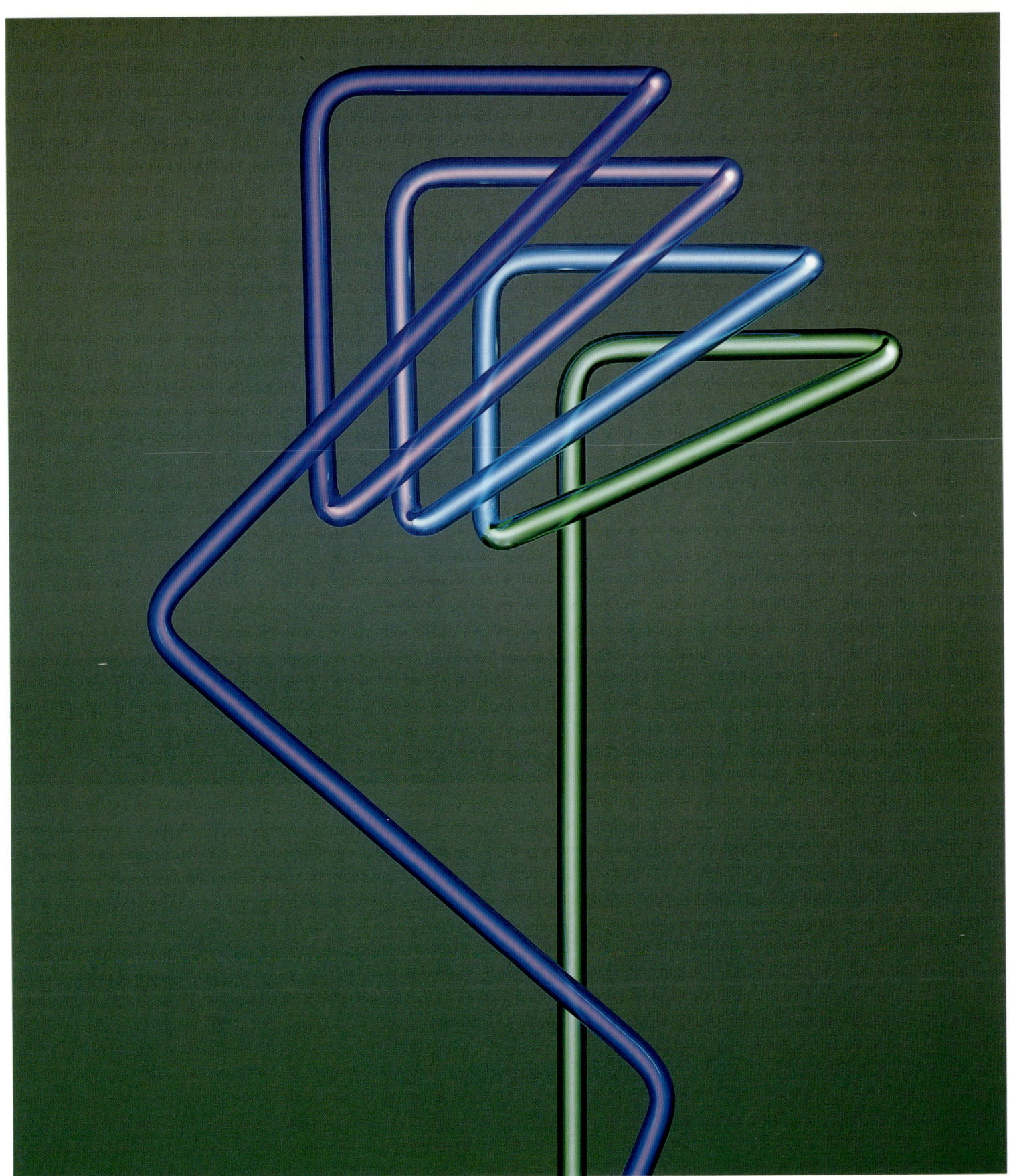

112 LIGHT WEAVE
Nobuyuki Sasaki, 1988
Dimensions: 450 mm high x 200 mm wide
Materials: 8 mm clear/argon
Photo: Takashi Kamagata

This Tokyo neon artist is involved with exploring many artistic applications through his company, Sun Neon. He is an excellent craftsman and makes beautifully poetic works.

CELIBATAIRES
Wolfgang Ernst, 1989
Dimensions: 193 cm high x 99 cm wide x 18 cm deep
Neon craftsman: Mario D'Ambrosio
Materials: door, metal plates, neon
Neon fabrication and installation: Neon Line, Vienna
Photo: Claude Buri, Louisa Haddu
Courtesy Dusty Sprengnagel

Dusty Sprengnagel has been encouraging the use of neon among artists in Vienna. He consults with them about proposed projects and finds ingenious methods of manufacture in keeping their creative intentions.

WAVES
Beverly Reiser, 1988
Dimensions: 14′ high x 35″ wide
Architect: R. Duell
Materials: sandblasted mirror and neon
Photo: Beverly Reiser
Commissioned for the Sandbard Lounge, Tropicana Hotel, Atlantic City, N.J.

This work has microprocessors which allow the various colors to dim and brighten in an infinitely varying pattern of color washes.

DANCER
Beverly Reiser, 1989
Dimensions: 4′ high x 3′ wide x 6″ deep
Materials: sandblasted mirror, neon, infrared sensor, microprocessor
Photo: Beverly Reiser

CLOUD SCULPTURE NO. 4/DOLL'S HOUSE
John David Mooney, 1982
Dimensions: 38" high x 50" wide x 20" deep
Materials: neon and wood
Photo: John David Mooney

The artist was commissioned by *"Architectural Design"* Magazine of London to create a "Doll's House." This sculpture was first exhibited at the Royal Institute of British Architects in London and then at The Art Institute of Chicago.

GATEWAY FOR A CLOUD
John David Mooney, 1982
Dimensions: 36" high x 48" wide x 20" deep
Materials: neon and wood
Photo: John David Mooney

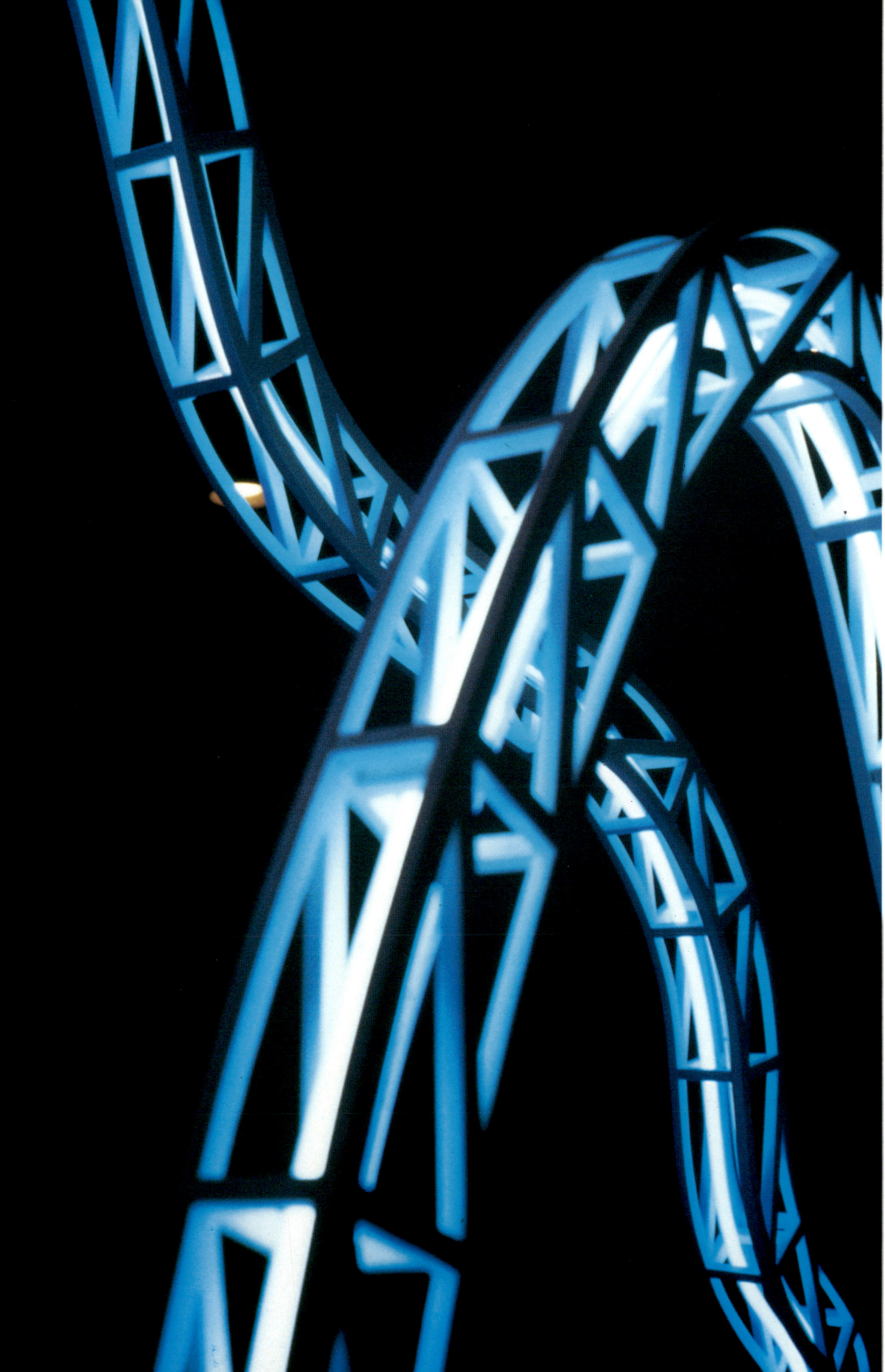

LET IT ROLL — FOR ALBERT AMMONS AND PETE JOHNSON
Cork Marcheschi, 1988, Jamaica, Queens, N.Y.
Dimensions: 6′ high x 108′ wide x 18″ deep
Materials: steel, paint, 1,200′ of neon and fading transformers
Photo shows only the blue outer phase.
Photo: Sarah Wells

Cork Marcheschi has been doing large scale projects with kinetic neon. He makes San Francisco his home base and travels around the country doing commissioned sculpture and architectural projects.

BRYANT'S ST. WALL WITH NEON
Bill Kane, 1979
Dimensions: 10′ x 20′ x 3″ billboard
Materials: photography on masonite, argon
Photo: Mark Rennie

"Bryant's St. Wall with argon is an affirmation of the human spirit in the urban environment. The decay of the city is represented by the photograph of the graffiti laden wall, torn and weathered. The dynamic human spirit is symbolized by the neon. Simply, man, in spite of himself, is a noble creature." Bill Kane

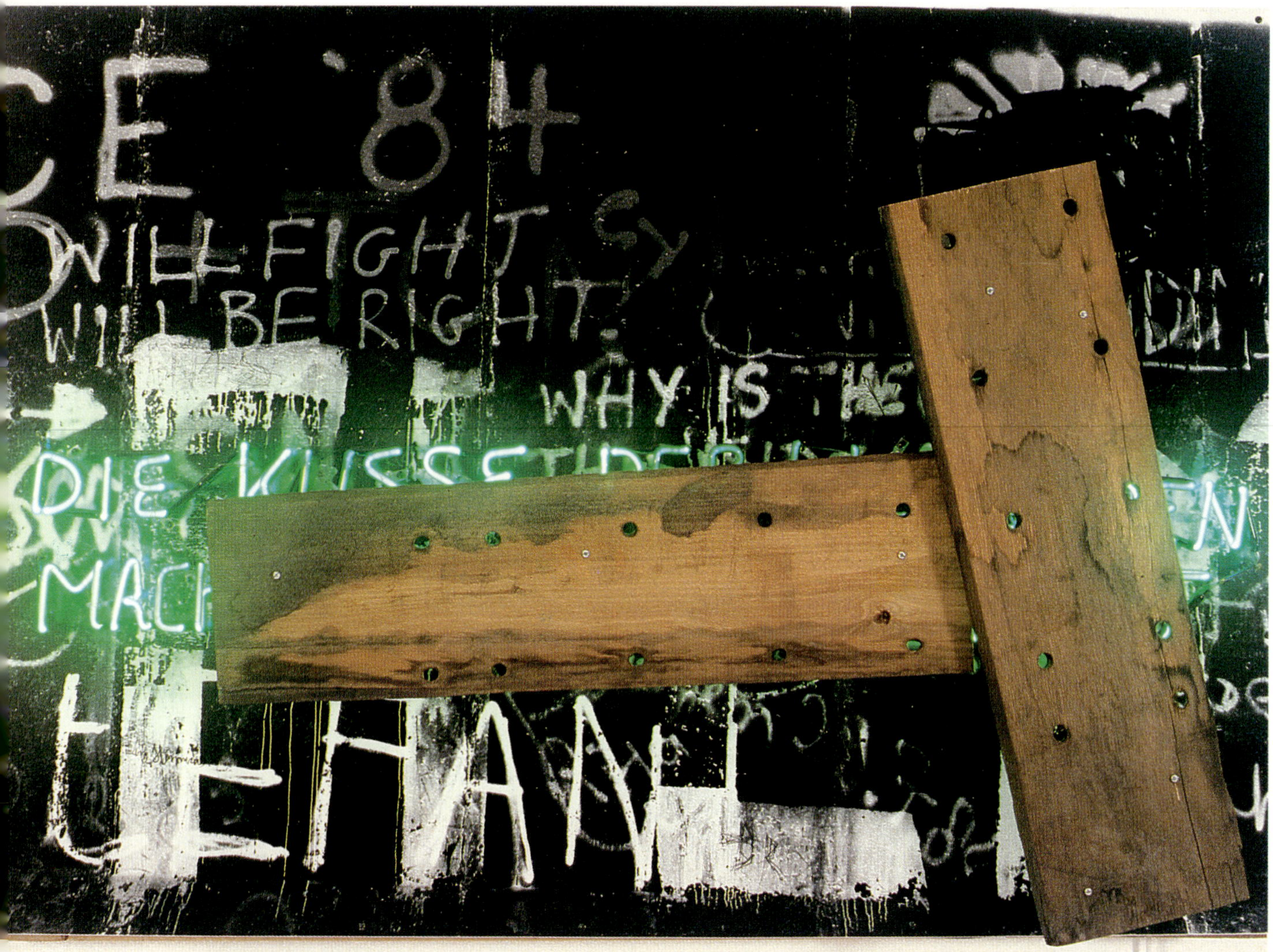
CE '84
WILL FIGHT
WILL BE RIGHT
WHY IS

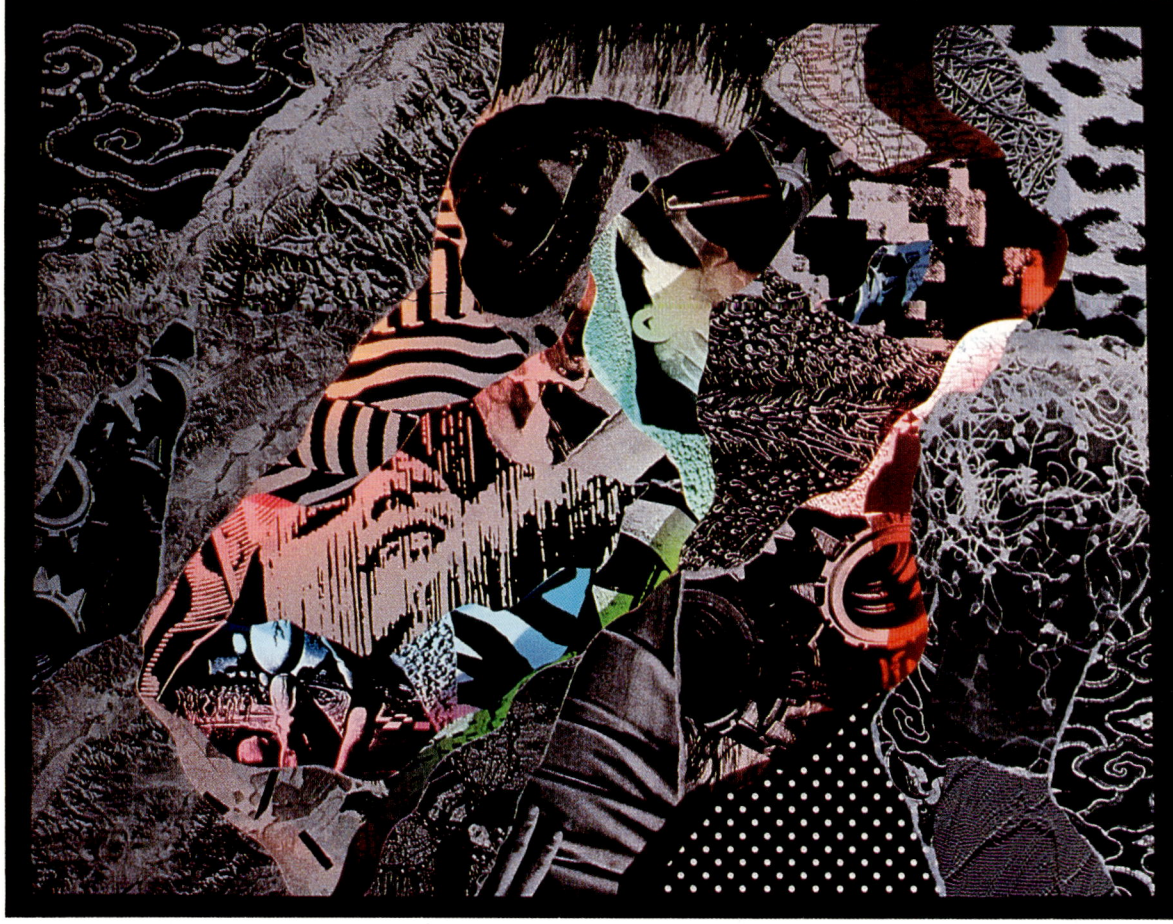

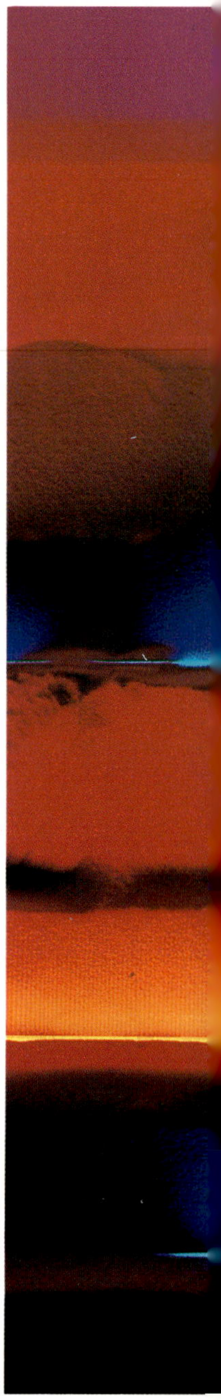

Top left:
THE KISSES OF LOVERS DO NOT SCARE ME
Bill Kane, 1987
Dimensions: 41″ high x 60″ wide x 9″ deep
Materials: photography, argon, wood, metal
Photo: Bill Kane

"This is from a series of works done on the Berlin Wall," the artist tells us. "The title is one line taken from a poem painted on the wall and recreated in neon on the artwork."

Bottom:
BUMP AND GRIND
Michael Rocco Pinciotti, 1988
Dimensions: 30.5″ high x 40″ wide x 5″ deep
Materials: neon and xerox on wood
Photo: Michael Rocco Pinciotti

"Over the years, exhibiting at galleries, cultural centers and neon art shows has allowed me to focus and flesh out many ideas and images. Exhibiting is important for both the artist and the public," says Mr. Pinciotti.

DETAIL FROM A SCENIC DESIGN FOR DEATH IN VENICE
Laddie John Dill, 1980
Dimensions: 30′ high x 60′ wide
Materials: neon, argon, sand
Fabrication and installation: Alert Lite Neon
Commissioned by the University of California in Long Beach
Photo: Laddie John Dill

One of the earliest sculptors to work with neon, Laddie John Dill began using the medium in New York in the 1960's. Living now in California, he has been doing commissioned projects.

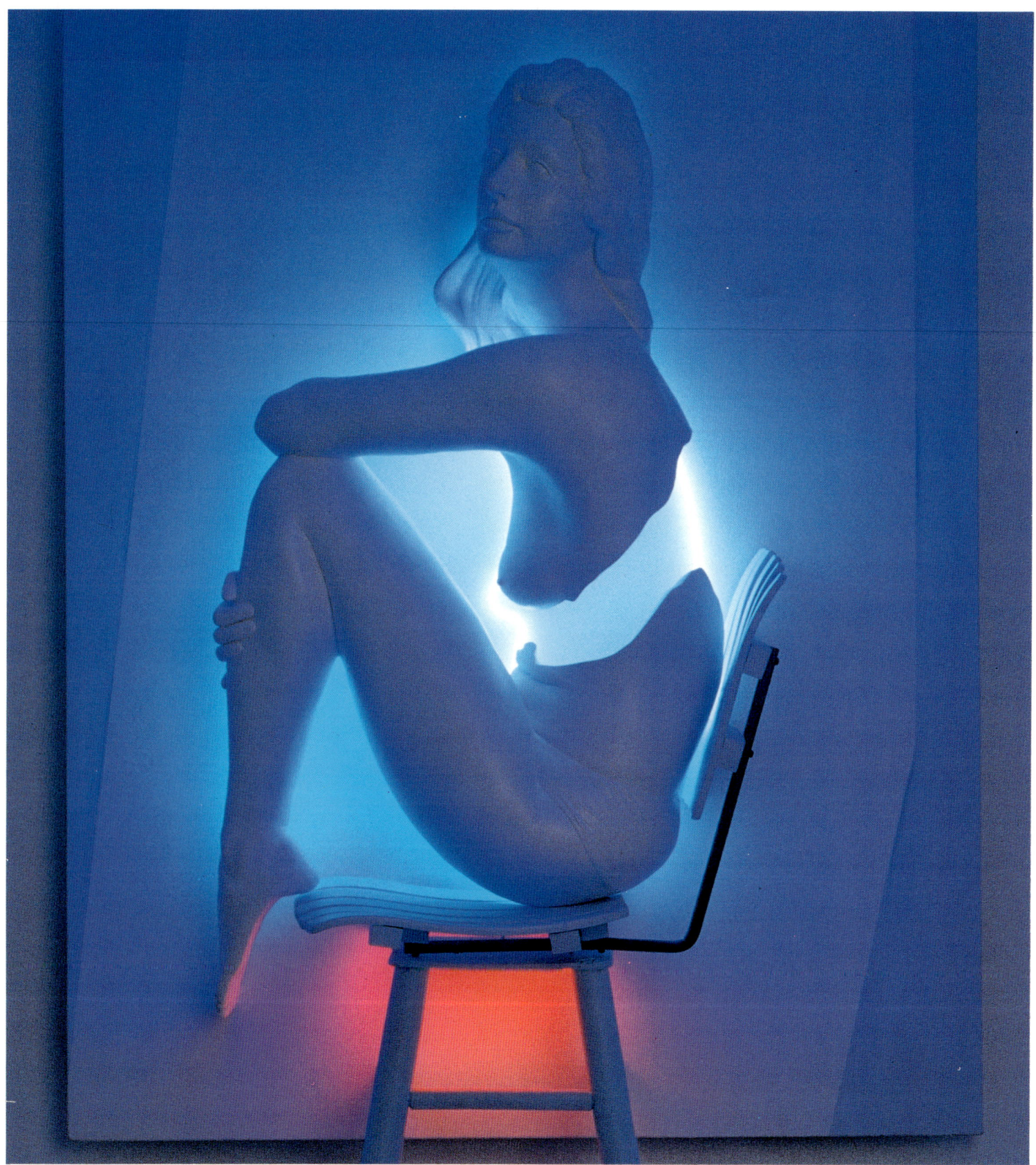

SEATED/UNSEATED WOMAN
Craig Kraft, 1989
Dimensions: 68" high x 33" wide x 14: deep
Materials: neon, canvas, wood, chair, densite
Photo: Craig Kraft

"Neon is one of the most mesmerizing yet least understood sculpture media. It is both a flat and dimensional line — a glowing tube, yet colored light itself. It communicates mundane and startling messages and can create surreal atmospheres. I have discovered myself trying to capture the gray zone of personal time and space where events are no longer what they have been, yet have not evolved into what they are about to be." Craig Kraft.

Right:
NICK'S LADY
Ellen Sandor in collaboration with G.E. Gondlach, 1980
Dimensions: 30" high x 40" wide
Materials: plexi and neon
Photo: Ellen Sandor and G.E. Gondlach

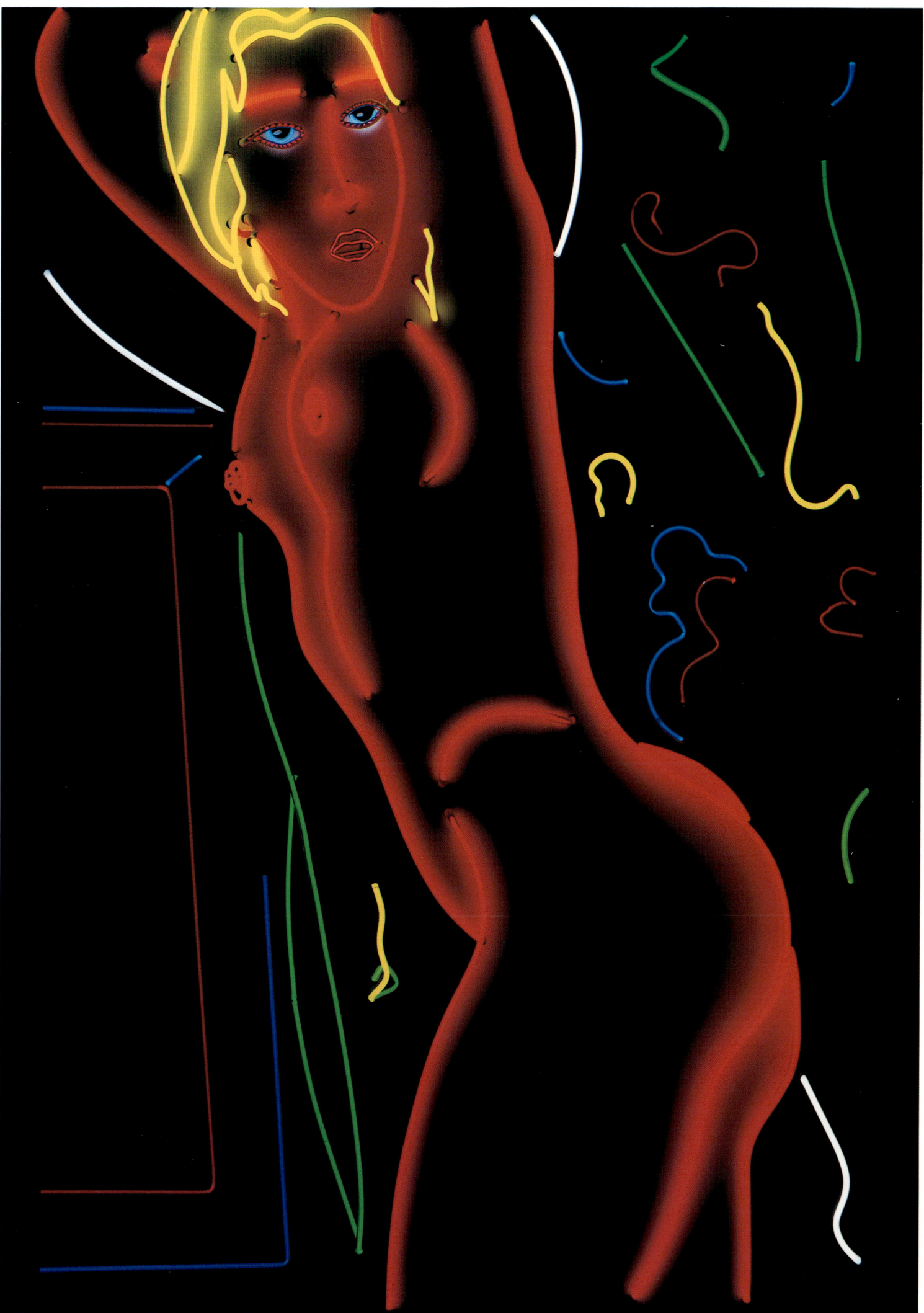

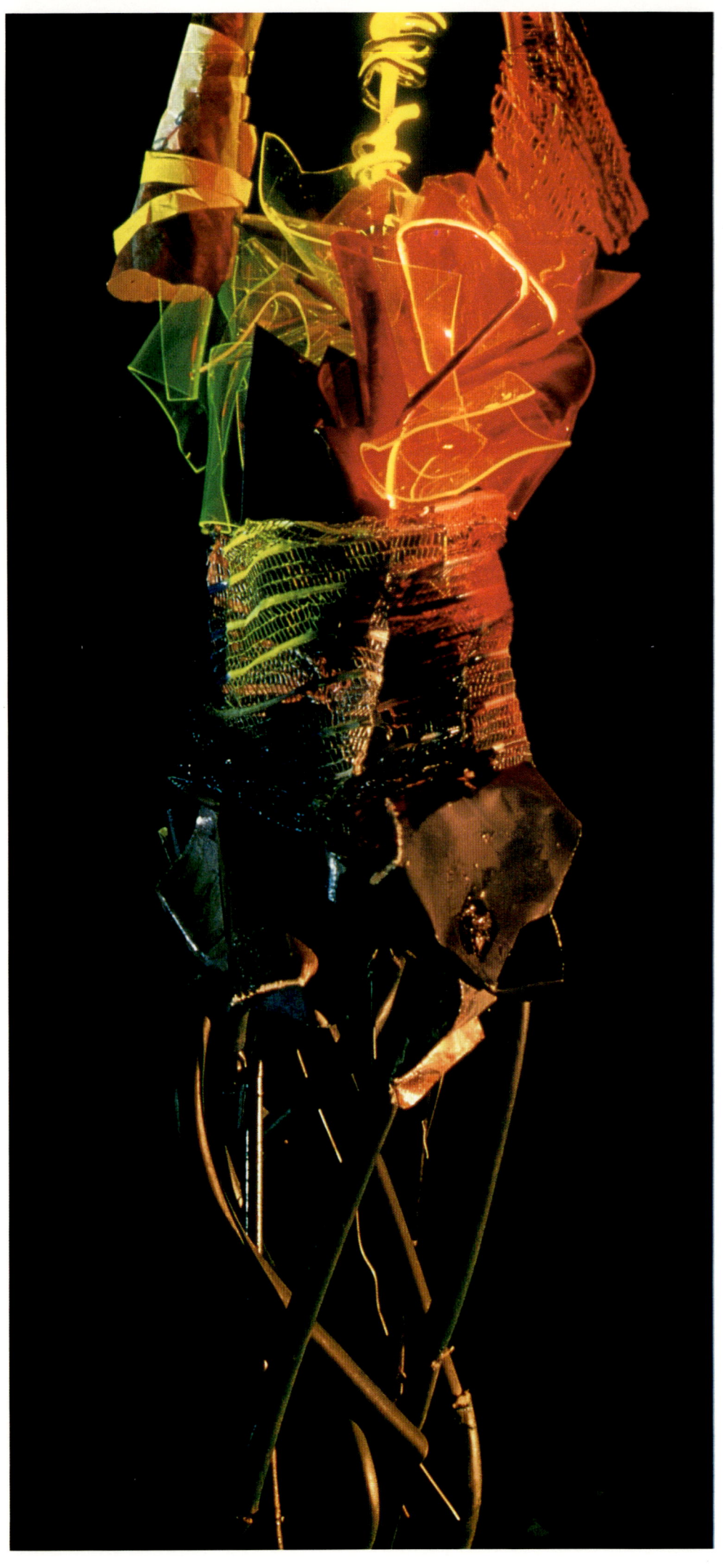

NEW GUINEA DANCE PARTY
David Morrison, 1990
Dimensions: 20″ high x 14″ wide
Materials: neon and plexiglas
Neon fabrication: David Morrison
Mask assembly assistance: Neon Design, N.Y.C.
Photo concept, photo and models supplied by Tom Sobolik

"I'd like to venture deep into an uncharted jungle and discover a primitive civilization that lived in caves and hunted with spears, yet somehow developed the technology to fabricate intricate and beautiful neon art." David Morrison.

Facing page:
DON'T LOOK BACK
Laurie Lea, 1989
Dimensions: 8′ high x 2 1/2′ wide x 2′ deep
Materials: neon, fibre optics, steel and plastic
Photo: Hiroshi Mishima

"Working with light is like playing with mystery . . . the invisible reality underlying appearance. Light illuminates form and space, affecting us psychologically. I am interested in using different types of lighting. . . as a means with which to deal with the world of ideas." Laurie Lea.

Overleaf:
I WANT YOU TO LOVE ME
Tom Gaddy
Dimensions: 96″ high x 48″ wide
Photo: Lightwriter's Neon

This sculpture is powered by 23 transformers and is animated by E-PROM integrated circuits. The 14 neon sections in the mouth are programmed to repeat the phrase "I want you to love me," while the eyes blink. The spirals oscillate between bright and dim asynchronously, while the hands slowly go back and forth emphasizing the whispered phrase.

Overleaf, far right:
THE ELVIS MACHINE
Joe Augusta, 1984
Dimensions: 48″ high x 36″ wide x 4″ deep
Collection: Rudi Stern
Photo: Sheila Augusta

The sculpture portrays a teenage Elvis Presley standing in front of a large machine-like head that is in fact the Elvis machine that created his persona. It has eyes that are squares within squares, a flattened nose, a 50's flat top, a mouth with teeth like one way doors. The waves on each side of the head are its fingers, about to scratch out its eyes in a gesture of horror. The machine has seen the future, and knows it must watch Elvis decline, decay and die.

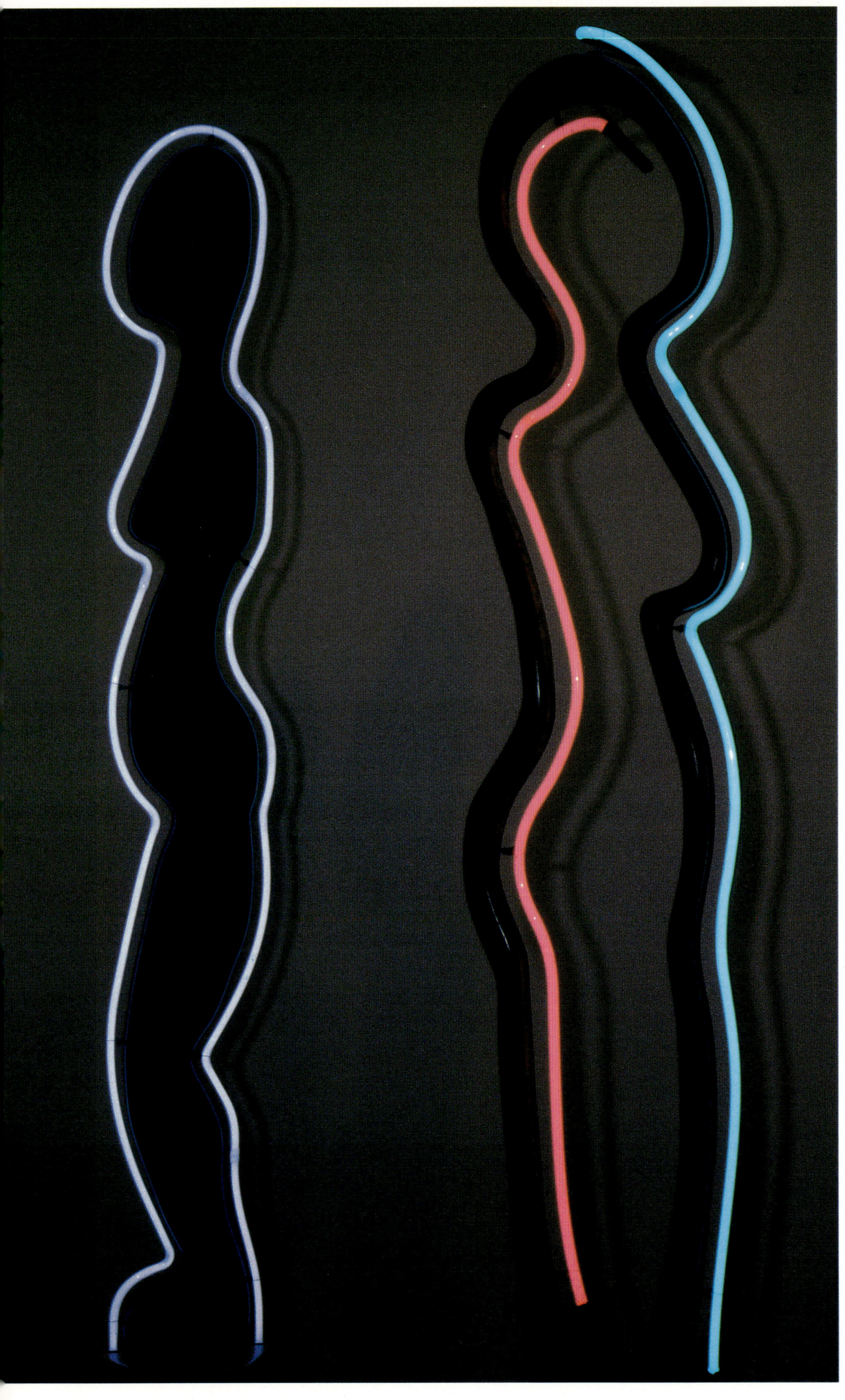

ELECTRO MAN
Michael Furey, 1986
Dimensions: 6' high x 3' wide
Materials: cement, glass, neon, ceramic insulators
Photo: Michael Furey

"Electro man is the result of my desire to create my own Frankenstein. He's 120 feet of red neon and approximately ten beer signs of brightness. He's dangerous, he sizzles and hums, and he is extremely difficult to look at." Michael Furey.

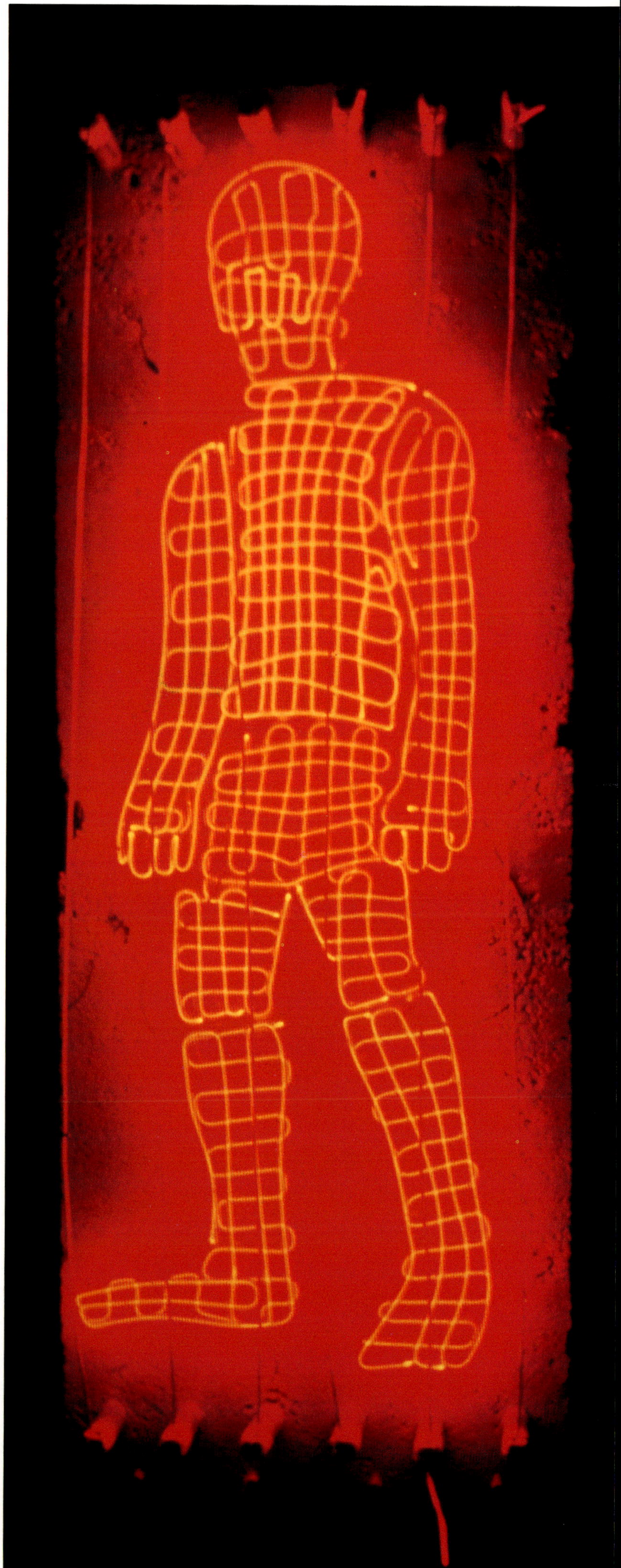

Left:
ILLUMINATED OUTLINE AND REFLECTED OUTLINE
Margery E. Goldberg
Dimensions: purple heart neon on birdseye maple base (left)
 — 6' high x 10' wide x 10" deep
paduk neon on birdseye maple base (right) — 10" high x 6 1/2" wide x 6 1/2" deep
Collaboration: Marty King of Light 'em Neon
Reflected outline collection: Andrea and Harvey Maisel
Illuminated outline collection: Vick Kamber
Photo: Ken Wyner

Margery Goldberg is the owner-director of the Zenith Gallery in Washington, D.C. She represents many neon artists and has been active in encouraging neon sculpture through lectures, panel discussions, tours, gallery talks and exhibitions.

Above:
GROUCHO MARX
Rob Robinson, 1990
Dimensions: 3'6" high x 2'6" wide
Fabrication: Rob Robinson
Photo: Rob Robinson

Groucho was the first in a series of figural "portraits" of well-known personalities as well as images of the common man.

JUS SUMMUM SAEPE SUMMA EST MALITIA
Ben Livingston, 1989
Materials: acrylic, wood, neon
Photo: Kevin Jordan
For the Bicentennial Exhibit: Jacques Prevert Centre Cultural, Cherbourg, France

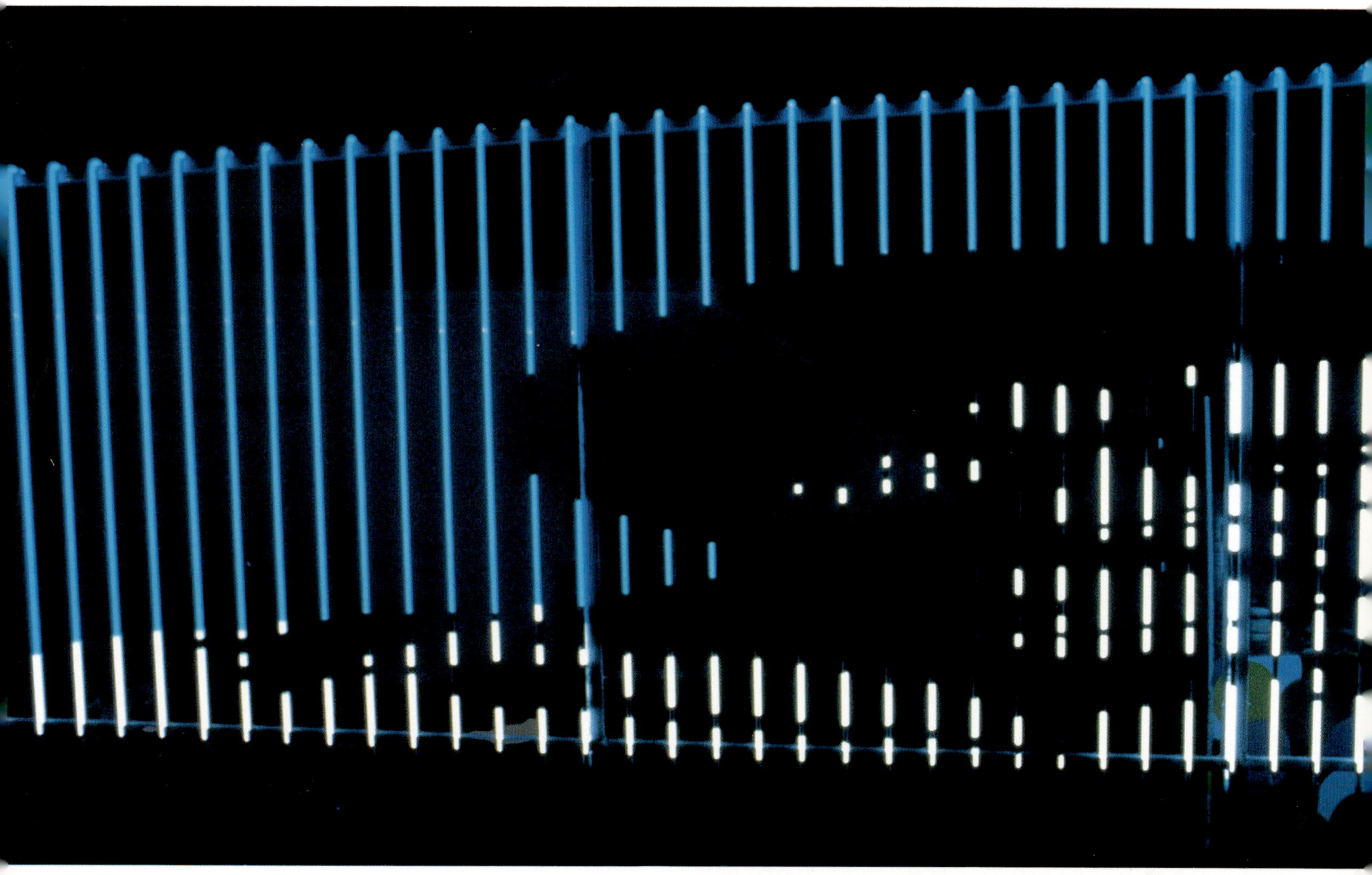

SELF-PORTRAIT, POINT OF PERSPECTIVE
Fred Elliott, 1988
Materials: aluminum, glass, argon
Photo: Tom Dorsey

The actual format is trapezoidal. It's twenty feet long, starts at four feet and increases to six feet. When viewed from twenty-five feet it appears to be rectangular and the portrait can be seen easily.

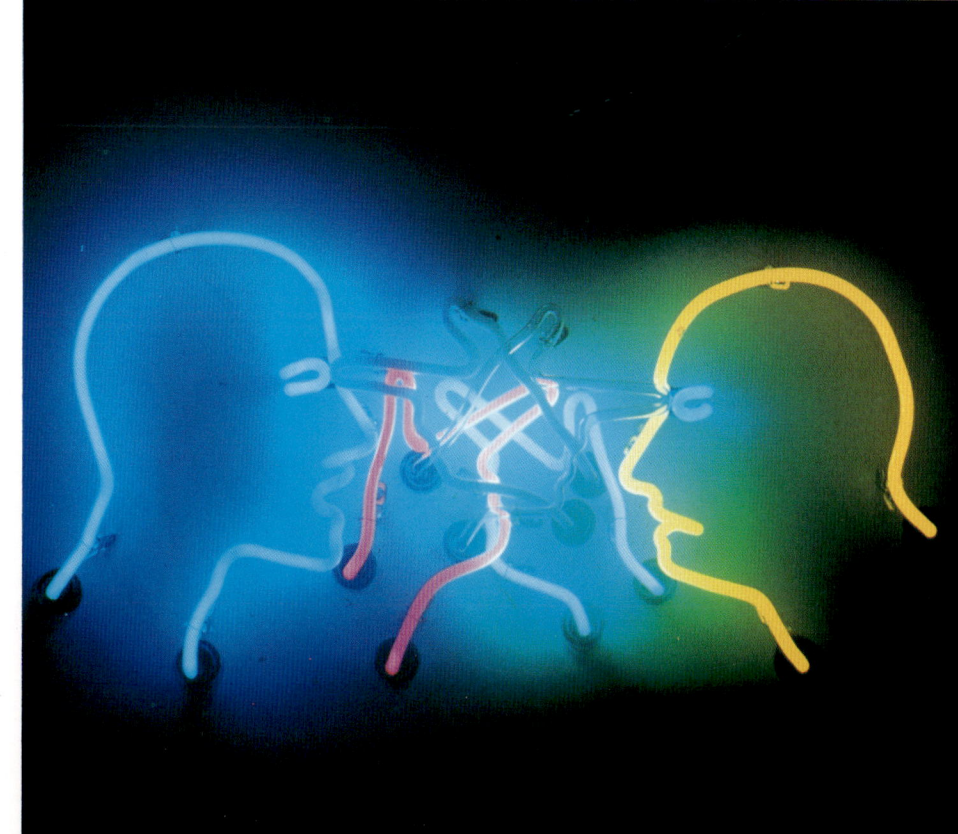

DOUBLE POKE IN THE EYE II
Bruce Nauman, 1983
Dimensions: 14" high x 28" wide x 6" deep
Photo courtesy Castelli Gallery

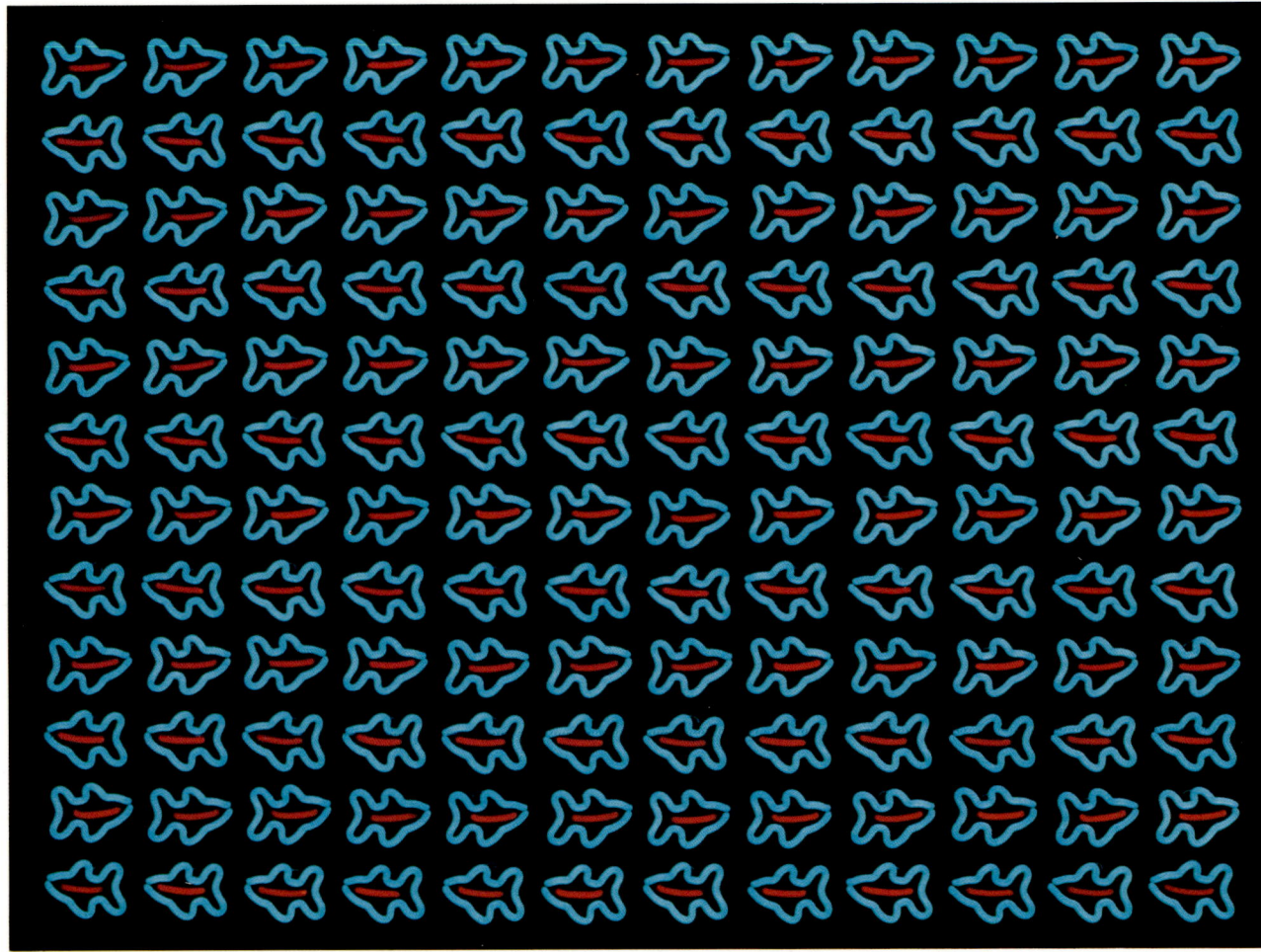

WALL-O-FISH
Karl X. Hauser
Photo: Karl X. Hauser

Wall-o-fish is an animated neon installation based on a modular grid of 144 neon fish, each complete with its own solid-state transformer and base. The animation, inspired by movie theatre marquees, runs through a number of varied sequences.

"I am a journeyman glassblower and have been making neon signs and art for the last 12 years. Currently I am working as an independent contractor for Brumfield Electric Sign Company in San Francisco." Karl Hauser

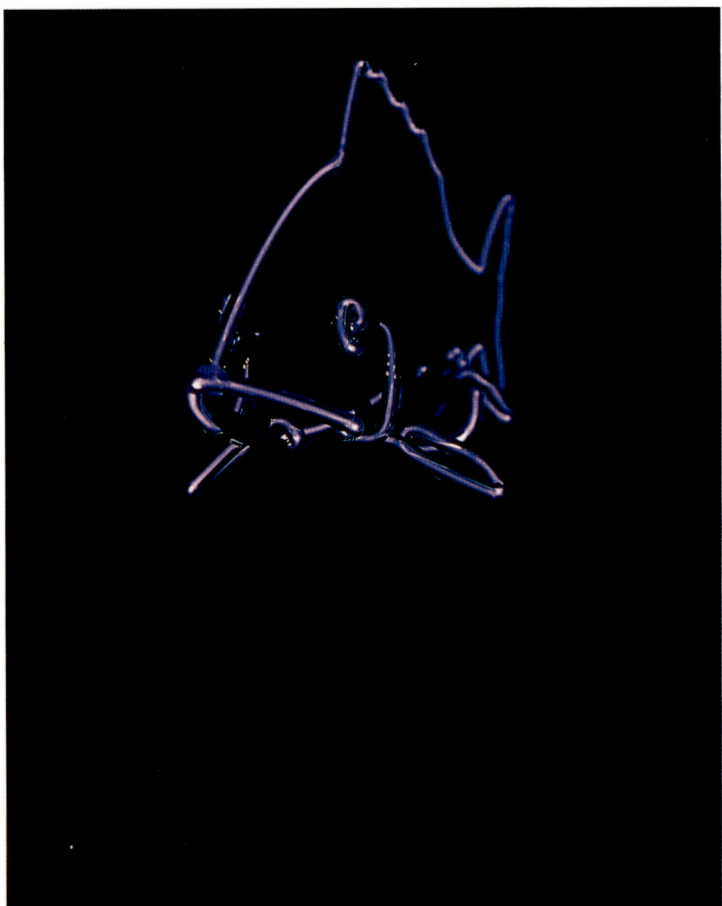

FISH
Michael Flechtner, 1989
Dimensions: 14″ high x 6″ wide
Photo: Michael Flechtner

ROCKER
Abe Rezny and Rudi Stern: Let There Be Neon, 1986
Dimensions: lifesize
Photo: Abe Rezny

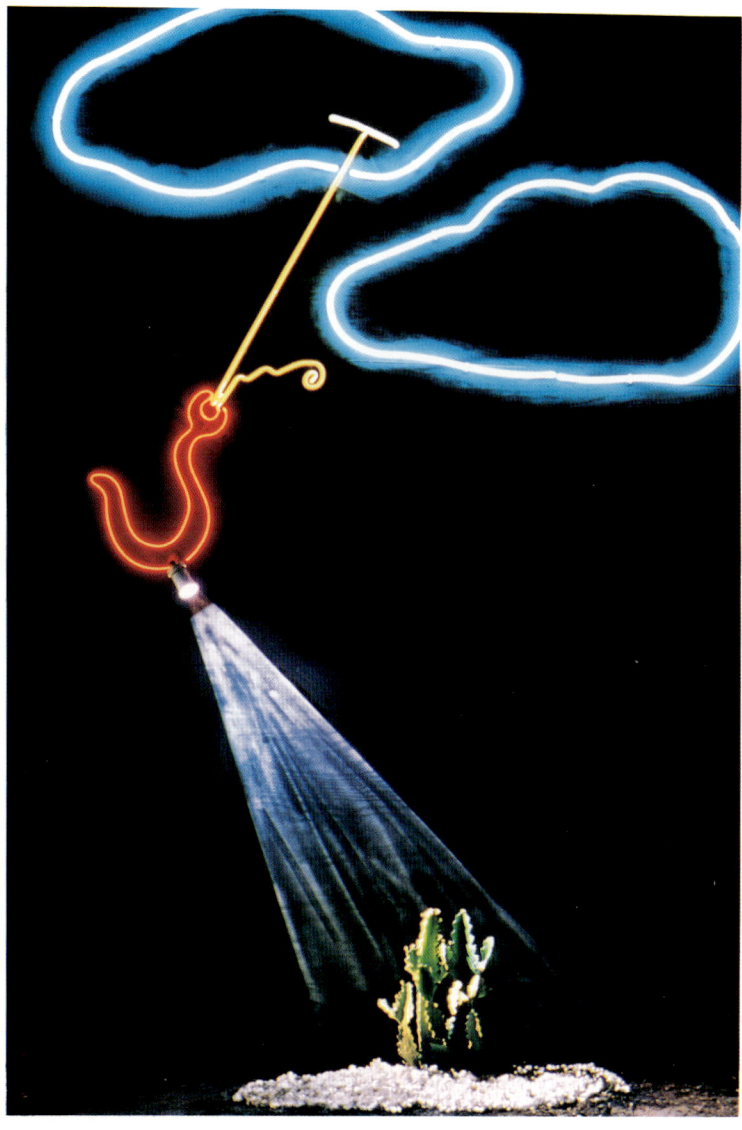

SKYHOOK
Ben Livingston, 1989
Dimensions: 12′ high x 8′ wide
Photo: Smiley N. Pool

Originally designed as an illustration for one of Jan Moyer's landscape lighting articles for "*Architectural Lighting*" Magazine, 1989.

LAST YEAR'S MODEL
Ben Livingston, 1990
Dimensions: 5′ high x 7′ wide x 7.5″ deep
Materials: neon and acrylic on framed canvas
Photo: Ben Livingston

BLUE CAR
Nils Eklund, 1982
Dimensions: 4′ high x 12′ wide
Neon: Let There Be Neon, New York, N.Y.
Materials: neon, 1956 'Vette
Client: Max Hasfeld, Amsterdam, Holland
Photo: Nils Eklund

Overleaf, top:
JEFFERSON'S TEMPLE
Michael Rocco Pinciotti, 1989
Dimensions: 28" high x 38" wide x 5" deep
Materials: neon, acrylic, oil, pencil on wood
Photo: Michael Rocco Pinciotti

Jefferson's Temple is one in a series of actual buildings captured in a loose drawing style and re-created as a three-dimensional, multi-layered sculpture. Neon is used in an imaginary monumental scale to highlight the surface and to accentuate the three-dimensionality of the piece.

Bottom, left:
TEMPLE OF THE HEART
Michael Rocco Pinciotti, 1990
Dimensions: 35" high x 28" wide x 6" deep
Materials: neon and mixed media on wood

"My neonized temples," says Mr. Pinciotti, "focus on the idea of man-made structures as revered objects. They reflect the poetry of place and incorporate precious and natural materials. Life, death, God and creation all revolve around the concept of light. Here, neon's sacred glow brings us into a place of respite and comfort while at the same time energizes us with its electrical warm glow."

FUN IN '56
Philip Hazard, 1989
Dimensions: 28" high x 67" wide x 5" deep
Materials: oil paint on black and white photostat with neon and argon
Photo: Philip Hazard
The art is is represented by Zenith Gallery, Washington, D.C.

Philip Hazard has been working with neon since arriving in New York in the early 1970's. He worked with Let There Be Neon for many years before starting his own company.

Above:
THE HOT JAZZ BAND
Richard Jenkins and his students at U.C.L.A. Extension Neon Design Class, 1986
Dimensions: 8' x 8'
Photo: Richard Jenkins

Hot jazz band plays krypton, neon, argon in animation which delights the eyes.

GROUND BREAKING CEREMONY NEON SCULPTURE
30' Vertical—Neon & Black Plexiglas
Replica of the Regent of New York, 1989
Developer: E.I.E. International
Public relations counsel: Howard J. Rubenstein Associates, Lloyd Kaplan, executive vice-president
Neon design, fabrication, installation: Let There Be Neon, Inc., Rudi Stern
Installation, June 1990 at the National Building Museum, Washington, D.C.

"The Regent of New York will — literally and metaphorically — light up East 57th Street. What better way to make that statement than with a neon sculpture of the building." Lloyd Kaplan.

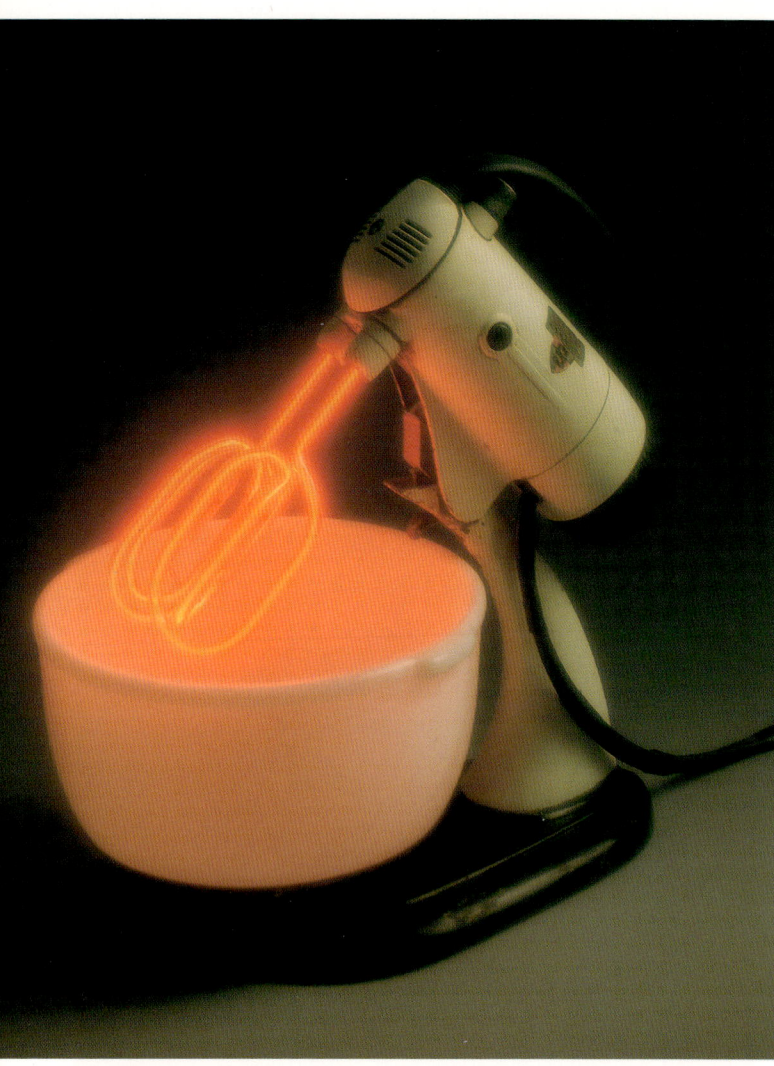

MIX MASTER
Robert Ziegler, 1983
Dimensions: 18″ high x 12″ wide x 12″ deep
Collection: Single Bullet Theory (Rock Band)
Photo: Robert Ziegler

MATT THOMPSON: NEON KITES 1990
Wing span of 8 feet
Neon and kite. The colors on the kite are deep green and ultra blue. The kite is a Hawaiian brand. It is a dual line stunt kite.
Photo: MAM Photography. Photographed at Sandy Beach on the Island of Oahu.

"An escape from the normal confines of neon art ... the beginning of a series with neon in flight."

CHAIR + TABLE TENNIS
Candice Gawne, 1984
Dimensions: 53″ x 66″ x 32″
Materials: neon, wood, paint, aluminum, table tennis paddles, balls and net
Photo: Larry Whitely

"I started working with neon about five years ago for the sheer joy of the glow. For me, neon is a very magical manifestation of light. Seeing neon, fireworks, stars, x-mas and freeway lights transport me to special places in myself, places of celebration, meditation, dreams, imaginary and unknown territories." Candice Gawne.

CLOTHESLINE
Robert Ziegler, 1980's
Dimensions: 5' high x 12' long x 1' deep
Materials: neon, rope, clothespins
Photo: Robert Ziegler

"I am an advertising photographer by profession, a 'fine-art' photographer and self-taught neon bender by avocation. I've been bending glass for about a dozen years," says Robert Ziegler.

NEON EGGS
Abe Rezny, 1978
Neon in eggs
Fabricated by: Let There Be Neon, New York
Photo: Abe Rezny

NEVER
Susan Firestone, 1986
Dimensions: 15 1/4" square cubes
Neon consultation and fabrication: Let There Be Neon, Inc., New York, N.Y.
Materials: clear plexi faces with black plexi sandwiching the neon. Tops are white plexi.
Photo: Dorothy Zeidman

"The traditional use of signage to communicate, to attract, to impact and to immediately inform, inspired my neon work. The intensity of its luminous color, the directness of its linear forms and its economy of graphic presentation suit the messages that I wish to convey. Electric urgency in a condensed language provokes an impression of today's pulsating street jive." Susan Firestone.

NEON SKATES
Moira North and Rudi Stern, 1986
Materials: battery operated neon skates for performances by The Ice Theater of New York, Moira North, Director
Photo: Morgan Kane

The choreography of the Ice Theater of New York creates kinetic light patterns on the ice as the skates and neon wands interact. The light patterns illuminate the ice dancers themselves as they weave and spin in the darkness.

NEW LANGUAGE
Paul Hartigan, 1982
Dimensions: 1200 mm x 1200 mm x 190 mm
Materials: neon on flat black painted metal background
Permanent collection: National Library of New Zealand, Wellington

The artist describes his work as "the spontaneous calligraphy of an illiterate graffitist or a New Language."

HUMAN NATURE/LIFE DEATH/KNOWS DOESN'T KNOW
Bruce Nauman, 1983
Dimensions: 107.5" high x 107" wide x 5.25" deep
Photo courtesy Castelli Gallery

Index

Abate, Romano, 163
Ablon, David, 104
Albright, Larry, 105
Allen Bank Associates, 26
Anthony, Tom, 84
Antonakos, Stephen, 50, 51
Augusta, Joe, 128, 129, 175
Bachure, Sharon, 91
Bane, Gary, 33
Bansbach Brothers, 85
Becker, Jeff, 147, 148
Berta, Jerry, 91
Beyer, Blinder, Belle, 78
Bressette, Patrick, 53, 120, 141
Bromley-Jacobson, 65
Brown/McDaniel, Architects, 58
Buchsbaum, Alan, 24
Bugrov, Valerij, 57
Burton, Dana, 32, 53, 81, 140
Campopiano, Remo, 15
Capers, Roddy, 134, 145
Cesentini Associates, 76
Chelsea, Dan, 86
Cicena, 83, 90
Coleman, Brian, 94, 97
Concannon, Bill, 19
David, Peter, 62, 107, 108, 109, 110
de Boer Lichtveld, Frans and Marja, 44
Design House, 24
Dill, Laddie John, 169
Dix, Dennis, 32, 53, 81, 140
Dunn Signs, 32
Eklund, Nils, 38, 87, 94, 182
Elliott, Fred, 179
Emmerson, Stephen, 74
Ernst, Wolfgang, 161
Evans, Janet, 136
Farcus, Joe, 56
Feith, Michel, 158
Ferren, Brian, 10
Firestone, Susan, 188
Flechtner, Michael, 180
Fowle, Bruce S., 77
Freeman, Christopher, 126, 150, 152
Frerichs, Steve, 106
Friedman, Jeff, 82
Furey, Michael, 144, 177
Gaddy, Tom, 174
Gaffney, Kyle, 91
Gassman, Stephanie, 53
Gawne, Candice, 186
Glick, Marvin, 66
Goldberg, Margery E., 176
Gough, Bryan, 11
Gundlach, G.E., 171
Hassman, Geoffrey, 61
Hartigan, Paul, 14, 54, 188
Hauenstein, Michael, 70

Hauser, Karl X., 180
Haverson, Jay M., 60
Havey, Maureen, 136
Hayden, Michael, 48-49, 68, 149
Hazard, Philip, 183
Heim, Jean-Pierre, 72
Hellmuth, Obata & Kassebaum, Inc., 63
Hepburn, Mundy, 99, 101, 102-103
Hibino, Katsuhiko, 17
Hillier Group, The, 64
Hoyem-Basso Associates, Inc., 58
Integrated Signs, 39
Jacobson, Don, 138
Janson, Andy, 33
Jenkins, Richard, 22, 62, 184
Johnson, Leland, 19
Jordan, M., 35
Kane, Bill, 167, 168
Kahn, Eve, 84
Kanter, Larry, 158
Kerns Group Architects, 64
Kowal, Kurt, 99
Kraft, Craig, 170
Kroeger, Wolf, 34
Kucera, H. Erwig, 24
Lacey, Bill, 63
Lakich, Lili, 36-37, 138, 139
Lambert, Denis, 23
Lea, Laurie, 172
Lee, Chung, 59
Let There Be Neon, 81, 185
Leverton, Jim, 62
Levitt, Robert, 84, 88
Livingston, Ben, 146, 179, 181
Macartney, Ian, 89, 107
Malamud, Marc, 57
Manstaduno, Joseph, 26
Marangoni, Federica, 156
Marcheschi, Cork, 67, 166
Matcovich, Liz, 82
McClain, Chuck, 84
McCoy, Nancy, 71
Michel, Simone and Olivier, 22
Miskinis, Jon, 134
Mooney, John David, 127, 164, 165
Morris Nathanson Design, 53
Morrison, David, 173
Motoko Ishi Lighting Design Inc., 52
Mount, Charles Morris, 60, 72
Muir, Ross, 78
Mulherin, Lori Gene, 137
Nakamura, Fumaki, 31
Nauman, Bruce, 156
Neon Line, 16
Neon Neon, 25
Ng Chun Man & Associates, 77
Noe, Jerry Lee, 123
North, Moira, 189

Norwood Oliver Design Associates, Inc., 33
Ohashi, Kunio, 117
Omuku, Masao, 28-29
Pannen, Brigitte, 36
Parker, Bill, 118, 119
Phoenix, Graham, 23
Pinciotti, Michael Rocco, 168, 184
Pirsig, Ted, 135
Pompei, Ronald Silvio, 55
Reiser, Beverly, 162, 163
Rezny, Abe, 181
Rivers, Victoria, 130, 131
Robinson, Rob, 178
Rockwell, David S., 60
Rose, Debra Lee, 75
Rozinski, Richard L., 137
Saccardo, Carmine M., 154, 156
Sandor, Ellen, 171
Saravay, Richard D., 71
Sasaki, Nobuyuki, 160
Scarff, Tom, 145
Schiess, Christian, 114, 115, 121, 122
Schneider, Christiän, 27
Seide, Paul, 111
Senkel, Helmut, 85
SGPA/Architecture and Planning, 39
Sicardi, Cristina, 140
Simmons, Jay, 82
Sina, Alejandro and Moira, 46, 112, 113
Smotrich, David, 71
Sonnier, Keith, 156
Spiers, Jonathan, 23
Sprengnagel, Dusty J., 24
Stern, Rudi, 38, 78, 87, 91, 181, 189
Stirnweis, Kevin, 144
Svenson, David, 106
Tanaka, Hiroki, 116
Tatman, Steven, 73
T.A.C., 65
Thomas, Stirling, 14
Tschida, Fred, 124, 151
van de Water, Hein, 69
van der Horst, Jozef, 157
van Munster, Jan, 45
Walenta, Ann, 135
Ward, Arthur, 33
Watkins, Candice, 105
Wesley Thuro, Div. of Luminescence, 47
White, James, 125
Withers, Gary, 79
Woloshin, Linn Westbay, 142-143
WZMH Group, 59
Yocum, Dave, 132, 133
Young, Michael, 70, 132, 137
Ziegler, Robert, 186, 187
Zimmerman, Eric, 46, 87, 89, 159

Acknowledgments

Grateful thanks to the following:

Tod Swormstedt of *Signs of the Times* so eager to share information and so enthusiastic about the future.

Jonathan Dolger, my good friend for the last 100 years.

Till Bartels, neon archivist from Berlin.

Mike Marklew, my fax pal in Tokyo.

Nobuyuki Sasaki, Sun Neon in Tokyo, good friend and fellow enthusiast.

Peter Mason, whose vision of neon keeps him forever young and dynamic.

Dave Caleno, at Masonlite, who kept sending wonderful examples and good cheer.

Debby Johnston, my assistant at Let There Be Neon, who is taking an intensive neon workshop and has been of great help in the process.

Burt Sobolik, my colleague, for his valuable suggestions.

Joan Levy, color doctor and new friend.

Milt Zlotnick, kind adviser—even if he still doesn't like neon.

Bernie Holland, for his support and encouragement.

Sylvia and Ben Weinstock, my neighbors, who provided good wine and great dinners at perfect moments.

Bernie Schleifer and his cat Gertrude who know where everything is all the time and have the same smile for anxious authors.

My friends, Federica and Gigi Marangoni in Venice, for their kind hospitality.

Dusty and Ylona at Neon Line in Vienna for their continuing enthusiasm and friendship.

In addition I would also like to thank the following:

Joe Augusta

Craig Carl

Chris Freeman

Midi and Giugliano at Montin's in Venice

Mundy Hepburn

Rocky Pinciotti

Danielle Wanders, Bart op het Veld, Carine and Lydian Eisjsbouts: My good Amsterdam friends for their help in the final stage of this project.

Tom Sobolik,
and all my friends and colleagues in the expanding neon network.

August, 1990 RUDI STERN